The social psychology
of religion

International Library of Sociology

Founded by Karl Mannheim

Editor: John Rex, University of Warwick

Arbor Scientiae
Arbor Vitae

The social psychology of religion

Michael Argyle

Department of Experimental Psychology
University of Oxford

and

Benjamin Beit-Hallahmi

Department of Psychology
University of Haifa

Routledge & Kegan Paul

London and Boston

First published in 1958 as Religious Behaviour
This wholly rewritten edition published
in 1975 by Routledge & Kegan Paul Ltd
Broadway House, 68–74 Carter Lane,
London EC4V 5EL and 9 Park Street,
Boston, Mass. 02108, USA
Set in 10 pt. Times New Roman
and printed in Great Britain by
Unwin Brothers Limited
The Gresham Press
Old Woking, Surrey
A member of the Staples Printing Group
© *Michael Argyle 1958 and 1975*
No part of this book may be reproduced in
any form without permission from the publisher,
except for the quotation of brief
passages in criticism

ISBN 0 7100 7997 4 (c)
ISBN 0 7100 8043 3 (p)

Contents

Preface

The first edition of this book, which came out in 1958 as *Religious Behaviour*, has been widely used as a reference work and a textbook. However, the growth of relevant literature in sociology and psychology over the last fifteen years has made it somewhat out of date, and provided many new methods and ideas. We therefore thought that it would be useful to bring out a new edition. We have made some changes in the basic structure of the book, and covered new areas. While our survey of the literature is not exhaustive, we have tried to keep our eyes open for any studies which may shed light on theoretical questions. The function of the book has remained that of a basic reference work, and the style is intended to make it usable by as wide an audience as possible.

Changes in the religious situation itself since the first edition came out have continued the slow trend towards secularization and the decline of religion both in Britain and the USA. At the same time interest in religion as a topic of inquiry in the humanities and the social sciences has greatly increased. A better understanding of religious ideas and traditions can come only from the efforts of all the human, and the humane, sciences, and we do not believe in the superiority of one single approach.

Since in our opinion this book falls within social psychology, it is appropriate to discuss its implications for that field. Compared with most of what is being done in social psychology today, this book can be regarded as an exercise in naturalistic observation. We have presented a large amount of data, collected in various ways, mostly in natural social settings. We have tried to offer generalizations regarding an area of behaviour which is social, human, and complex. By looking at the context of religious behaviour, we have attempted to show certain regularities in its relationship to other human behaviour and attributes. Without an understanding of these natural regularities we believe that a social-psychological understanding of religion will be quite handicapped. One major conclusion of our exercise in observing religious behaviour is the interrelationship of religious beliefs and behaviours and other kinds of social behaviour.

The authors and the publishers thank the following for permission to reproduce copyright material: American Council on Education for data in Table 3.2; American Personnel and Guidance Association for Table 3.5; American Psychological Association for Table 10.13 (copyright 1972); American Sociological Association for Tables 2.7, 2.18, 3.1, data in Table 6.2 (Jackson, Fox and Crockett, 1970) and Tables 7.4, 10.1 and 10.3; American Sociological Association and the authors for data in Table 6.2 (Crespi, 1963; Glenn and Hyland, 1967) and Tables 6.3, 6.5, 7.6, 7.7 and 10.5; Associated Book Publishers for Table 8.7; Association Press, New York, for data in Table 5.3 (Ross, 1950) (copyright 1950); *Behavioral Science* for Table 5.5; British Psychological Society for Table 6.8; Catholic Hospital Association for Tables 6.6 and 6.7; Center for Family Planning Perspectives and the authors for Table 9.1 (reprinted from *Family Planning Perspectives*, vol. 4, no. 4, 1972); Clarendon Press for Table 7.3; Columbia U.P. for Table 8.8; F. A. Davis for Table 8.4; Doubleday for Table 7.10 (copyright © 1963 by Gerhard Lenski); *Fortune Magazine* for Table 6.4 (reprinted from the June 1954 issue of *Fortune Magazine* by special permission, © 1954 Time Inc.); Gallup Poll for data in Tables 2.3, 5.1 (BIPO), 5.2 (Gallup Poll and BIPO); A. Godin and the International Center for Religious Education for Table 11.11; Geoffrey Gorer for Tables 3.11 and 3.13, data in Tables 5.1 and 5.3 and for Table 10.10; Hamlyn Publishing Group for data in Tables 5.2 and 5.4 (Odham, 1947); Harper & Row for Table 2.11 and Figure 2; Harvard U.P. for Tables 5.6 and 10.4; Hawthorn Books for Tables 2.14 and 3.3; Hodder & Stoughton for data in Table 3.7; Institute of Social Research for Table 7.13; Institutes of Religion and Health for Table 2.13 (from vol. 8, no. 4, *Journal of Religion and Health*, New York 10001); Journal Press for Table 4.1 and UK data in Table 4.2; Journal Press and Dr J. M. Gillespie for data from Allport, Gillespie and Young, 1948, in Tables 3.2, 3.12 and 5.3; Liverpool U.P. for Table 5.7; Dr D. C. McClelland for data in Table 6.1 and for Figure 3; Macmillan, London and Basingstoke, and St Martin's Press, New York, for Table 7.2 and Figure 4; Meredith Corporation for Table 7.1; National Council for the Churches of Christ in the USA for data from *Yearbook of American Churches*, in Tables 2.4, 2.15 and 10.12 (© 1955, 1957 and 1967, National Council of Churches, New York); New Science Publications for data in Table 2.1; Northwestern U.P. for Table 7.8; Oxford U.P.

for Tables 8.9 and 11.2; Parapsychology Foundation and Mrs Walter Pahnke for Table 3.10; Pergamon Press for Table 8.1; Princeton U.P. for data in Tables 2.10 (Cantril, 1951) and 3.12 (Stouffer, 1949) and for Tables 9.2 and 9.6; Random House for Tables 2.6, 2.8, 2.9 and 3.4 and for data in Table 2.10 (Gallup, 1972) (copyright © 1972, by the American Institute of Public Opinion); Religious Education Association for US data in Table 4.2; Religious Research Association and *Review of Religious Research* for Tables 3.6, 6.2, 7.12, 8.3 and 9.5; Royal College of Psychiatrists for Table 8.5; Charles Scribner's Sons for Table 9.4; Science Research Associates for Table 4.4; *Social Science Quarterly* and the authors for Tables 3.8 and 10.11; Society for the Scientific Study of Religion for data in Table 3.2; Society for the Scientific Study of Religion and the authors for Tables 2.12, 7.9, 7.11, 10.2 and 10.9; *Sociological Analysis* for Tables 7.5, 10.7 and 10.8; Dr Leo R. Srole for data in Table 8.2; Turnstone Books for Table 3.9; University of California Press for data in Table 6.2 (Lipset and Bendix, 1959) (reprinted by permission of the Regents of the University); University of Chicago Press for Table 4.3, data in Table 6.2 (Goldstein, 1969) and for Table 11.3; University of London Press for data from Social Surveys, 1964, in Tables 5.3 and 5.4 and for Tables 9.3 and 10.6; Weidenfeld & Nicolson for Table 2.16.

We are grateful to secretaries who typed the chapters: Ann McKendry, Wenda Jean Ulmer, Sanna A. Baker and Linda Marra.

MICHAEL ARGYLE
BENJAMIN BEIT-HALLAHMI

1 Introduction

Scope and aims

What we shall do in this book is to present the main empirical findings from social surveys, field studies and experiments about religious behaviour, beliefs and experience. We shall use these findings to test psychological and sociological theories about the origins, functions and effects of religious behaviour. We shall confine ourselves to religion in Britain and the USA between 1900 and 1973, which is where most of the research has been done.

We should define what we mean by 'religion'. Several social scientists today offer definitions of religion which are very broad and include most systems of beliefs, philosophy or ethics. We decided to use a straightforward, everyday, limited definition of religion as a system of beliefs in a divine or superhuman power, and practices of worship or other rituals directed towards such a power.

Much of this research is about the antecedents of religious behaviour and beliefs; that is, the conditions under which they occur. These conditions in turn may be used to decide which of various possible psychological processes is responsible for producing religious behaviour. These conditions and processes can be regarded as the causes of religious activities, but they need not be regarded as the whole explanation.

A second kind of research is concerned with those correlates of religious behaviour in other spheres of behaviour, which can be regarded as the effects of religion. The basic question here, is 'Does religion make a difference?' (cf. Bouma, 1970). The answer is given in terms of both individual and social behaviour. The main difficulty is in isolating the influence of other variables such as social class and education. Lenski (1963) attempted to show that there was indeed

1

an independent religious factor, which affected other social institutions and could be isolated from their influence. We shall examine the influence of the same religious factor, while holding constant other factors in social behaviour.

Some readers may be more concerned with individual religious beliefs and actions, and may worry that the individual believer may disappear behind the generalizations. This danger exists with any kind of systematic social-psychological inquiry. Our basic premiss is that individual behaviour cannot be isolated from its social environment. Our generalizations, when we formulate them, are intended to apply to individuals and their actions. Naturally they cannot predict every case of individual action, but if they have any value at all, they should help us to understand most cases.

Measurements and indices

In this section, the most important indices of religious activity will be described, and in each case two questions will be discussed: how satisfactory the index is as a criterion of religious activity; and how accurate the measurement is likely to be in terms of actual, as opposed to merely reported, behaviour.

Church membership is a widely used index. As an index it is rather unsatisfactory since it tells us very little about how active a person is or what he believes. Some members may have lapsed in enthusiasm while remaining on the books; others may be keen but never actually become church members. This index is often used for the study of changes in time, since the records are readily available for many years past. However, the criteria for membership tend to change with time: in the USA some churches concealed increases of membership before 1936 in order to evade taxes, while in the early years of the century some Protestant churches did not count children, and others did not even count women! Again, care must be taken in making any interdenominational comparisons, since the criteria vary from church to church. The Catholic church attaches a rather broad meaning to membership, and counts all who are baptized in the faith living in the area. The Church of England counts Easter communicants—rather more than the number of communicants on a normal Sunday. Other Protestant churches include only those over thirteen or fourteen who have made the effort to be accepted as members and placed on the roll of the church.

The usual way of studying membership statistics is via records, based on returns from individual clergymen and published in the yearbooks of individual churches. These are summarized in *Whitaker's Almanack* for Great Britain and in *The Yearbook of American Churches* for the USA. The figures go back to 1900 and beyond. Another way is to ask respondents in a sample social survey if they are church members. Rather larger estimates result from doing this. In 1954 in the USA, 79 per cent of people questioned in a Gallup Poll claimed to be church members (Rosten, 1955, p. 239), while the membership returns for that year only totalled 60·3 per cent (National Council of Churches of Christ in the USA, 1955). This may be because people tend to exaggerate their religious activities (as, it will be shown, in the case of church attendance) and because 'membership' is a rather vague term. It may be confused with occasional churchgoing or with 'affiliation'.

Frequency of church attendance is another valuable index. It has the advantage over membership that its significance is the same for different dates and denominations. On the other hand, it may be argued that the Catholic church puts on greater pressure for sheer attendance than some other churches. There may be some church attenders who have no real religious beliefs or feelings. However, these people would not be expected to be active in more private kinds of worship, such as saying prayers or reading the Bible. The usual way of studying overt religious activity is by asking people how often they go to church. It is probably better to be specific and ask them if they went last Sunday; the concrete question put like this leaves less room for distortion. It was found in one English survey (Odham, 1947) that people who claimed to go to church 'weekly' actually missed an average of seven Sundays a year. In the case of church attendance it is also possible to count the number of people who go to church, and this has been done in a number of local studies by sociologists.

The saying of private prayers, and other forms of private religious act, can be ascertained from answers to questions, but not easily validated against direct observations of behaviour. As an index of genuinely religious activity, this particular criterion is a good one since non-religious motives are less likely to interfere; as a measurement it is unsatisfactory because of the impossibility of checking and the likelihood of exaggeration. All that is generally asked is the frequency with which prayers are said; the answers could be made much clearer by also inquiring into the duration of such prayers. As things are, it is difficult to interpret the very high frequencies reported: about 46 per cent of people in England report the saying of prayers daily, though about 14 per cent go to church weekly.

Attitudes towards religion or towards the church provide another index. By an 'attitude' is meant the extent to which a person is favourable or unfavourable to the organization or set of practices as judged by his verbal expressions. Some writers use 'attitude' to refer primarily to overt behaviour, in which case verbal measures

3

must be validated, or checked against more direct measures. However, since attitudes are invariably assessed by verbal methods, and since attitudes measured in this way often differ from actual behaviour, it is probably best to treat them independently.

The objection to attitudes as an index of religious activity is that a person may be favourable to religion without either holding the beliefs or engaging in the practices. There is some evidence that this does not often happen. The importance of attitudes is that considerable progress has been made with refined means of measurement; this is one of the most effective kinds of measurement in psychology. One of the best known of all attitude scales is that originally devised by Thurstone and Chave (1929) for attitudes towards the church. Another widely used instrument is the Allport-Vernon-Lindzey Study of Values (Allport, Vernon and Lindzey, 1960; Hunt, 1968) which compares the relative strength of interests in six areas: religious, aesthetic, social, political, economic and scientific. Examples of attitude scales measuring religious attitudes are found in Shaw and Wright (1967), and Robinson and Shaver (1972).

Specific beliefs can be assessed only by asking single questions, and the precise wording of these is important. It is important that surveys should not be compared unless the wording of questions is identical. On the other hand overall measures of the extent to which a person accepts orthodox religious beliefs can be obtained by the construction of lists of items, on the attitude scale model. Kirkpatrick (1949) and others devised series of items to measure 'religionism', consisting of questions covering a wide range of conventional beliefs and having a high degree of internal validity. The use of open-ended questions can be illuminating: Gorer (1955), for example, asked his respondents to describe what they thought the after-life would be like. The answers to open-ended questions need coding or classifying before any statistical results can be obtained, and such questions also take longer to answer. It is more usual to give subjects a series of definite alternatives, though sophisticated people often find it difficult to agree with any of these: Leuba (1934) found it impossible to report the religious beliefs of philosophers because they could not understand the questions or agree with any of the answers. The kind of question which goes 'Do you believe in God? Yes, No, Don't Know' can be improved by specifying different forms or degrees of belief.

An important recent development in the measurement of religious beliefs is the application of the Semantic Differential, Q-sorts and similar measures. These enable an individual's perception of God to be compared with his perception of, for example, mother, father, doctor, or policeman.

Religious experiences have been asked about in a number of studies. Although relatively uncommon, they are of great interest, and are thought by some to be of great importance. Bourque (1969) used the question 'Would you say that you have ever had a religious or mystical experience, that is a moment of sudden religious insight or awakening?' About 32 per cent of the US adult population said 'Yes' to this question. Others have suggested that larger percentages will admit to religious experiences if references to mysticism or sudden conversion are omitted (Havinghurst and Keating, 1971).

Further indices that have been used in the investigation, and will be reported later, include *professional employment* as a clergyman, church worker or theological student—which can presumably be accepted as a good index, though the psychology of these people may well be different from that of the keen follower—and two sociological indices: *contributions to church funds*, and the *publication of articles about religion*. The first must, of course, be corrected for changes in real value and the level of wages. A suitable index is perhaps the average donation per head as a percentage of the average wage. Publications have been analysed by Hart (1933) and others in studies of changes with time. It may be objected that publications only reflect the opinions of a small minority, though of course publishers and editors have to stay in business, and to some extent give the public what they think it wants. In some analyses periodicals were weighted by the size of their circulations, so that some measure of the number of people actually reading the articles is included in the final index.

Multi-dimensional measures of religiosity have become widely accepted in recent years. Since it has become clear that being religious involves several discrete kinds of behaviour, which are possibly measurable as dimensions, the idea that a good measure of religiosity has to include several criteria has gained popularity.

Glock (1962) suggested the following five dimensions: ideological, ritualistic, experiential, intellectual, and consequential. The ideological dimension covers religious activities such as prayer and worship. The ritualistic refers to church attendance of various kinds. The experiential dimension covers intense religious experiences such as conversion, 'speaking in tongues', or mystical experiences. The intellectual dimension measures knowledge of religious dogmas and practices, and the consequential dimension deals with the effects of religiosity on conduct in other spheres. The measurement of these dimensions is done by using questionnaire items. Despite its theoretical refinement, this approach shares the problems of all questionnaire methods in relating to actual behaviour. Most studies using the multi-dimensional approach (e.g. Glock and Stark, 1966) measured these attitude dimensions and then correlated them with other attitudes. In a number of studies very low correlations have been found between the five Glock dimensions (e.g. Fukuyama, 1961).

Religious affiliation, or denominational membership, can be used as a dependent variable or as an independent variable, to predict or explain behavioural differences. Ideas about how members of various denominations differ stem from historical traditions, theological writings, or assumed psychological differences resulting from the first two. Examples of predictions based on denominational differences in traditions and practices are found in Lenski (1963), Johnson (1962), and others. One problem in conceptualizing the importance of denominational differences is the weight given to other factors, such as social class and education. Another problem is that of historical and social changes, which tend to modify or blunt denominational distinctions.

Limitations and caveats

We would like to spell out some of the possible limitations of our presentation, and to suggest some appropriate caution in using it. First, most of the studies we called upon were done in Great Britain and the USA. We relied on the copious published behavioural science literature in these two countries, where research techniques are most advanced. This limitation of our sources sets the boundaries for our generalizations. We can generalize from our findings to the situation in other English-speaking countries, and with less certainty to other Western countries. Since we are discussing societies which are advanced, industrialized, mostly secular, but with a predominantly Christian heritage, it is not easy to generalize about more traditional, non-Christian societies. Nevertheless, the findings and the theories presented here may be a source of ideas and hypotheses for further explorations in other cultures. Especially when we deal with general theories of religious behaviour, the ideas offered may be, and should be, tested, in a variety of social contexts.

We are also limited to a particular historical period, 1900–73. One may ask: 'If things are changing so much, how can we generalize or predict anything?' Some readers may be concerned over how much of what we report is already history. Since we are reporting changes and trends over two-thirds of a century, some of what we report is undoubtedly and deliberately historical. This is true of other findings in the social sciences. The changing structure of society affects behaviour at many levels, including the religious one. We are not necessarily trying to show universal and stable characteristics of behaviour, unless they are supported by empirical findings. We are certain that some readers will conclude that religious behaviour has enormously changed, while others will be impressed by how much continuity and stability are in evidence. Certainly some of the functional relationships which emerge appear to have a good deal of stability.

2 Religious activity in Great Britain and the USA, 1900–73

We shall not attempt to provide a complete history of religion in Great Britain and the USA during the twentieth century. We are concerned with absolute changes in religious activity, and with delineating historical trends, which set the stage for our discussion in the following chapters. In order to appreciate best some of the findings presented later, it is important to be aware of general levels of religious activity and how they change. The presentation in this chapter will lead us to a comparison between the two countries and to an analysis of the meaning of religious activity in each one.

Religious activity in Great Britain

Church membership

The criteria of membership are different for different churches, so that they have to be considered separately. Furthermore there is no national reporting organization of religious bodies, as in the USA.

The Church of England keeps careful records; perhaps the most useful is the number of communicants during Easter week. The changes since 1900 in this number, expressed as a percentage of the population of England over the age of fifteen, are shown in Figure 1. It can be seen that there is a considerable decline, from 9 per cent in 1900 to 5 per cent in 1970, despite temporary revivals in 1920–30 and 1950–5.

The Roman Catholic church does not keep comparable records, though the *Catholic Directory* reports estimates of the Catholic population by local priests. Between 1894 and 1903 the estimate for England and Wales was 1·5 million (4·6 per cent of the population). This rose to 6·4 per cent in 1951. The method of reporting changed in 1955, and this had the effect of increasing the figures to 7·1 per cent in that year, rising to 8·3 per cent in 1970. If the figures for Scotland are included, 9·0 per cent of the British population were Catholic in 1970. These estimates include a lot of inactive Catholics: in 1962 only 53·5 per cent of the Catholic population attended mass, and about 40 per cent attended weekly. However, there clearly has been an increase in the proportion of Catholics: the percentage of Catholic marriages in England and Wales rose from 4·1 per cent in 1901 to 11·2 per cent in 1967; the proportion of children born who were baptized as Catholics rose from 7·7 per cent in 1911 to 16·1 per cent in 1963 (Currie and Gilbert, 1972; Martin, 1967).

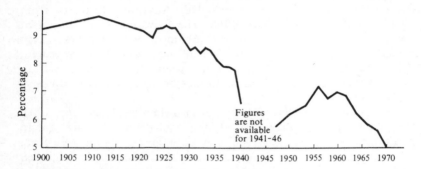

FIGURE 1   *Easter week communicants in the Church of England, as a percentage of the population aged 15 and over, 1900–70*

Source: Church of England (1965).

The Roman Catholic increase is partly due to Irish and Polish immigration; there are 14 per cent Catholics in the north-west as compared with 3 per cent in the south-west (Gorer, 1955). Other factors are larger families, conversions and the Catholic rule about children of mixed marriages. Conversions are reported as between 9,000 and 14,000 per year during recent years (Spencer, 1966).

The nonconformist churches show a similar pattern to that of the Church of England. For example, communicating members of the Methodist church for Britain fell from 3·1 per cent of the population over fifteen in 1901 to 1·7 per cent in 1966. The Baptists and Congregationalists show a similar decline. The Methodists have been losing about 3,000 per year; there have been fewer young people joining, so that they have an ageing population structure, the opposite of the Catholics (Martin, 1967).

The main churches in Scotland are the Church of Scotland (which amalgamated with part of the United Free Church of Scotland in 1929) and the Roman Catholic church. Membership of the Church

9

of Scotland increased from 22·4 per cent of the population of Scotland over fifteen in 1901, to 31·9 per cent in 1967. During the same period the Presbyterian church in England lost ground. It is probable that the success of the Church of Scotland is partly due to its appeal to Scottish nationalist feelings. On the other hand, the Baptists and Congregationalists have kept up their strength better in Scotland than in England and Wales.

There have been increases in the membership of some of the small sects. The Jehovah's Witnesses increased from 5,033 in 1931 to 65,693 in 1972; they have been comparatively static since World War II, apart from increases due to West Indian immigration. The Mormons have increased from half a million in 1916 to 3·4 millions in 1971. The Seventh Day Adventists increased from 1,160 in 1903 to 11,666 in 1968. The Salvation Army increased from 13,317 in 1904 to 31,916 in 1961, most of the increase taking place by 1920. Recently a number of new sects have appeared, like the Jesus Movement, and a variety of Eastern, mystical, and meditative groups. The total membership of these groups is small as yet.

The total membership of churches in Britain has fallen since 1900. Membership of all Protestant churches fell from 20·4 per cent in 1901 to 12·1 per cent in 1966; the Catholic population rose from 5·9 per cent to 9·2 per cent; overall church membership thus fell from 26·3 per cent to 21·3 per cent. In Scotland total membership is considerably higher: in 1966 31·9 per cent belonged to the Church of Scotland, 15·9 per cent were Catholics, and total church member-ship was about 53 per cent (Currie and Gilbert, 1972).

The records of church membership thus show a marked decline in membership of Protestant bodies, except for the Church of Scotland and certain small sects, together with a steady growth in the Catholic church. There have been a number of interesting fluctuations, such as general expansion of membership between 1900 and 1915, and between 1948 and 1961. The Church of England, and some other churches, had another period of growth between 1920 and 1930. The periods of most rapid decline were during the depression years, during World War II, and since 1960.

Church attendance

This has been studied in a number of local surveys, and more recently by reported church attendance in social surveys. The local surveys are more accurate, but there are wide variations from one area to another, and it is difficult to extrapolate from them. There are also difficulties about the proportion of people who go twice on Sundays. Social surveys cover larger areas, but are subject to quite large sampling errors, and there are discrepancies between different surveys in the same year.

Since there were no social surveys at the turn of the century, we must depend on counts of attendance in particular areas. Counts in 25 English cities found an average Sunday attendance of 38 per cent of the population in 1881 (Chadwick, 1966). Correction for those who went twice, estimated at 40 per cent, reduces this to 27 per cent. Later counts in other cities, corrected in a similar way, show that about 25 per cent of the adult population attended in Liverpool in 1902 (Jones, 1934), and 25 per cent in York in 1901 (Rowntree and Lavers, 1951).

The level of church attendance in recent years can be obtained from social surveys, though the percentages obtained vary with the area covered (the inclusion of Scotland raises it, for example), and the time of year. A good survey of people in Britain aged over twenty-one was conducted for *New Society* by the National Opinion Poll in 1965, and was reported by Goldman (1965). This showed that 16·9 per cent of the sample had been to church in the previous week. Other surveys found 14–15 per cent attendance. There appears to have been a decline of weekly church attendance from 25 per cent for England in 1900 to about 15 per cent in 1965.

TABLE 2.1   *Church attendance in Britain in 1900 and 1965–70 for different denominations (in percentage of the population)*

	1900 for one Sunday	1965–70 previous week	1965–70 previous 3 months*
Church of England	10	5	24·1
Nonconformists (inc. Church of Scotland)	11	4	9·4
Roman Catholics	3	5	6·7
Jews		0·2	0·8
Other religions		0·8	1·5

From various sources.
*From Goldman (1965).

This decline has varied between denominations. In Table 2.1, the figures for 1900 are estimated from a variety of local studies, some of which were mentioned above (for others see Martin, 1967). The figures for 1965–70 are derived from the National Opinion Poll survey (Goldman, 1965) and other surveys. We concur with the estimates made by Martin (1967).

Part of the decline in church attendance is due to a change in the frequency with which individuals go to church. The proportion of those who went twice on a Sunday fell from about 40 per cent in 1909 to 8 per cent in 1947, and is now probably lower still, following the decline of Evening Service. The Church of England has a large proportion of members who go less than once a week, as Table 2.1 shows. In addition, 68 per cent of the population of England and Wales are married in church, 80 per cent are baptized, and 67 per cent claim to belong to it.

Radio and television provide another way of attending services. On any Sunday about 24 per cent of the adult population watch BBC religious programmes, and 18 per cent see ITV programmes; as many as 45 per cent make a point of watching or listening to broadcast services. The most popular programme was 'Songs of Praise', watched by 35 per cent of the population (*Social Surveys*, 1964; ITA, 1970). Of course the level of attention may not be very high, since some people simply leave their sets switched on, more or less permanently.

Other religious behaviour

Sunday Schools   There has been a big decline in Sunday School membership since 1900. At that time 30 per cent of children belonged to Church of England Sunday Schools alone (three times the rate of adult attendance). This had dropped to 13 per cent by 1960. Nonconformist Sunday School membership has fallen in a similar way. On the other hand family services have become more common. Sixty-nine per cent of parents still wanted Christian religious education in schools in 1965 (Goldman, 1965).

Prayer   About 44 per cent of the adult population claim to pray every day, mostly before going to bed (Gorer, 1955). This rather high percentage is supported by a number of other surveys. What they pray about are family and friends, especially for those who are ill, happier family life, peace, and help for self in crises (ITA, 1970; Mass Observation, 1947). An even larger number, about 58 per cent, teach their children to pray.

Bible reading   This is much less common: about 11 per cent read it regularly at home, nonconformists more than others.

Church groups   About 22 per cent belong to church groups, 33 per cent for nonconformists (Social Surveys, 1964).

Beliefs

Since social surveys have been carried out only during recent years, it is not possible to trace changes in beliefs very far back.

12

Belief in God   There have been a number of surveys since 1947. Since there are a variety of results at each period it is impossible to distinguish between historical shifts and sampling errors: between 1947 and 1965 about 80 per cent of the British population said they believed in God. Of these about half believed in a God who is a kind of person who watches over each of us, and half in 'some sort of spirit or vital force which controls life' (Social Surveys, 1964; ITA, 1970). This second image of God was more prevalent in later surveys, for younger people and members of the Church of England.

Belief in an after-life   Between 1947 and 1965 a number of surveys found that about 45 per cent of the British population believed in an after-life. Gorer (1955) found from a large English volunteer sample that 47 per cent believed in an after-life. When asked what it would be like, of those who believed in it 13 per cent referred to a scriptural heaven and hell, with judgment, plus another 9 per cent without judgment; 15 per cent had very material ideas of heaven as being like this life with the unpleasant features omitted and with endless leisure (e.g. no washing-up); 25 per cent believed in some kind of reincarnation; and 12 per cent looked forward to rejoining loved-ones; some used more than one category.

Other beliefs   Representative and averaged findings from recent social surveys are as shown in Table 2.2.

TABLE 2.2   *Religious beliefs in Britain*

Jesus Christ is the Son of God	64%
Jesus can save sins	'certain' 30%, plus 'probably' 36%
The Devil	18%
	(higher for Catholics: 67%)
Hell	20%
The miracles in the Bible really happened	'certain' 25%
Literal truth of the Bible	10%

There is little information about changes in these beliefs. The number of people believing in the Devil appears to have declined from 34 per cent in 1957 to about 24 per cent or less now (ITA, 1970, and other sources).

It is interesting to find that there is often inconsistency between these beliefs, or between beliefs and practices. Mass Observation (1947) found, for example, that over 25 per cent of those who did

13

not believe in God prayed occasionally, and some believed in the divinity of Christ; many who went to church and believed in God did not believe in an after-life, or that Christ was more than a man. This may be thought to cast some doubt on the value of social survey data in this field. On the other hand, the same kind of inconsistency has also been found for political attitudes (Butler and Stokes, 1969).

Donations

In 1962 donations to the Church of England were 2s. 7d. per week for each member of the electoral rolls, about 1·6 per cent of income.

Summary

There has been a definite decline in religious activity in Britain, in terms of church membership and attendance. This is more marked for the nonconformist churches than for the Church of England, while the Catholics and certain sects have shown continuous expansion. In recent years some of the practices of these sects have been adopted by the larger churches. Pentecostalism is reflected in the 'charismatic movement' found in the Roman Catholic and some Protestant churches. Although only about 15 per cent of the population go to church weekly (compared with about 25 per cent in 1900), many others go less often, watch services on television and claim to pray daily. The Church of England in particular has a lot of members who attend regularly, but less than once a week. A high proportion continue to hold central beliefs, though there is evidence of some shift towards seeing God more as a spirit than as a person, and of a decline of belief in the Devil. Most people want their children to be taught Christian religion in schools. Many more send them to Sunday School, and teach them to pray, than go to church or pray themselves. Overall there has clearly been a decline of religious activity since 1900, but this has been partly a decline in the number of services religious people attend, and a shift to more passive forms of worship.

This gradual decline has been interpreted by some observers in terms of 'secularization' (Wilson, 1966). By this is meant a continual reduction in the influence of religion on society and people's lives as the result of the rise of science and technology, the replacement of village life by city life, and other such factors. In Britain religion has become a 'compartmentalized marginal item in the society' (Wilson, 1966, p. 114). Another aspect of this is the clergy's loss of status and power. A recent survey found that few people would turn to a clergyman in distress, except for two kinds of problem: marital problems and fear of death (ITA, 1970).

A British poll dealing with the decrease in religious influence was conducted twice, in 1965 and 1967. The results are reported in Table 2.3. However, as Martin (1967) points out, the majority of

TABLE 2.3   *Replies to the question: 'Do you think that religion as a whole is increasing or decreasing its influence? (Percentages in a sample of British adults)*

Reply/year	1965	1967
Increasing	11	9
Same	20	19
Decreasing	55	65
Don't know	14	8

Source: Gallup Polls, 1965, 1967.

people still retain central Christian beliefs and go to church occasionally. Although committed religious people are few, there are many more who are nominally Christians, though it probably has little effect on their lives.

Religious activity in the USA

We have evidence on several indices of religious activity levels in the USA during all or part of this period. The different measures will be presented separately, and the overall conclusions will be discussed at the end.

Church membership

As a percentage of the general population this rose from 36 per cent in 1900 to 62 per cent in 1972. However, as has been observed earlier, the notion of 'member' has been variously defined over this period, and has tended to become more inclusive. Before the USA government Census of Religious Bodies in 1926 the basis for reporting membership in religious bodies was different. Several churches before 1926 used to report only heads of families as members, while others counted all baptized persons, including infants, as members. Thus, general membership figures for the years before 1930 are not computed on the same basis as those for the years since 1930. Table 2.4 presents church membership figures as a percentage of

15

the USA general population, based only on statistics supplied by the various religious organizations in the USA, which have used their own criteria for the definition of membership. The religious organizations reporting included Protestant denominations, the Roman Catholic church, Eastern Orthodox churches, and Jewish congregations.

TABLE 2.4 *Percentage of the US population who were church members 1900–72*

1900	1910	1920	1930	1940	1950	1955	1960	1962
36	43	43	47	49	57	60·9	63·6	63·4

1963	1964	1965	1967	1968	1969	1970	1972
64	64·9	64·3	64·4	63·2	63·1	62·4	62·0

Source: National Council of Churches of Christ in the USA, 1957–73.

A study of other data suggests that this apparent increase in church membership may be due to the inclusion of different age-groups at different periods. A better index is the percentage of people aged thirteen and above who are church members. This has the additional advantage of putting different denominations on the same footing, since the proportion of members under thirteen reported by different churches varies greatly. This calculation has been carried out for several years, and the results are presented in Table 2.5.

TABLE 2.5 *Percentage of the US population aged 13 and over who are church members*

1906	1916	1926	1930	1935	1940	1950	1960	1970	1972
55	55	52·7	53·4	52·1	50·7	61	64	64	62·4

Source: *Yearbook of American Churches.*

The figures in Table 2.5 show a different trend from that presented in Table 2.4. It becomes clear that the level of membership at the beginning of the century was actually much higher, and the overall gain is smaller. Instead of a continuous increase, there is actually a slight decline between 1900 and 1940, and since then a sharp rise. The figures here support the notion of an American revival after

1940. Lipset (1959) opposed the notion of a post-World War II religious revival in the USA, and suggested that American religious institutions have been marked by their stability over time. He emphasizes the unreliability of religious statistics as measures of long-term trends. Demerath (1968) concludes that most religious growth in the USA in recent decades occurred in conservative Protestant groups and small sects. This is in accordance with the general explanation given by Wilson (1966) for the viability and development of sects in modern society.

Reported frequency of church attendance

This has been obtained through public opinion polls since 1939. Table 2.6 shows the percentage of adult interviewees replying affirmatively to the question 'Did you, yourself, happen to go to church this last Sunday?' over a period of 31 years, between 1939 and 1970. This rather unreliable measure shows a trend of increase during the 1950s, with the peak in 1958, and a decline since then.

TABLE 2.6   *Percentage of the US adult population reporting weekly church attendance 1939–71*

1939	1940	1942	1947	1950	1954	1955	1956	1957	1958	1959
41	37	36	45	39	45	49	66	47	49	47

1960	1961	1962	1963	1964	1965	1966	1967	1968	1969	1970	1971
48	47	46	46	45	44	44	45	43	42	42	40

Source: Gallup, 1972.

The limited reliability of public opinion poll data and the respondents' tendency to exaggerate become clear when we are able to check responses against another source. One example was provided by a Gallup Poll in June 1954, which asked respondents to indicate whether they were church members: 79 per cent replied affirmatively (Gallup, 1972), while on the basis of official church statistics for the same period (National Council of Churches of Christ in the USA, 1955) we would expect only about 60 per cent to report membership. Nevertheless, the partial validity of reported attendance figures is shown by the changes they show over time, and the differences among denominations reflected in them. For example, the decline of 12 per cent in reported attendance between

17

1958 and 1969 was not equally felt by the different denominations. Decline among Catholics during those eleven years was 11 per cent, while for Protestants it was only 6 per cent; for Jews, 8 per cent.

TABLE 2.7   *Religious participation by religious affiliation in a sample of white American men, 1966*

Religious Group	Attend church once a week or more*	Highly devotional†
	%	%
Protestant	27·5	32·7
Congregational	40·0	30·0
Episcopal	20·5	20·6
Presbyterian	25·3	32·0
Non-denominational	20·0	11·1
Methodist	22·8	31·9
Lutheran	33·6	41·3
Protestant, no denom.	9·4	21·9
Baptist	26·0	33·4
Church of Christ	56·3	31·3
Other fundamentalist	53·4	53·3
Roman Catholic	71·2	53·6
Eastern Orthodox	33·3	33·4
Jew	3·4	17·2
No preference, other	0·0	5·2
Percentage of total sample	44·1	40·2

* Respondents were asked: 'Now referring to religion again, about how often, if ever, have you attended religious services in the last year?' For each group, the proportion of people who answered 'more than once a week' or 'once a week' is given.

† Devotionalism, following Lenski (1963, pp. 25–6, 57–60), was measured by summing up the answers to two questions: (1) 'When you have decisions to make in your everyday life, do you ask yourself what God would want you to do—often, sometimes, or never?' (2) 'Which of these described most accurately how often you yourself pray? (*a*) more than once a day, (*b*) once a day, (*c*) once or twice a week, (*d*) rarely, (*e*) never.' Respondents were considered highly devotional who said they prayed at least once or twice a week and considered God's wishes often or that they considered His wishes sometimes and prayed daily.

Source: Laumann (1969).

There are differences in religious participation according to religious affiliation, as Table 2.7 shows. These differences in religious activities are consistent with those reported in other studies (e.g. Lenski, 1963), and reveal interesting differences among denominations. It can be observed that Jews are extremely low on measures of religious participation, followed by Protestants without denomination. Catholics and members of Protestant fundamentalist groups are the highest on church attendance and 'devotionalism', and can be regarded as less secularized. It is likely that religious factors will be more influential in affecting behaviour in these groups.

Attitudes towards the church

These have been assessed in repeated surveys on several occasions. Roper (cited by Herberg, 1955, p. 64) carried out national surveys in 1942, 1947 and 1950 on attitudes toward religious leaders. The percentage of people saying that these leaders were doing the most good for the country at the present time (as compared with government and business leaders, etc.) increased from 17·5 to 32·6 per cent and 40 per cent for the years mentioned.

A measure of public attitudes toward religion as a social institution was obtained by repeated public opinion surveys (Gallup, 1972), which asked the respondents to reply to the question: 'At the present time, do you think religion as a whole is increasing its influence on American life, or losing its influence?' Table 2.8 shows the percentage of those answering 'losing' to this question, over a period of fourteen years.

TABLE 2.8 *Is religion losing its influence on American life? Percentage of those answering affirmatively*

1957	1962	1965	1967	1968	1970
14	31	45	57	67	75

Source: Gallup (1972).

Given other indications of religious beliefs and practices, and even considering the limited validity of the findings, the changes over fourteen years are striking. They may indicate that Americans are able to differentiate between their beliefs and practices, and the real impact of religion as a social institution.

Beliefs

These have also been repeatedly surveyed by several investigators. Public opinion surveys provide findings on the reported frequency of holding the main religious beliefs. Tables 2.9 and 2.10 show the prevalence of beliefs in God and the after-life in the American population, and indicate wide acceptance of both.

TABLE 2.9 *Percentage of US adult population replying 'Yes' to the question: 'Do you personally believe in a God?'*

	1944	1948	1954	1968
	96	94	96	98

Source: Gallup (1972).

How are we to interpret these findings, and how shall we use them? Demerath and Hammond (1969) suggest that the high percentages of positive answers to the 'belief in God' question in public opinion polls in the USA 'may mean only that more than nine out of ten answer questions from strangers, so as to avoid the stigma of a nonconformist, atheistic No' (p. 123). They also suggest that in the USA 'many feel obliged to scoff publicly at disbelief even though they themselves are disbelievers in private' (p. 123). Thus, these high percentages indicate the existence of a strong norm which calls for public manifestations of religious beliefs (cf. Demerath and Levinson, 1971). The use of public opinion data is meaningful for our purposes in the light of two considerations. First, as suggested above, they give us an indication of the degree to which certain beliefs are considered important or authoritative. Second, when comparative data are available, as in the next section, these findings are significant in indicating differences in national norms of legitimate and acceptable public beliefs.

TABLE 2.10 *Percentage of US adult interviewees who replied 'Yes' to the question: 'Do you believe there is a life after death?'*

	1936	1944	1948	1960	1961	1968
	64	76	68	74	74	73

Sources: Gallup (1972); Cantril (1951).

More sophisticated analyses reflected in Table 2.11 and Table 2.12 show that the certainty with which Americans hold their basic religious beliefs depends on their denominational membership, among other things. All the respondents whose answers are recorded in these tables were active church members. However, there were clear differences in the degree of certainty or doubt which they expressed regarding beliefs in God, the Devil and after-life.

TABLE 2.11 *Belief in God, the Devil, and life beyond death, by denomination, in a nationwide American sample, 1966*

	'I know God really exists and I have no doubts about it.'	Absolutely sure there is a Devil	Absolutely sure there is a life beyond death
	%	%	%
Unitarian (9)	22	0	0
Congregational (44)	63	7	26
United Presbyterian (75)	67	20	36
Protestant Episcopal (56)	72	21	35
Methodist (217)	78	33	42
Presbyterian Church USA (40)	70	35	43
Disciples of Christ (42)	73	29	42
American Lutheran bodies (146)	70	31	52
Total moderate Protestants [628]	**72**	**27**	**41**
Lutheran, Missouri Synod (45)	70	44	50
Evangelical and Reformed (28)	71	39	50
American Baptist (91)	82	47	41
Southern Baptist (187)	93	55	65
Other Baptist bodies (90)	86	55	59
Sects (128)	90	61	67
Total conservative Protestants [569]	**86**	**53**	**59**
Total Protestants (1,197)	79	40	50
Catholics (507)	85	36	48

Source: Glock and Stark (1966).

TABLE 2.12 *Responses to the question: 'How strongly do you feel about your religious beliefs?' by religion, for white American adults, 1965*

Religion	Very strongly	Strongly	Moderately	Less than moderately	N
	%	%	%	%	
Protestant	42	23	28	7	830
Catholic	50	21	24	5	332
Jewish	25	19	45	11	36

Source: Alston (1973).

Several longitudinal and comparative studies of religious attitudes and beliefs in college students over the last few decades are available. College students were used because of their ready availability to the researchers, and do not represent the general population. Nevertheless, changes in religious attitudes over a long span of time should be significant and possibly reflect changes in the wider society. For example, Heath (1969) measured religious attitudes in the entering class of a small liberal arts college between 1948 and 1968. The data over twenty years show a clear decline in religious orthodoxy and a decline in positive value given to the religious way of life. Table 2.13 presents some of Heath's findings.

TABLE 2.13 *Percentages of believers in three religious tenets, in 1948 and 1968, among American freshmen*

	1948	1968
Belief in God	79	58
Belief in life after death	46	34
Belief in the Second Coming of Jesus Christ	29	20

Source: Heath (1969).

Hoge (1971a, 1971b) carried out the most extensive replication study of religious attitudes and beliefs in American students. Between 1966 and 1968 he carried out replications of earlier questionnaire studies, some dating back to 1906, in twelve American colleges and universities. The longest time period between the first and second survey was sixty-two years, the shortest nineteen years. The results in all groups were summarized as indicating a long-term liberalization of religious attitudes and a decrease in traditional religious activity.

Donations

As a percentage of individual incomes these show a sharp fall between 1929 and 1943, followed by a steep rise from 1943 to 1952 (Information Service, 1954). This is further evidence for a revival at this period, and dates its onset as 1943–4. In view of the widely voiced allegation that American religion is shallow and does not affect people's lives, it is interesting to see how much money people give to churches. In 1966–7, 1·4 per cent of income, for the whole population, was given to churches; church members gave an average of $127 per year; different surveys found that 8–15 per cent of various groups gave 10 per cent or more of their income to churches. The amounts given varied between denominations, as shown in Table 2.14.

TABLE 2.14 *Weekly donations to American churches in 1966–7*

	Over $15	*$4–15*	*$1–4*
	%	%	%
Roman Catholics	2	20	63
All Protestants	10	39	40
Southern Baptists	32	35	20
Sects	28	44	18
American Baptists	15	57	19
Disciples of Christ	12	50	32
American Lutherans	8	40	39
Episcopalians	7	33	46
Presbyterians	6	36	49
Methodists	6	39	41
Congregationalists	1	47	42

Source: Moberg (1971).

Articles in periodicals

Analysis of periodical articles shows a gradual decline in the proportion between 1905 and 1931 that were favourable to religion (Hart, 1933). Another way of analysing periodicals is to study the number and favourability of articles on particular aspects of religion. Several separate changes took place in the first thirty years of the century. (1) There was a decline of interest in traditional dogmas. For example, articles about the after-life fell from 0·057 to 0·015 per cent during this period, and of these the percentage of favourable articles fell from 78 to 7 per cent. Similar results obtain for other theological matters such as atonement, the divinity of Christ, the Bible, baptism and the Devil. (2) Interest in the church declined.

23

In particular, articles on church work in women's magazines disappeared between 1905 and 1932. The proportion and favourability of articles on the church, church unity, missions and Sunday Schools all declined considerably. (3) There was an increase in the number of articles on the connection between religion and ethics, politics, social problems and war. This reached a peak of $0 \cdot 14$ per cent of all articles during the depression of 1932, compared with $0 \cdot 017$ per cent in 1929 and $0 \cdot 043$ per cent in 1935. (4) A similar increase was observed in the number of publications on the relation between religion and science. Science is no longer regarded as an enemy of religion. (5) Finally, there was an increase in articles about prayer, spiritual life and worship, the parts of religion that are based on personal experience.

Similar results were obtained by Crawford (1938), who compared hymns used in 1836 with those used in 1935. Hymns on the subject of fear were replaced by others on love and gratitude; hymns on traditional dogmas fell from $44 \cdot 6$ to $11 \cdot 7$ per cent of the total; hymns on the humanity of Jesus rose from $1 \cdot 9$ to $8 \cdot 5$ per cent.

In brief, there seems to have been a change between 1900 and 1930 in the direction of a more open-minded religion based on personal experience rather than on dogma, and allowing the questioning and examination of beliefs and their social consequences (Hart, 1933, 1942).

Denominational changes

The distribution of church membership as analysed in Table 2.15 shows a steady increase in the number of Catholics until 1960, when the position began to stabilize.

TABLE 2.15   *The relative percentage of Protestants, Catholics and church members in general, as percentages of the US population, for selected years*

	1926	1940	1950	1960	1965
Protestants	27·0	28·7	33·8	35·4	35·6
Catholics	16·0	16·1	18·9	23·3	23·8
All church members	45·0	49·0	57·0	63·0	64·3

Source: National Council of Churches of Christ in the USA (1967).

The main Protestant denominations have increased in size, but not in proportion with the population. However, if the small Protestant sects are taken separately, a very different picture emerges.

Many of these sects—the Pentecostal, Holiness, Nazarene churches and others—have increased enormously in proportion to their size during this period (cf. Table 2.16). The charismatic movement in the main American churches is probably stronger than in Britain.

TABLE 2.16   *The growth of Pentecostal sects in the USA*

1906	1916	1926	1936	1956
1,000	22,000	126,000	350,000	1,500,000

Source: Wilson (1970).

Summary

Since 1900, there has been little change in church membership and attendance, though there was a revival between 1945 and 1960. The beliefs of students have become more liberal, fewer believing in traditional dogma; however, most of the population still hold the main Christian beliefs. It is now widely thought that religion is losing its influence, and many observers think that much American religion is less 'religious' than it was, a kind of passive acceptance that does not influence conduct. There have been changes in denominational composition, with a steady increase in Catholicism, a rapid increase of some of the small sects, and little change among the main Protestant bodies.

Comparison of religious activity in Great Britain and the USA

Surveys of religious beliefs and practices in Great Britain and the USA have been carried out during the same period with exactly the same questions put to representative samples of both populations. The period 1962–70 will be taken, since a number of reliable surveys were conducted in each country during those years. Table 2.17 gives the results of these surveys, including only those items for which exactly comparable data exist, and taking averages where more than one result is available.

It is clear that in terms of membership and attendance there is much more religious activity in the USA than in Britain. There are comparable differences for beliefs in the Devil and hell, while belief in God is more similar in the two countries. These clear differences need an explanation. The fact that the two countries share to a large extent a common cultural and religious heritage, and the fact that both are advanced industrial societies undergoing secularization, are going to make our explanatory task more demanding and complex. Historical, sociological and psychological elements must play a role in causing these differences. Both the history and current functions of religious behaviour should be considered.

The difference in patterns of church attendance and church membership between the USA and Great Britain fits with the general pattern of secularization in Europe, described by Berger and Luckmann (1963), as follows: 'In Europe, despite the survival of various degrees of legal establishment in various countries, popular participation in organized religion lags considerably behind the conspicuous piety of the [trans] Atlantic masses' (p. 417).

TABLE 2.17 *Comparison of Great Britain and the USA on several indicators of religiosity*

	Great Britain	USA
	%	%
Church members	21·3 (1966)	62·0 (1972)
Weekly attendance	15	42 (1970)
Frequent prayer	44	63
Belief in God	74 (1973)	98 (1968)
Belief in after-life	37 (1973)	73 (1968)
Belief in hell	20 (1973)	65 (1968)
Belief in the Devil	18 (1973)	60 (1968)
Donations (% of income)	1·6 (1962)	2·3 (1966–7)

From various surveys, cited in the text.

What needs explanation is the consistently higher level of religiosity in the USA, on every measure used. Historical and sociological factors used in explaining the level of religiosity in the USA include immigration and ethnicity, and the characteristics of American urbanization and secularization. Psychological factors, which are related to the ones mentioned above and result from them, include the needs of individuals in American society for security and identity. Religion as an identity component for the individual is mentioned more often in connection with the situation in the USA because of the many religious groups, with different national origins or racial composition.

Wilson (1966) states that religious statistics in the USA and Great Britain can hardly be compared, since they do not have the same meaning in both societies. He offers a historical-sociological explanation of the differences in the secularization processes in both countries, starting with the fact of an Established Church in England, and the strict separation of church and state in the USA. Secularization in England, according to Wilson, took the form of a decline in religious activity and church membership. In the USA it took the form of the absorption of churches by society, with the loss of distinctive religious content, and with membership becoming a matter of social conformity and respectability; there is less denominational loyalty in the USA, and much more mobility between denominations, than there is in Britain.

Luckmann (1967) provides a clear formulation of the differences in the secularization process in the USA and in Europe, which helps us explain these differences. According to Luckmann, traditional church religion in Europe kept its religious functions and was pushed to the periphery of modern life, while in the USA church religion has undergone a process of internal secularization, which has kept it 'modern' and visible. Most of the functions—be they social, psychological, or cultural—fulfilled by American churches should be considered secular rather than religious in the traditional sense (Berger, 1961).

The relationship between religion and political symbols in the USA is a paradoxical one. Despite the strict separation of church and state, references to religion by public officials in a direct and ceremonial way are frequent, forming what has become known as a 'civil religion' (Bellah, 1967), or a 'civic religion' (Parsons, 1966). Political leaders also make public statements which favour religiosity and religious activities. Thus President Eisenhower suggested that it is more important to have 'a deeply felt religious faith—and I don't care what it is' (quoted in Herberg, 1955, p. 84). Another president, Richard Nixon, called for a renewal of 'our faith in God' in a political speech to the American nation (Nixon, 1973, p. 7).

The existence of Socialist parties in Great Britain has been suggested as a partial explanation for the lower church attendance among the poorer classes there (Glock and Stark, 1965). It is clear that more people in Great Britain than in the USA identify themselves as members of the working class, and most of them support the Labour Party. As Table 2.18 shows, there is a relationship between party preference, social class identification, and church attendance. The lowest percentage of attenders is among those who identify with both the working class and the Labour Party. Glock and Stark (1965, p. 199) concluded that 'the strength of lower-class radicalism in Great Britain partly accounts for lower-class religious apathy'.

It is highly probable that Socialism in Great Britain has been one of the forces which have shaped the course of secularization there. Wilson (1966) points to the historical tie between political dissent and religious nonconformity in England, which gave rise to several working-class religious movements, before the rise of a working-class political movement. The Labour Party was described by Wilson (1966) as 'a party inheriting something of the old Nonconformist conscience as well as a certain secularist tradition' (p. 60). No secularist movement of any consequence has ever existed in the USA.

The psychological satisfactions provided by church activities in the USA are discussed by Herberg (1955) and Wilson (1966). In an impersonal, tension-ridden society the local church provides a supportive community and a temporary, even illusory, shelter from the rough, rational and demanding society around it.

TABLE 2.18   *Subjective class, party preference, and church attendance in Great Britain, 1957*

Class	attending at least 'now and again'		Other and don't know
	Tory	Labour	
	%	%	%
Upper	82 (17)	* (1)	* (8)
Upper-middle	74 (96)	* (13)	79 (29)
Middle	62 (255)	40 (94)	53 (124)
Lower-middle	56 (101)	47 (120)	57 (62)
Working	54 (122)	33 (449)	43 (177)

* Following the usual convention, no cell with fewer than 15 cases has been percentaged.

Source: Stark (1964).

A related explanation for the greater level of religious affiliation and religious activity in the USA has been that of the 'third generation return' (Bender and Kagiwada, 1968). This notion of the changes in religio-ethnic behaviour in immigrant groups has been formulated as: 'what the son wishes to forget the grandson wishes to remember', known as Hansen's law (Hansen, 1952). Herberg (1955) applied Hansen's law to the revival in religious activity following World War II. According to this view, churches were seen as the embodiment and the source for religio-ethnic identity. Lenski (1963) found some indications of growing religiosity in the third generation, but without a decline in the second generation. The data seemed to indicate a consistent increase in religious activity across successive generations. Lazerwitz and Rowitz (1964) also found some support for the successive growth notion, but indicated that the generational index was insufficient to measure religious change.

At the individual level, the 'triple melting pot' (Protestant-Catholic-Jew) is reflected in the pressure to maintain a religious affiliation as a part of one's identity and one's close relationships. The individual identifies himself within a religio-ethnic sub-group within the larger society, and most of his intimate relationships are included within the sub-group (Lenski, 1963). According to Herberg (1955) identification with religious groups is increasing in the USA because Americans feel alienated and unidentified unless they belong to one of the major religious divisions.

Church membership in the USA has the connotation of respectability, status and belonging, and serves as a way of identification with the middle class (Berger, 1961; Herberg, 1955). It is part of the respectable middle-class life-style in the USA, and religious activity then becomes part of the sought-after social status. As the data show (see Chapter 10), there is indeed a pattern of religious activities which typifies those who are more prosperous economically, and may be regarded as more 'respectable'.

As a result of the various factors described above, religious participation on the part of the individual, and the family, becomes a means of affirming and maintaining both a culturally prescribed and a sub-cultural identity. By going to a particular church the individual is both a 'good American' and a good member of his particular religio-ethnic group.

In the light of the findings and the discussion presented so far, it is plausible to assume that there is a real difference in the character of religious activity between the two countries. Religion in America has become an American religion, which is mostly secularized, middle-class and supportive of an individual and national 'good image', while religion in Great Britain has maintained its traditional character, and changes in the world around it have brought about its decline.

3 Environmental and situational factors

Parental attitudes

There can be no doubt that the attitudes of parents are among the most important factors in the formation of religious attitudes. In several surveys of students in which subjects were asked what had been the most important influence on their religious beliefs, 'parents', 'home' or 'mother' were the most frequent answers given (e.g. Cavanaugh, 1939). These reports are substantiated by correlations with the actual beliefs of parents. Newcomb and Svehla (1937) gave Thurstone scales to the parents and children of 548 families, the ages of the children ranging from 14 to 38 (see Table 3.1).

TABLE 3.1   *Parent-child correlations in religious and political attitudes*

	Church	Communism
Fathers-sons	0·64 (0·18)	0·54 (0·08)
Fathers-daughters	0·65 (0·21)	0·62 (0·47)
Mothers-sons	0·58 (0·24)	0·58 (0·50)
Mothers-daughters	0·69 (0·46)	0·49 (0·24)

The partial correlations eliminating the effects of the other parent are given in brackets.

Source: Newcomb and Svehla (1937). Reproduced by permission of Professor Newcomb.

Factors affecting parental influence

The effects of parental attitudes and beliefs on those of their children vary with a number of factors.

30

Denomination There are clear differences among denominations in the effectiveness of religious training. We can measure this effectiveness by looking at the endurance of beliefs, or the percentage of those who are still loyal to their parents' religion when they come of age. Table 3.2 summarizes the results of three studies which asked respondents to report on both their parents' and their own religious affiliation.

TABLE 3.2   *Percentage of young adults who reported the same religious affiliation as their parents*

Study Religion	Bell (1938)	Allport et al. (1948)	Stark (1963)
Catholic	92·7	85	85
Protestant	69·0	40	71
Jewish	62·0	40	65

As Table 3.2 indicates, Catholic religious training seems to be the most successful in terms of endurance, and Jewish training the least successful. The respondents in all three studies had been exposed to additional influences, such as education, and the results show how well the religious training withstood the effects of time and other influences.

It seems likely that effectiveness of socialization is related to the amount of initial emphasis put by the parents on religious training. Some relevant data were obtained by Srole *et al.* (1962) in a survey of New York residents. Respondents were asked about the importance of religion to their parents. 67 per cent of Catholics, 40 per cent of the Protestants and only 31 per cent of the Jewish respondents described religion as important to their parents. We may also hypothesize that religious training in Catholic families starts earlier than in other groups.

Relationship between parents and children Children who like, identify with, or have a close relationship with their parents, are more likely to adopt parental attitudes. Erickson (1962) found that the religiosity of children was a joint effect of parental religiosity and identification with parent.

First-born children have on average a closer relationship with their parents than other children. MacDonald (1969) found that first-born children were more often religious, as compared with later-born children. Weigert and Thomas (1972) found that a high degree of parental support was associated with conformity and

31

TABLE 3.3   *Mean religiosity scores of 198 students as a function of parental religiosity and identification with parents*

		Identification with parents	
		high	low
Parental	high	2·72	2·03
religiosity	low	1·56	1·31

Source: Erickson (1962).

religiosity in adolescents, and that Catholic American ado lescent reported attending church to satisfy parental expectations.

Living at home   In the Newcomb and Svehla study the high correlations are partly because most of the children were still living at home. Other studies of young people who have left home produced rather lower correlations, e.g. 0·29 (Hirschberg and Gilliland, 1942), 0·39 (Woodward, 1932). Chesser (1956) found the religious practices of single women more similar to those of their parents than was the case with married women: this presumably reflects the results of living at home.

Influence of mother versus father   Comparing the influence of the two parents, a number of studies show the greater impact of the mother. In the surveys of Catholic students at Notre Dame University Cavanaugh (1939) found that twelve times as many named their mother as named their father as the greatest influence on their religious beliefs. Newcomb and Svehla (1937) give separate correlations with each parent, and also partial correlations, holding the attitude of other parent constant. These are shown in Table 3.1. While there is only a slight difference in the uncorrected correlations, the partial correlations for the mother are considerably higher, this being largely due to the strong mother-daughter relationship.

Relations in the family   The effect of parents is greater if they hold the same religious beliefs (Lenski, 1953; Putney and Middleton, 1961). When parents disagree about religion, the children are more likely to rebel in this sphere, and more likely to follow the mother than the father (Bell, 1938), as would be expected from the findings about the greater influence of the mother.

Parents influence the religious outlook of their children in a second quite different way, through their methods of child-rearing. There

32

appears to be some evidence for a direct connection between child-rearing and beliefs. In two cross-cultural studies of primitive societies, it has been found that when parents are punitive people believe in punitive gods, while where parents are kinder they believe in loving gods (Spiro and D'Andrade, 1958; Lambert *et al.*, 1959). In another cross-cultural study, Terry (1971) found that monotheistic beliefs were associated with strong independence training. However, it is not clear from these studies which is the direction of causation; child-rearing does not necessarily generate the beliefs.

Later we shall review research on the similarity between images of God and images of parents (p. 183f).

Educational influences

Several studies have been made of the effects of American parochial schools. Johnstone (1966), in a study of Lutheran schools, found that these schools had little effect on religious knowledge and behaviour, if parental attitudes were held constant. However, the schools did have some effect for parents who had little contact with the church. On the other hand, Greeley and Rossi (1966) found that Roman Catholic schools did have an effect independent of that of the parents.

Similar considerations apply to the effects of Sunday School. In Woodward's study (1932), later conservatism of belief correlated 0·43 with Sunday School attendance and only 0.39 with measures of parental religious activity. If Newcomb and Svehla's suggestions (1937) are correct the Sunday School would be one of the main religious institutions to which parents introduce their children. Several British studies cast some doubt on this hypothesis. Cauter and Downham (1954) found no difference at all between parents who did and did not go to church in the proportions sending their children to Sunday School. Gorer (1955) found that the religious practices of parents affected whether they taught the children to pray, but had little effect on whether they sent them to Sunday School. Chesser (1956) discovered that about half the married women in his sample imposed their own churchgoing habits on their children, the rest either sent the children more often than they went themselves (25 per cent), or less often (16 per cent). Hyde (1956) reports a survey of 500 Free Church (i.e. nonconformist) Sunday Schools: it was found that the younger they joined, the later the pupils stayed; only about 14 per cent of the members eventually joined the church; 'Family churches', in which church and Sunday School are combined and where more parents attend, retained children for longer, and more joined the church.

A higher level of formal education has been found to be positively related to formal church membership and church attendance (Cantril, 1943), because of its effect on a person's social class, and to be negatively related to the holding of traditional beliefs (Ford, 1960), because of the presumed liberalizing effects of education. The positive relationship between education and church attendance is presented in Table 3.4.

TABLE 3.4 *Education and weekly church attendance in the USA, 1947-70: percentage reporting church attendance in the previous week*

Educational Level	1947	1954	1957	1964	1967	1970
College	49	51	53	50	48	46
High School	45	47	52	44	44	41
Grade School	43	43	48	43	43	41

Source: Gallup (1972).

The effects of education on specific beliefs has been studied most extensively in the case of college students. During their years at college many students become more religious, less religious, or religious in a different way. A large number of studies have been carried out, mostly in the USA; some of them were follow-up studies, others were comparisons of students at different stages, in different colleges and universities. It is usually found that there is an overall shift towards less religious attitudes and beliefs, but that this is composed of a greater number of changes in opposite directions. For example, Ferman (1960) compared the beliefs about God of 895 Cornell students in their first year in 1950, and in their second year in 1952. The last three columns of Table 3.5 compare the numbers who later adopted each belief (recruits) with those who abandoned it (defectors). Although quite a number of students were recruited to believe in a 'Power greater than myself', nearly as many abandoned this belief.

If the overall average changes are examined, there is a highly consistent trend towards a lower level of church attendance and a lower level of religious beliefs and attitudes. These studies show that students in their later years are less orthodox, less fundamentalist, less likely to believe in God and to think of him as a person, more liberal in religious beliefs, less moralistic, less favourable to the church; and they attach less importance to religious values (Feldman, 1969a). Similar changes are found in British studies, e.g. Poppleton and Pilkington (1963).

TABLE 3.5   *The beliefs about God of 895 Cornell students when in their first and third years at college*

	1st year %	3rd year %	defectors (N)	recruits (N)	recruits / defectors
Divine God	40	30	113	70	0·62
Power greater than myself	31	33	110	127	1·12
God as humanity	5	7	30	49	1·63
Natural Law	8	8	39	42	1·08
Not quite sure what I believe	12	13	74	88	1·19
Atheist	2	2	13	9	0·69
Other/agnostic	2	2	15	12	0·80

Source: Ferman (1960).

On the other hand, the number of students who become atheists or agnostics is small (see Table 3.5). They are more likely to modify their beliefs, in many cases to 'a God so tenuous and vague that, like certain very rare gases, it becomes highly enigmatic to say that He is "here at all" ' (McNees, in Leary *et al.*, 1960). Allport *et al.* (1948) found that 68 per cent of Harvard students and 82 per cent of Radcliffe students felt that they needed some form of religious orientation in order to achieve a fully mature philosophy of life. The most recent studies have found rather smaller shifts away from religion over the college year, possibly, because the attitudes of freshmen are more negative to start with (Jones, 1970).

These changes are not simply a result of general changes due to ageing: control studies of young people not at college show that similar changes occur, but to a much smaller degree. However, follow-up studies of alumni fifteen years or so later show that these effects are reversed. This may be the result of general ageing processes (see p. 65f); but, in the USA, if graduates are compared with non-graduates, the graduates are somewhat more active in religion. Thus, Feldman and Newcomb (1969) concluded that college brings about only a temporary decline in the orthodoxy of students' religious beliefs.

The norms of religious behaviour and beliefs vary considerably among colleges. For example, the percentage of students who go to church once a week varied from 49 per cent at Fisk to 20 per cent at Dartmouth; the percentage scoring high in a scale of religion (based on frequency of attendance, strength of belief and self-evaluated religiousness) varied from 96 per cent at the College of Our Lady of the Elms to 6 per cent at Amherst; the percentage reporting daily prayer varied from 74 per cent at Marquette to 7 per cent at Reed (Feldman, 1969b, from various sources). The effects of college norms on individual students is greater at small, homogeneous colleges or Catholic and other denominational colleges. Students at different colleges already vary between colleges when they first arrive; when they graduate there has been an accentuation of initial differences.

Religious changes also depend on the field of study. The results of a number of surveys of students of different faculties are shown in Table 3.6.

TABLE 3.6 *Religious values and orthodoxy for students in different fields*

	Religious value (Allport-Vernon)	Religious orthodoxy
Natural science	Low (except chemistry and biochemistry)	low
Humanities	medium and high	medium and high (except English)
Art, music, etc.	high	high
Social studies and psychology	low	low
Business administration	low	high
Engineering	high (2 studies only)	high
Education	high	high

Source: Feldman (1969b).

These results can partly be accounted for by variables which have not been held constant. For example, females are both more religious, and more likely to study arts, humanities and education than natural science or business administration. On the other hand, many women study social science and psychology. But do students study psychology because they are agnostics (or have associated characteristics), or do they become agnostics as a result of studying psychology? Several studies have found that initial differences between fields of study become accentuated (e.g. Arsenian, 1943), showing that both processes operate. Such differences are perpetuated within disciplines by direct or indirect influences. We discuss the religious beliefs of scholars and scientists in different fields later (p. 87f).

A number of other variables modify the effects of college on students: *denomination*: Roman Catholics change least, and least of all when at Catholic colleges; *sex*: Females are less likely to decrease in religiosity while at college, but are also more likely to move towards the college norms; *background factors*: It seems likely that changes are greatest when there is an intermediate degree of diverseness between the student background and the characteristics of the college, in social class, religious outlook and other respects (Feldman and Newcomb, 1969).

What is the explanation for the effects of college on religious behaviour and beliefs? The teaching and the attitudes of the teachers may be one factor. While there is no intention on the part of most colleges to oppose religious beliefs, they do encourage logical consistency, independence of authority and a sceptical attitude. There is a general shift towards more liberal and sophisticated views about religion and politics, and this is part of the student self-image. 'To be in step with these social expectations means for many of them a moving away from the moralism, the political cautiousness and the religious piety of the mass culture. Seen in this light, the loss of orthodoxy may be better understood as a rejection of the uncriticized norms of the wider culture and an embracing of those of the academic élite, than as a rejection of religion' (Havens, 1963, p. 57).

In particular colleges and fields of study, there are more specific educational goals and influences which may affect religious beliefs directly or indirectly. In some small colleges there is increased homogeneity of religious attitudes as students pass through; in others this does not happen, though attitude scores may bunch in a bi-modal or multi-modal distribution. This indicates the formation of two or more sub-groups within the college community with diferent norms about religion.

Changes may also be taking place at deeper levels of the personality. Intellectual conflicts, for example between science and religion, are often reported, especially by students in their first two years. The lower level of religious belief on the part of science students reflects this. In their later years at college, religious conflicts over behaviour and self-image become more common (Havens, 1963). Studies of values show that there is a widespread conflict between a concern with success and a concern with altruism and religion, both of course having extensive support in the culture (McCann, 1955). Conflicts about values and self-image become particularly important in the first year, when career decisions have to be taken. Webster, Freedman and Heist (1962) conclude from their study that students change towards freer expression of impulses, greater nonconformity and greater independence of authority. They may rebel against parental and religious authority, but they still feel the need for a religious outlook and have a concern for altruism as well as for success. Meanwhile they are exposed to a variety of intellectual and social influences, in a social setting in which beliefs are explicitly verbalized and consistency respected. They have the

37

difficult task of working out their own compromise solution to problems which the culture has not been able to resolve.

Social influence

There is evidence from a variety of sources showing that social influence by friends can affect religious beliefs. For example, 42 per cent of Starbuck's subjects (1899) said that they were converted as a result of social pressure or imitation. The importance of personal contact and emotional attachments as part of the religious conversion process was suggested by Lofland and Stark (1965). Whitam (1968b) performed a follow-up study in 1963 on teenagers who had 'decided for Christ' at a Billy Graham meeting in 1957. He found that the most important factor in the retention of religious commitment was the acquisition of new friends, and the second most important factor was parental reaction. Studies of college students show that many move towards the norms of their colleges or fields of study (p. 36), and that many more acknowledge the influence of other students on their religious activities (e.g. Smith, 1947).

The acceptance of specific persons or organizations as sources of authority is part of religious faith and part of the religious socialization process. This selective acceptance of authority has been demonstrated in experimental studies. Burtt and Falkenberg (1941) gave a religious attitude scale to 213 church members; subjects were told of the majority opinion, or of the views of a group of clergymen; both majority and expert opinions had a significant effect on opinions expressed during a second administration of the scale. Brown and Pallant (1962) found that Methodist Bible Class children were more influenced by the supposed opinions of a Methodist minister than by those of a Catholic priest.

Pallone (1964) showed that among Catholic subjects visual judgment can be influenced by the presence of religious authority surrogates. Landis (1949) in a study of the parents of 4,000 college students found that in a third of marriages between people of different religions one partner changed to the other's belief; it is interesting to note that the divorce rate was lower when this happened. Chesser (1956) found that married women resembled their parents in religious attitudes less than did single women: married women have left the influence of the parental group, and are influenced by their husbands.

The findings mentioned above show that religious attitudes are susceptible to social influences just like other attitudes and beliefs. The detailed empirical conditions for such attitude changes have been much studied, though rarely with religious attitudes. Whenever religious attitudes or beliefs have been used, they have been found to follow exactly the same empirical laws as other attitudes or beliefs.

Social influence is greater when the group is a reference group for a person, i.e. when he is keen to be accepted as a member of the group. Newcomb (1943) found more political conformity at Bennington College for the girls who were more concerned with acceptance at college than with acceptance at home. Brown and Freedman (1962), however, found a rather different pattern of influence operating at Vassar: the peer-orientated group did not change their religious and other attitudes so much as did those who were more involved with the faculty and their own future careers, in some cases because their backgrounds made them less acceptable to other students. At Vassar, unlike Bennington, faculty and student norms were different, with the result that overall attitude change was less (Havens, 1963).

Smith (1947) found that 48 per cent of theological students surveyed regarded their fellow students as a negative influence in religious matters, while only 5 per cent regarded them as a positive influence. These results would be accounted for by assuming that the subjects in each case were becoming more orthodox as a result of adult influences. Then the students might tend to conceal their growing orthodoxy from one another and thus exert a negative influence. In the Notre Dame surveys (Cavanaugh, 1939), student influence was mentioned most often as the cause of more frequent taking of communion. No mention was made of the teaching staff, as in the studies of Protestant students. There is usually more than one potential reference group in any environmental setting, and quite complex social psychological factors are relevant to how influential each will be.

Some people are more susceptible to social pressures than others: those who are very keen to be accepted by the group in question, with intermediate levels of intelligence and self-esteem, and without a clear structure of ideas in the relevant area (cf. McGuire, 1969). Smith, Bruner and White (1956) distinguish those people whose attitudes are primarily an adjustment to group standards from those whose attitudes are based on more internal personality dynamics. The former change their beliefs rapidly as they join new groups, whereas the others do not.

Groups can exert more influence over activities that are publicly observable by the group members, as several experiments show. Sometimes views are expressed in public which are different from those held in private: Schanck (1932) studied a Methodist community where people disapproved of tobacco, alcohol and cards, although many of the members indulged privately in these same things. It is noteworthy that religious beliefs are strictly unobservable since it is literally impossible to discover if a person really believes something or not.

39

Although people may first acquire attitudes through overt conformity to group standards, after a time internalization takes place; then private as well as public attitudes are affected. Kelman (1961) distinguished an intermediate stage between public compliance and internalization, which he called 'identification'. By this he meant a changed attitude or belief, which depends for its maintenance on a continuing relationship with the source of influence, such as a religious leader or a brainwasher.

Social influence is greatest upon beliefs which are vague and unstructured, and on matters about which the subject is ignorant. The contents of religious beliefs are extremely vague, as is shown by the diversity of interpretations given to the idea of the after-life (Gorer, 1955). Matters of religious practice—ritual, organization, etc.—are much more definite, and it would be expected that agreement over them would be more difficult.

It has never been satisfactorily explained why people should want to influence deviates or particular potential converts outside the group. Festinger et al. (1956) suggested that such people are motivated to manufacture social support for their own uncertain beliefs. One can imagine that, for example, the inmates of an old people's home would not be very happy with the views of a deviate who thought that there was no life after death. Festinger et al. studied an 'end of the world' cult, which twice revised the date of the end and set about finding new members, when their predictions had been proved false. This did not happen a third time, and has not happened in other cases. Nor do religious evangelists give the impression of being uncertain of their beliefs. However, we shall see later that individuals with orthodox religious views are often dogmatic and intolerant of other views about religion. They may also be genuinely concerned about the spiritual condition of others, and such concern has support in theology and the traditions of some churches, especially evangelical churches and certain sects.

Why do people change their mind as a result of social influence? The main factors are: (a) fear of being rejected as a deviate; (b) belief that others are experts; and (c) gradual cognitive changes as a result of exposure to a particular way of thinking and talking.

Social influence in the religious sphere is likely to take place under several conditions. First, a person may to some extent belong to a religious group, and accept the group or its leaders as sources of influence. Second, a person may join a religious group for other than religious reasons—he may like some of the members, for example. He will then be exposed to strong pressures towards conformity. Third, he may be influenced by other members of non-religious groups to which he belongs, such as work groups or educational groups; this is a more common situation, but here the pressures will be weaker since religion is not relevant to the group purposes.

Evangelistic meetings

In the early days of revivalism in America, and in campaigns like John Wesley's in England, wild emotional scenes were frequently reported. The evangelist would preach in a way calculated to produce great anxiety (Pratt, 1924, p. 178):

I preach hell because it arouses their fears, arrests their consciences and causes them to reform their lives and habits . . . . Hell has been running for six thousand years. It is filling up every day. Where is it? About eighteen miles from here. Which way is it? Straight down—not over eighteen miles, down in the bowels of the earth.

The emotions were further stirred by the singing of very moving hymns. The result was often devastating. Hundreds of those present would speak with tongues or bark, display violent jerking and twitching, while many collapsed senseless on the ground (Davenport, 1906). No figures are available, but the reports of these meetings indicate that a high proportion of those present were affected in the ways described and were converted, temporarily at least.

The most spectacular examples of this kind of evangelism in England are the three campaigns of Billy Graham in 1954–5, about which a certain amount of statistical and descriptive evidence is available.* The most startling aspect of these campaigns is the number of people affected: about $5\frac{1}{2}$ million attended the three campaigns, though some went more than once; it was estimated that half the audience were new at each meeting, which would cut the above figure to half. About 120,000 came forward and made 'decisions for Christ', of whom 75 per cent were making their first public decision and 61 per cent were not already church members, although according to Herron's survey (1955) only 48·6 per cent were genuine non-churchgoers. Thus about one person in fifty came forward, one in a hundred being a genuine convert; this percentage is probably much lower than for the earlier evangelists, supporting Sargant's hypothesis (see p. 44) although the total numbers were large. Two-thirds of those making decisions were women, and 60 per cent were under nineteen. Only 16 per cent regarded themselves as belonging to small sects or evangelical churches; 47 per cent were nonconformist, 37 per cent Church of England.

* We are indebted to Dr Erik Routley of Mansfield College, Oxford, for giving access to his collection of newspaper cuttings on this subject.

TABLE 3.7 *Percentages of audiences responding at Billy Graham's meetings*

	Average size of meeting	Number of meetings	Percentage making decisions
Graham's Harringay meetings 1954. First four weeks	11,600	33	2·30
Relay services during 1954 campaign	930	430	0·44
Meetings addressed by members of Graham's team 1954	410	425	1·15
Graham's Glasgow meetings 1955	16,000	16	2·39
Graham's Wembley meetings 1955	56,000	8	5·30

Computed from various figures given in Colquhoun (1955) and from figures released by the campaign organization.

Graham's campaign in New York in 1957 was similar. About 2 million people came to his meetings in Madison Square Garden, which has 19,000 seats; 56,246 made decisions (2·8 per cent) (Lang and Lang, 1960). Analysis of samples of those who came forward by Whitam (1968a) showed that those who made decisions mainly came from middle-class homes and were of white Anglo-Saxon or European origin. They belonged to the main Protestant churches, and 75 per cent were already regular church attenders. There were few blacks, Jews or members of other ethnic groups (Table 3.8). Thus about 50 per cent of British 'converts' and about 75 per cent of the Americans were already going to church regularly. Whitam concludes that most of those 'making decisions' were not being converted at all, but merely engaging in a religious ritual. However, as Glock (1962) points out, they may have shifted to a deeper level of emotional commitment, or to a changed set of beliefs. We can divide up those who made decisions into (*a*) the 50 per cent British and 25 per cent American who were not already churchgoers, though they were mostly nominal members of Protestant churches; (*b*) churchgoers who became more committed; and (*c*) those engaging in a religious ritual.

The next question to be raised concerns the permanence of evangelical conversions. Two careful follow-up studies have been carried out of Graham's campaigns, and these will be discussed first. Highet (1957) carried out censuses of church attendance in Glasgow before and after the campaign. Weekly attendance rose by 10,575 from 7·6 to 9·2 per cent of the adult population just after the campaign, and 4,197 new members came on to the church records during the next few months. However, a census of attendance carried out a year after the campaign showed that only 54 per cent of the new attenders were still going to church. Herron (1955) sent a questionnaire to 1,500 vicars listed by the Graham organization, after the Harringay campaign. Of these, 520 replied giving details of 3,222 individuals for whom cards had been received. It was found that 64 per cent of the people who had previously not been churchgoers were still attending about eight months after the campaign. This is consistent with the first in suggesting that about half the real converts are active a year later.

TABLE 3.8 *Comparison of religious identification among 'deciders' in Billy Graham's New York campaign, 1957, with religious identification and affiliation data for the New York metropolitan area, 1958*

Religious group	Religious identification metropolitan region 1958	Religious affiliation metropolitan region 1958	Religious preference of 'deciders'
	%	%	%
Protestant	28·0	16·0	90·7
Catholic	52·0	30·0	3·5
Jewish	18·0	18·0	0·3
Other	2·0	2·0	—
No affiliation or preference	—	34·0	5·5
TOTALS	100·0	100·0	100·0

Estimates of religious characteristics of NYC metropolitan region are from Protestant Council of the City of New York, Department of Church Planning and Research, *Religious Affiliation, New York City and Metropolitan Region*. Source: Whitam (1968a).

Starbuck (1899) reported that 87 per cent of a group of ninety-two revival converts had lapsed within six months, compared with 40 per cent of a group of 'gradual' converts. Wilson (1955) reports that at Elim Foursquare Gospel meetings in England after the War, about one in six of those converted actually become members of the church. This is consistent with Starbuck's finding that about one in eight is left after six months. We may suggest that just as a higher percentage of people respond at these highly emotional revival meetings, so these conversions are more short-lived.

43

Factors accounting for attitude change

The results discussed above can be explained in terms of the variables and processes known to account for attitude change in general. When changes of religious beliefs have been studied experimentally, the same principles have been found to apply.

Emotional v. *rational* Experimental studies find that emotional propaganda is more effective than rational, as for example in Hartmann's study (1936) of political propaganda. Sargant (1957) puts forward the interesting hypothesis that the most effective techniques first create states of emotional exhaustion in the hearers, and that people are extremely suggestible when in this condition. He lists the different methods of producing such exhaustion in different religious groups: the prolonged rhythmic dancing and drumming of Voodoo, the handling of poisonous snakes in Tennessee snake cults, and the deliberate concentration of excited evangelists on intended converts in small Protestant sects. Sargant maintains that people are suggestible to anything when emotionally fatigued, and reports that certain young men attend snake-cult meetings in order to seduce girls who have just been saved; they are just as easily seduced as saved at this juncture.

The combination of a high level of arousal and strong social pressure is effective in changing attitudes in a number of settings—brainwashing, psychotherapy, and religious healing—as well as religious conversion (Frank, 1961). At Graham's meetings, considerable use was made of music, highly emotional gospel hymns sung by the many thousands present, assisted by a choir of 1,500 and by various American singers. This partly explains why a much lower percentage of people came forward at the relayed meetings (Table 3.7).

Anxiety arousal It is found that up to a point the arousal of anxiety produces greater attitude or behavioural change, especially if specific requirements are stated (Leventhal *et al.*, 1965). But if too much anxiety is generated, as it may be for more anxious people, there may be avoidance of the message. Graham's forty-minute addresses avoided hell-fire and were less emotional than those of many evangelists; however, he was much concerned with sin and worldly pleasures, made use of the fear of death ('in ten years a quarter of you will be dead'), and indulged in repetition and other oratorical devices; he gave a strong impression of sincerity and conviction.

Public commitment Public commitment, by making public decisions, or speaking in defence of new beliefs, has an effect on attitudes. This

44

is partly because thinking out the arguments produces greater understanding of the beliefs, partly because guilt is generated by awareness of inconsistency, or by persuading others of a belief if one suspects it is not true (Nel *et al.*, 1969). Graham's converts had to come forward and make a public decision and they had already committed themselves by taking part in the service.

Lang and Lang (1960) used 44 student observers in their research on Graham's New York campaign. One result of this research was that several of the observers were converted. Johnson (1971) suggested that the crucial factor here was role-playing, i.e. behaving like a genuinely involved member of the congregation. He carried out a study using 46 students as active participants at a Graham meeting, 46 passive observers, and a control group; members of the experimental groups thought that they were acting as observers. There was very little difference between the two experimental groups in the effect of the meeting, and the majority were unaffected. On the other hand, 9 of the 92 subjects made decisions at the meeting, though their questionnaire replies did not indicate any change of beliefs; perhaps the measuring instruments were not sensitive enough.

Personal influence This has been found to play an important part in attitude change. Often there are two stages for those affected: exposure to the new ideas, and the adoption or trying out of new ideas or behaviour. While the first may come from the mass media or a public speaker, the second stage usually needs personal contact with friends or acquaintances whose opinions on the matter in hand are valued (Weiss, 1969). In Graham's campaigns those going forward are interviewed by very persuasive counsellors, and put in touch with the appropriate local clergyman, who is supposed to integrate them with the church. Many people went with friends, family or a church group. Whitam (1968b) followed up 3,000 Graham converts, and found that the acquisition of new friends was the most important social factor; reactions of parents were also important, but those of peers were not.

Characteristics of speaker Many studies show that public speakers have more effect if they have prestige, are regarded as experts, are liked and admired, are thought to be members of the same group as the listeners, and are regarded as sincere and concerned with the welfare of their listeners. Before Graham's campaign in Britain, there was an elaborate public relations campaign by posters and other publications, by a film, and via the churches. The prestige built up for him was no doubt a factor in the higher percentage of converts at his meetings as opposed to those by other members of his team (Table 3.7). About half the seats were booked by parties, mostly from churches, and many people went with the intention of making a public decision.

It is often supposed that simple one-sided messages are the most effective. Cantril (1941) stresses the oversimplifications used in successful movements such as the Kingdom of Father Divine and the Townsend plan. It may be the case that such simple solutions are eagerly accepted by many people who find the true situation too puzzling. However, there is some evidence from research on international attitudes that presentation of both sides of the case is more effective with those who are initially opposed to the case being presented, and also with the more intelligent.

Public meetings v. *other media*   Attitudes and beliefs can be influenced by verbal communications: these can be delivered face-to-face at public meetings or via the mass media of radio, television and print. Although the mass media reach a wider audience, the effect on that audience is less than at public meetings, the traditional vehicle for religious evangelism. Wilke (1934) measured the attitudes of 341 students towards the existence of God before and after they had heard a ten-minute speech. Those students who had heard the speaker in person changed their attitudes considerably more than others who heard the same speech through a loudspeaker or read it in print.

Studies of Billy Graham's campaign in London found that while 2·3 per cent came forward at the proper meetings, only 0·44 per cent of those who had heard relayed services came forward. As Hovland suggests (1954), the superiority of face-to-face presentation could be due to the added visual element, to a greater flexibility through observation of the audience's response, to the better attraction of attention, or to the increased pressure due to personal contact. There are probably advantages in large meetings, as Table 3.7 suggests. There is evidence of massive social support for the movement, while those going forward (preceded by a large group of counsellors) have a powerful suggestive effect.

The effects of drugs and meditation

One of the central features of religion is the experience of the holy, a non-rational feeling of awe and mystery (Otto, 1958). This is experienced most vividly by mystics, while lesser forms of it are brought about in various ways at religious services—by the use of music, bells, incense, darkness, and other influences. In a number of cults drugs are regularly used at religious rituals, not as a result of psychological research but since it was found that certain substances enhanced religious experiences.

A number of drugs have psychedelic properties, i.e. can create altered states of consciousness, where subjective experiences are made more intense in various ways. Mescaline, found in the cactus peyote, was used by the Aztecs in 300 B.C., and is used today by 50,000 Indians in the Native American church for religious purposes. Aldous Huxley (1954) described the effects of mescaline and popularized its use. Psilocybin has been used for centuries in Siberia, and by the Aztecs, and is used today in Mexico. Marihuana is used in a secular way, but also in parts of India for religious purposes. LSD is a manufactured drug, but has become the basis of a cult, partly through the influence of Timothy Leary. Yage grows naturally, is similar to LSD, and is widely used in South America to produce 'dreams' rather than religious experiences. Alcohol is not usually regarded as a psychedelic drug, but it is used for religious purposes by the Sufis in India and Persia, as well as in Christian and Jewish rites. The psychedelic drugs have somewhat different effects. For example, mescaline makes ordinary objects appear abnormally clear, while LSD produces visual hallucinations. However, the effects experienced are very much a function of the beliefs and expectations of the drug-taker, in turn a function of the preparation and social setting (Aaronson and Osmond, 1971; Tart, 1969).

When people take psychedelic drugs, some have experiences which they regard as mystical, while others do not. Masters and Houston (1973) give the proportions of people reporting religious experiences in a number of LSD studies. The proportion is much higher in a religious setting, as Table 3.9 shows.

TABLE 3.9   *Religious experiences under* LSD

	Non-religious setting (N = 74)	Some religious stimuli (N = 96)
	%	%
Felt it (LSD) was the greatest thing that ever happened to me	49	85
A religious experience	32	83
A greater awareness of God or a Higher Power, or an Ultimate Reality	40	90

Source: Masters and Houston (1973).

There are a number of close similarities between drug experiences in the laboratory and mystical experiences: feelings of timelessness, of depersonalization, of being in touch with basic reality, and very vivid sense perceptions, for example. We describe later an experiment showing that drugs can enhance religious experience in many respects (p. 49). It has been objected by Zaehner (1957) that there are several different types of mystical experience: nature mysticism, monistic or pantheistic (as in Buddhism and Hinduism), and theistic, involving love and communion with God (as in Christian and Muslim mysticism). While mescaline experiences are often like nature mysticism, and LSD experiences are like pantheistic mysticism, drugs do not usually produce theistic Christian experiences. However, both mystical and drug experiences are difficult to describe, and there have been individuals who have described their drug experiences in Christian terms. Members of the Native American church, who take peyote, often have theistic experiences. Peyote is also used by some Mexican Indians who have been converted to Catholicism, and they have corresponding religious experiences, such as visions of the Virgin Mary (La Barre, 1938). The effects of drugs vary greatly, and can include demonic experiences and highly destructive behaviour (Stark, 1965).

Schachter (1967) found that the same drug (adrenalin) could produce emotions which were experienced either as euphoria or aggression, depending on the environmental setting. It looks as if psychedelic drugs generate religious and other experiences in a similar two-factor way. In order to have a mystical experience a person needs both a particular physiological state, which may be induced by certain drugs, or perhaps by prayer and fasting, and also a set of religious beliefs and expectations, which result in his interpreting, experiencing and describing the state in a religious way. Clark and Raskin (1971) found very little relationship between the amount of drug taken and the intensity of experiences. They suggest that the drug acts as a kind of trigger.

As yet we do not know why these physiological states can be the basis of religious experiences. In the case of mescaline, one of the main effects is to change the way ordinary objects are perceived. This also can occur under various natural conditions, and is often reported by nature mystics. Other psychedelic drugs affect different parts of the brain.

It is sometimes objected that drug experiences differ from mystical experiences obtained in other ways, in that they do not have any beneficial effects on the life of the recipient (Zaehner, 1972). In all the classical traditions of mysticism, whether Christian, Zen, or others, there was always a demanding discipline of training, and this may be essential for the positive effects on behaviour. Evidence on this point is provided by the celebrated experiment by Pahnke (1966), on the religious effects of psilocybin. Twenty theological students attended a $2\frac{1}{2}$-hour Good Friday service; half had been given psilocybin, half had been given a placebo; the two groups had been matched beforehand. The subjects completed a lengthy questionnaire, provided free descriptions, and were interviewed six months later. Combined scores were calculated on a number of dimensions of religious experience, devised by W.T. Stace (and mainly reflecting the pantheistic type of mysticism). The theological students who were given psilocybin had more intense experiences along all of the dimensions.

TABLE 3.10   *The effects of psilocybin on mystical experience*

Category	*Percentage of maximum possible score for 10 Ss*		
	Exp.	Control	p*
1. Unity	62	7	0·001
(a) Internal	70	8	0·001
(b) External	38	2	0·008
2. Transcendence of time and space	84	6	0·001
3. Deeply felt positive mood	57	23	0·020
(a) Joy, blessedness and peace	51	13	0·020
(b) Love	57	33	0·055
4. Sacredness	53	28	0·020
5. Objectivity and reality	63	18	0·011
6. Paradoxicality	61	13	0·001
7. Alleged ineffability	66	18	0·001
8. Transiency	79	8	0·001
9. Persisting positive changes in attitude and behaviour	51	8	0·001
(a) towards self	57	3	0·001
(b) towards others	40	20	0·002
(c) towards life	54	6	0·011
(d) towards the experience	57	31	0·055

* Probability that the difference between experimental and control scores was due to chance. Source: Pahnke (1966).

The greatest effects, and the greatest agreement between different measures, was for dimensions 1(a), 2, 6, 8, 9(a) and 9(c). The follow-up six months later showed the lasting changes summarized under category 9. In this case subjects had received religious training before the drug experience. What the drug did was to magnify the immediate experience and its long-term effects. There has been disagreement over whether drug experiences lead more often to withdrawal or to positive social action. There is no doubt that very often they lead to withdrawal (Spangler cited by Clark, 1971). On the other hand, they can have therapeutic effects.

LSD has been used in the treatment of alcoholics and criminals, but again it has been found that the drug alone has no effect. If there are any lasting effects, psychotherapy is needed as well (Hoffer, in Aaronson and Osmond, 1971). Abramson (1967) also reports that for LSD to have therapeutic effects, there has to be the support of an institution and a disciplined way of life. The use of LSD for therapy has been abandoned since some people have very unfavourable reactions, such as becoming psychotic, committing suicide, or suffering injuries from acting on their hallucinations, such as walking out of windows.

In the past, mystical experiences have been induced by meditation and associated exercises. All religious traditions have methods of meditating, prescribing how the subject shall control his thoughts and imagery, and, in the case of yoga, his body. Transcendental meditation (TM) based on Vedic teaching has become popular in the West, and research has been carried out on its physiological effects. The technique briefly is to 'turn the attention inwards towards the subtler levels of thought until the mind transcends the experience of the subtlest state of the thought and arrives at the source of the thought' (Mahesh Yogi, 1966).

It is now known that TM has definite physiological effects. Wallace (1970) studied fifteen students who meditated in this way for 30 minutes, with rest periods before and after. He found that during TM there was a rapid drop in oxygen consumption of about 20 per cent, and an increase in skin resistance of about 100 per cent, compared with the resting state. Both changes were greater and faster than the similar changes with sleep. The heart rate dropped by five beats per minute. The electro-encephalograph (EEG) changed towards larger and slower alpha-waves, with periods of cessation, and replacement by theta waves. Studies of Zen monks have produced similar results. The state induced by TM is different from sleep in its EEG pattern, and is equivalent to a very low level of arousal.

Meditation is now widely used by people who do not regard the experience as religious. However, as in the case of drugs, there are clear similarities between the effects of secular meditation and mystical experience. Deikman (1963) asked eight subjects to meditate on a vase for a series of 15-minute sessions. The subjects all experienced (a) more vivid perception of the vase, e.g. increased colour saturation; (b) personal attachment to the vase; (c) increased ability to keep out distracting stimuli; (d) time shortening; and (e) felt that the experience was pleasant and valuable. Some subjects had more intense experiences, such as seeing the object radiating or transfigured, or a merging of self and object. Meditation was able to generate some of the components of mystical experience.

The only long-term consequences from TM which have been reported are that tension and blood-pressure can be reduced. It is possible that other positive effects on behaviour may result if meditation is combined with training or other forms of influence.

Marital status

A number of surveys which provide separate statistics for the married and the single indicate a much lower level of church attendance on the part of married people. Chesser (1956) found that 30 per cent of single female respondents were regular churchgoers compared with 16 per cent of the married. Considering that married people are older than single people on average this is even more striking, since older people (after 30) are more religious. Fichter (1952), reporting a survey of American Catholics, found single people more active on several criteria, though each involved church attendance of some kind.

TABLE 3.11 *Marital status and religious activity in Great Britain, 1955*

	Denom. affil.	Weekly attend.	Daily prayers	Believe in after-life	Believe in devil	Spiritualists
Single	75	21	44	48	21	2
Married	76	12	41	46	19	3
Widowed	76	26	71	62	24	10
Divorced or separated	65	12	49	44	20	7

Source: Gorer (1955).

Whether taking care of children keeps parents away from church is unclear. Some evidence from the USA (Nash and Berger, 1962) indicates that it is the children who take their parents to church, at least in some cases. Table 3.11 gives Gorer's data (1955) on the connection between marital status and religious activities. While single people go to church much more often than married, they are only slightly more active in prayer and belief. It seems that single people are consistently more religious than married, but that the difference is only marked for church attendance, though correction for age would probably increase the differences.

Widowed people show a rather higher rate of activity than single or married, particularly on saying daily prayers and believing

51

in the after-life. They are older on average and this may account for the difference. However, the widowed also tend to believe in spiritualism and to believe that they will rejoin loved ones in the after-life (Gorer, 1955).

Divorced and separated people will be older on average than married people, probably not much younger than the widowed. On an age basis alone we should expect them to be intermediate between married and widowed. In fact, they are similar to married people except that they pray more often and belong to a church less frequently. They also have the same low rate of church attendance as married people. The explanation may be that some churches condemn or discourage divorce, so that divorced people only engage in private religious practices. Karlsson (1957) found that recently separated women in Sweden were more religious than married women; other studies show that happily married people are more religious, so that Karlsson's result is probably due to the need of separated people for religious consolation.

Glock, Ringer and Babbie (1967) found that unmarried and childless church members were more involved in church activity. Their interpretation was that church activities provided for these people the satisfactions that were available to other people in their family life. Glock (1959) suggested that the church serves for these people as a family substitute.

Life crisis and stress situations

The most interesting problem here concerns the impact of stress in battle on religious behaviour. Valuable evidence is provided by Stouffer and his colleagues (1949) who report on the surveys carried out in the American Army during World War II. About 75 per cent of men were helped 'a lot' by prayer 'when the going was tough', which was higher than the percentage mentioning other responses such as thinking of not letting the other man down, feeling hatred for the enemy, or thinking about what they were fighting for. The men who were most exposed to stress in battle were helped by prayer in a higher percentage of cases: infantrymen mentioned this more than men in other branches, as did those who had seen friends killed or who had been shelled or bombed by their own side. There was some evidence that men whose resources for dealing with stress were less adequate were more helped by prayer: replacements, who would have less group support, said more frequently that prayer helped them. Similarly, men who were most frightened in battle said they were helped by prayer in 72 per cent of cases, as compared with 42 per cent for those least frightened; this was also true for the men with least confidence in battle, those who were least willing to take part in more fighting, and those most concerned about becoming a casualty.

As the authors point out, it is possible, though unlikely, that the use of prayer made the men more afraid, instead of the reverse. It seems most likely that both objective and subjective stress are related to prayer as a response. Men in the ranks prayed rather more than NCOs or officers, but educational differences did not affect the use of prayer. It is interesting that other mental adjustments to stress, such as the thought of not letting the other man down, followed a quite different statistical pattern: this was less often mentioned by men who had been under stress and who showed neurotic symptoms.

Since prayer was found helpful in battle by so many soldiers, it would be expected that ex-servicemen would be more religious than before. Table 3.12 shows the results of three surveys in which soldiers were asked if their war experiences had made them more or less religious.

TABLE 3.12   *The effect of war experience on religion*

A Being religious	More religious	No effect	Less religious
	%	%	%
Princeton Students (Crespi and Shapleigh, reported by Allport *et al.*, 1948)*	25·1	53·3	18·6
Harvard Students (Allport *et al.*, 1948)	26·3	54·5	19·2
US Army Survey (Stouffer *et al.*, 1949, p. 187)			
(1) Men with combat experience	29	41	30
(2) Men without combat experience	23	42	35

B Interest in problems of religion	More interested	No effect	Less interested
Harvard Students	58·4	36·7	4·9

C Belief in God	Increased faith	No effect	Decreased faith
US Army Survey			
(1) Men with combat experience	79	2	19
(2) Men without combat experience	54	29	17

* 3 per cent of Princeton sample had no opinion.

One striking result is that similar experiences can have opposite effects on different men. Allport *et al.* (1948) report some of the reasons given by their subjects for changes in religious beliefs. Those who had become less religious said that the horrors of war, together with seeing churchgoers killed, had made them sceptical; those who had become more religious referred to the help they had had from prayer in battle. About equal numbers in these surveys claim to have become more and less 'religious', but comparisons of ex-service students with others show that the former have a less favourable attitude towards the church (Telford, 1950), attend church less frequently, and hold less orthodox religious views (Allport *et al.*, 1948). When we look at other criteria, different results appear. According to the Army survey, there is an increased belief in God, and the Harvard students said they were more interested in problems of religion than before. Allport concludes that although war experience weakens traditional church religion, it increases the concern with basic religious ideas. The previous findings on prayer receive some confirmation in that men who had been in action reported that they were more religious and had an increased faith more often than those who had not been in action (Table 3.12C).

Finally, we can inquire how far national interest in religion was affected in wartime. The best available data are for the USA during World War II. As shown previously, church attendance was lower during this period than either before or after, as were donations to church funds. The revival in American religion appears to date from the War, whereas there had been a continual decline since the turn of the century (see p. 15f). It is possible however that this is part of a larger trend due to quite different sociological causes. In Great Britain there has been a gradual decline since 1920. Data for the 1914–18 war are not very accurate, but there is no evidence in either country of any marked effect.

The occurrence of a major crisis in an individual's life has traditionally been described as an occasion for religious reawakening and an impetus for religious commitment. Religious literature supplies us with many case histories in which a crisis brought about a strong religious commitment or conversion. There are a few systematic studies, most of which do not report much change in religiosity as a result of life crises. Nash and Berger (1962) found no connection between increased religious involvement and the occurrence of life crises. Loveland (1968) reported that recently bereaved persons reported more frequent prayers for consolation compared with a control group, but there were no significant changes in any religious beliefs among the bereaved. Croog and Levine (1972) studied 324 American men recovering from a heart attack, and examined patterns of religious activity before and after the attack. The men were followed for a year after the crisis, and during that period there were no changes in religious beliefs or religious activities. Beliefs about the causes of the crisis were totally secular, and very few men sought contact with clergy. Additional findings on religion as a factor in adjusting to life crisis is found in Chapter 8.

We report below (p. 67f), that old people are more likely than others to believe in an after-life, to pray, and read the Bible, and are more concerned about religion. Anxiety about death, and what happens after it, is widespread; is there any connection between this anxiety and religious beliefs? Studies of old people have found that the more religious have less fear of death. Swenson (1961) studied 210 people over 60, and found that both church attendance and fundamentalism correlated with looking forward positively to death, as opposed to a negative and evasive attitude. The religious people were much more likely to say 'I look forward to death', or 'it will be wonderful', or to associate it with 'glorious happy life'. Jeffers *et al.* (1961) studied 260 people over 60, and found that belief in an after-life and frequency of Bible reading correlated with a lower fear of death.

Martin and Wrightsman (1965) studied 58 Protestant church members with an average age of 44. The correlation between fear of death and religious participation was strongly negative: $-0·42$ on one scale. Studies of the general population, or of students, on the other hand, have produced inconsistent findings (Lester, 1972).

If there is a link between religion and reduced fear of death, which causes which? One possibility is that those who are most anxious about death become religious in order to reduce their anxiety. An experiment to test this hypothesis was carried out by Osarchuk and Tate (1973). They induced fear of death experimentally by a taped communication about the dangers of accidents and diseases, accompanied by dirge-like music and slides of corpses. This produced substantial increases in a questionnaire measure of belief in an after-life, but only for those who already had a fairly high degree of belief in it. Other evidence supports the hypothesis that fear of death affects religion. As we have seen, belief in an after-life and prayer increase rapidly with age, and reach nearly 100 per cent as death approaches. Soldiers when in great danger are very likely to pray, and often become more religious afterwards (p. 53).

Another explanation of the link between religion and fear of death is that religious teaching reduces the fear. There are denominational differences in belief in an after-life, as shown in Table 3.13. There are also denominational differences in what members believe the after-life will be like. Gorer found Jews, Spiritualists, Presbyterians and Congregationalists the least likely to believe in hell, while

55

Spiritualists were most likely to believe in rejoining loved ones. (The last result in particular is probably partly due to people joining the denomination because of its beliefs.) There is clearly evidence that denominations influence the amount and type of belief in an after-life, and this in turn could affect the amount of anxiety on this topic.

TABLE 3.13 *Denomination and belief in an after-life*

	%
Spiritualists	90
Baptists	71
Presbyterians	65
Roman Catholics	62
Small sects	62
Methodists	55
Church of England	46
Jews	32

Source: Gorer (1955).

Some people do not report any fear of death, but are found to avoid the subject, or provide other evidence of 'blocking', 'denial' or 'repression' during clinical interviews. This is more common in non-religious people. Alexander and Adlerstein (1959) studied 25 religious and 25 non-religious students and suggested that religious students tend to escape to the satisfying concept of after-life, while non-religious subjects are likely to banish the topic of death from their consciousness altogether.

Feifel and Jones (1968) studied the attitudes to death of 371 people, including 92 seriously ill and terminal patients, other patients, and controls. The seriously ill and terminal patients were less able to conceptualize death and made more use of denial and avoidance of this topic, while the healthy subjects used intellectualization. Those with terminal illnesses, who knew they must die from their illnesses, made more use of denial than the seriously ill, and had a more urgent desire for home and family. A study of 81 doctors of various kinds, of average age 39, found that they had more fear of death, and that fewer of them believed in a religious solution, than either patients or healthy people; the doctors had encountered death at an earlier age than other people (Feifel *et al.*, 1967).

In Chapter 8 we shall examine the relationship between religious activity and adjustment in old age.

Despite the low rate of church attendance in Britain, at least 95 per cent of those who die have a religious funeral. A person's death causes deep depression and distress, particularly to members of the immediate family. Death of a spouse is very disturbing and leads to the longest period of mourning. Death of a child creates perhaps even more long-lasting distress; Gorer (1965) reports that parents never recover from it. Death of a parent can create long-standing psychological disturbance in children. The various rites of passage help relatives to recover: the religious ceremony, the family gathering, and the period of public mourning (Gorer, 1965). The stress of bereavement is probably a source of belief in an after-life in which loved ones will be seen again, a belief which is most common among Spiritualists. Wilson (1966) suggests that it is because religion can provide these supportive rituals that the bereaved turn to it. In a British survey it was found that 'death' made 64 per cent of respondents think about God (v. making love 2 per cent, holidays 2 per cent, etc.); 44 per cent said they would talk to a clergyman if they were afraid of death (v. wife 15 per cent, doctor 8 per cent); this was the main problem on which the clergy were consulted (ITA, 1970). It looks as if in Britain today religion is seen by many people primarily as a means of dealing with death.

4 Age and religion

Here we shall consider changes in religious activities and religious beliefs throughout the life cycle, using age as an independent variable. Changes in religious behaviour at different ages will be discussed in connection with the other psychological processes typical of that age period.

Childhood: 3–12 years

A number of studies have been concerned with the development of religious thinking during this period. Harms (1944) asked several thousand children to draw their idea of God, and to give written or spoken comments. While no statistical analysis was done, Harms concluded that there were three stages:

3–6   fairy-tale stage. God is regarded as in the same category as giants and dragons, but bigger and wearing flowing robes;

7–12   realistic stage. God is seen as a father, as a real person; many orthodox ideas are accepted;

12–   individualistic stage. Here there are a variety of interpretations, mystical or conventional.

Later research has followed Piagetian ideas. For example, Goldman (1964) asked 200 children to discuss three Bible stories, and found that they followed the Piaget age sequence. It is not until 13–14 that physical interpretations of God and other aspects of religion are abandoned in favour of analogical and abstract ideas. This corresponds to the Piagetian idea of 'formal operations', when abstract thought is first possible.

From 3–6 years, children accept religious ideas readily, they like Bible stories, accepting them as fairy tales. They will say prayers,

58

usually asking for the gratification of childish desires (Kupky, 1928). In the period 6–12 there is a lot of questioning, not in a sceptical sense, but to find out exactly what God, heaven, etc., are like (Lawrence, 1965). Children acquire an increasingly accurate knowledge of local religious concepts (Bose, 1929). After 12, serious doubts about religion begin. Children between 5 and 12 acquire a clear idea of what is meant by belonging to a particular denominational group, at first in terms of practices and sacred objects, later in terms of specific beliefs (Elkind, 1964).

Long, Elkind and Spilka (1967) interviewed children of different ages about prayer, factor-analysed the results, and found the following stages.

5–7   vague understanding, linked with verbal formulae;
7–9   verbal requests;
10–12 private conversation with God, sharing of confidences, less egocentric.

The effects of religious training on non-religious behaviour of young children were shown in several studies. Ezer (1962) found that children from religious families tend to use more often animistic and anthropomorphic concepts to explain physical causality. Crandall and Gozali (1969) found that children from religious families tended to score higher on a measure of social desirability, i.e. presenting a more socially acceptable front when asked about unacceptable behaviour.

Adolescence: 12–18 years

The period 12–18, which we shall label 'adolescence', is of great interest. It is the age of religious awakening, during which time people either become converted or decide to abandon their childhood faith, if they had one.

While most studies of religious behaviour in adolescents refer to 'religious conversions', the experience referred to should more properly be described as a heightened commitment to an already known religious belief system. The proper use of the term 'conversion' should be limited to cases of a complete change and transfer of commitment from one belief system to another. Despite the fact that the term 'conversion' is so commonly used in connection with adolescence, we shall put it in quotation marks to remind the reader of its inaccuracy. Many of these 'conversions' can be understood in the context of a rebellion against the parents, which is expressed in a 'holier than thou' demonstration against their superficial religiosity. Interpretations of the adolescent 'conversion' experience from a psychodynamic viewpoint have emphasized the importance

59

of relationship with the parents and their psychic representations (Allison, 1969). It is found that 10–30 per cent of religious people have had a more or less sudden 'conversion' experience; the others became religious gradually over a longer period. Sudden conversions are less common than at the beginning of the century.

The violent 'conversion' experience has been described by the earlier writers. James (1902) and other authors have used literary sources to give examples of famous conversions. James supported his method by arguing that 'we must make search for the original experiences which were the pattern-setters to all this mass of suggested feeling and imitated conduct' (p. 8). As is pointed out later in this book (p. 190), the social learning hypothesis cannot account for such things as the age of 'conversion' or for other systematic variations of religious phenomena with empirical variables, although there is considerable evidence that social learning is one factor. The use of literary sources results in examples of 'conversion' which are atypical in several ways. (1) These are often conversions of outstanding religious leaders or were sufficiently extraordinary to have been placed on record. (2) They were usually sudden, not gradual conversions. (3) They were generally conversions of adults, whereas conversion is far more common among adolescents. It thus appears that literary methods of inquiry may actually fail to describe the normal as opposed to the exceptional or pathological phenomenon. Systematic research can show the frequency of each type of event as well as the empirical conditions under which each occurs.

However, both views agree about the description of the sudden adolescent conversion—a morbid and unrealistic sense of sin and guilt suddenly changes to an ecstatic sense of peace and virtue.

There has been little recent research on the topic of 'conversion', probably because the phenomenon itself has become rarer. Many adolescents adopt beliefs, clothes or practices (e.g. drugs), which contrast with those of their homes, and which are shared with members of peer-groups outside the home. New beliefs and attitudes are usually involved, and sometimes these are religious. Some groups such as the Jesus Movement appeal specifically to this age-group.

Loveless and Lodato (1967) found that adolescence brings about a relative convergence of values in individuals from different religious groups. This reflects the declining influence of the parents and the growing influence of the peer group. We have already seen the powerful effect of group membership on religion (p. 38f). Another source of influence is an older sibling, as Debord (1969) shows. Adolescent boys with older brothers exhibit low church-attendance rates, while adolescent boys with older sisters exhibit the highest attendance rates.

Another problem about 'conversions' is the age at which they occur. The greatest number take place in the sixteenth year for boys, the fifteenth for girls, according to many studies (McKeefery, 1949). Age distributions of several typical investigations are given in Figure 2.

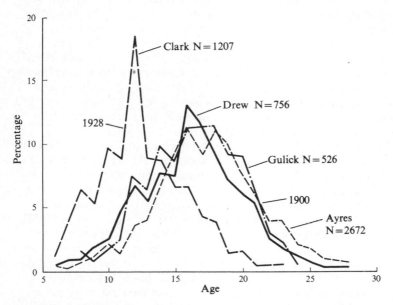

FIGURE 2   *The age of 'conversion'*

Source: Pressey and Kuhlen (1957). Reproduced by permission of Harper & Row.

It will be seen that the majority fall between 10 and 20, though 'conversions' do occur later; since college students or other young people are often the subjects for these inquiries, later 'conversions' are not reported. Jones (1937) took older people, many of them clergymen, and found some 'conversions' at over 40, though these were much less common. Clark (1929), in a careful study of over 2,000 cases, found an average 'conversion' age of 12·8 with a mode at 12, from which some writers have drawn the conclusion that the conversion age had declined since the turn of the century. However, later American work has not confirmed this trend (McKeefery, 1949), and the modal age of Billy Graham's British converts in 1954 was about 15 (Colquhoun, 1955).

The same person may be 'converted' more than once. Olt (1956) found subjects reporting up to six 'conversions', while nearly a third of his subjects reported two. The typical sequence for these was for a 'conversion' to last two years, being succeeded four years later by another. As was shown above (pp. 41f) many crisis 'conversions' at revival meetings tend to be temporary, and people who experience a gradual 'conversion' are more religious later on.

There is some evidence concerning the conditions under which people are likely to have a sudden 'conversion'. (1) Certain sects encourage this kind of 'conversion'—Evangelical Protestantism, American revivalism in the nineteenth century—while some small sects actually require it as a condition for membership. (2) Those people who have not been to Sunday School or had any church connections are more likely to have a crisis 'conversion'; the others have a gradual one. (3) These 'conversions' typically occur at revival meetings, though this is becoming less common. However, about 120,000 people made decisions at Billy Graham's recent campaigns in Great Britain (p. 41).

The relation of the age of 'conversion' to the age of puberty is of some interest in the light of theories relating religion to the sexual instinct. The physical changes comprising puberty may take place at any age between 10 and 17; the distribution is symmetrical and has a peak of $13-13\frac{1}{2}$. Although girls are the first to show the acceleration in growth, the age of first menstruation is slightly later than the corresponding changes in boys. There is some evidence that puberty in girls is now about a year earlier than it was a generation ago (Garrison, 1951). From Figure 2 it seems that about 10 per cent of 'conversions' should take place before puberty—unless those with an early 'conversion' also have an early puberty. Thirty per cent of Starbuck's subjects however (1899) claimed to have been converted before puberty, and the distribution curve for conversions shows many 'conversions' after 17.

The foregoing investigations have all been conducted by the questioning of religious people about their experiences during adolescence. The studies now to be discussed compare the average religious activity of different age-groups between 12 and 18. An interest in religious and cosmic problems appears at about the age of 12. Associated with an increased intellectual interest in religious affairs comes doubt of what was uncritically accepted earlier. MacLean (1930) found doubts appearing at about the age of 12–13. Hollingworth (1933) found that the awakening of intellectual interest and doubt occurred at a *mental* age of 12, so that more intelligent children start questioning earlier; for example, children of IQ 150 come to this stage at the age of 8. Fritsch and Hetzer (1928) studied the diaries of German adolescents and found that doubts were first concerned with church practices and later with the contents of beliefs; this suggests a relation between the growth of doubt and the growth of understanding, since Bose (1929) found that the more abstract religious notions only came to be described correctly towards the end of the period 8–15, while concrete matters of practice—church festivals and the like—were understood much earlier. Bose found that understanding correlated both with age and IQ (i.e. with mental age), just as Hollingworth found that doubt increased with mental age. Fritsch and Hetzer (1928) found evidence of conflict between an emotional attachment to the religion of childhood and intellectual doubts—faith versus reason—and that this was generally resolved one way or the other by the age of 20, the height of the conflict coming at 17.

TABLE 4.1   *Changes in specific religious beliefs during adolescence*

Statement	'Believe'			'Wonder about'		
	12 years	*15 years*	*18 years*	*12 years*	*15 years*	*18 years*
	%	%	%	%	%	%
God is a strange power working for good rather than a person	46	49	57	20	14	15
God is someone who watches you to see that you behave yourself and who punishes you if you are not good	70	49	33	11	13	18
I know there is a God	94	80	79	2	14	16
Catholics, Jews and Protestants are equally good	67	79	86	24	11	7
There is a heaven	82	78	74	13	16	20
Only good people go to heaven	72	45	33	13	27	34
Hell is a place where you are punished for your sins on earth	70	49	35	13	27	34
Heaven is here on earth	12	13	14	18	28	32
People who go to church are better than people who do not go to church	46	26	15	17	21	11
Young people should belong to the same church as their parents	77	56	43	10	11	11
The main reason for going to church is to worship God	88	80	79	4	7	6
It is not necessary to go to church to be a Christian	42	62	67	18	15	8
Only our soul lives after death	72	63	61	18	25	31
Good people say prayers regularly	78	57	47	13	13	27
Prayers are answered	76	69	65	21	25	27
Prayers are a source of help in time of trouble	74	80	83	15	10	9
Prayers are to make up for something that you have done that is wrong	47	24	21	18	17	9
Every word in the Bible is true	79	51	34	15	31	43
It is sinful to doubt the Bible	62	42	27	20	26	28

Source: Kuhlen and Arnold (1944). Reproduced by permission of the Journal Press.

Kuhlen and Arnold (1944) surveyed over 500 children grouped around the ages of 12, 15 and 18; the results of this study are given in Table 4.1. It will be noticed that many specific traditional beliefs are discarded between 12 and 18. For example, 72 per cent of the 12-year-olds believed that 'only good people go to heaven', as compared with 33 per cent of the 18-year-olds. Beliefs became more abstract and less concrete, and there was more toleration for the ideas of others. There was only a slight increase in the percentages of young people 'wondering about' these topics, though the number reporting definite beliefs declined. The topics most 'wondered about' were sin, heaven and hell, science versus religion, and what happens after death.

Further evidence is provided by a survey of 500 Harvard students by Allport, Gillespie and Young (1948). Asked if they had ever 'reacted either partially or wholly against the beliefs taught', 73 per cent of the Protestants and Jews and 62 per cent of the Catholics said they had; the median age of rebellion was 15½ for men, 14½ for women. Since the parents would tend on average to be fairly religious, if these young people were to rebel at all it would have to be in an irreligious direction: therefore we cannot tell whether the rebellion or the doubt was the primary factor.

TABLE 4.2   *Adolescent religion*

	Britain	USA
	%	%
Weekly church attendance	40 (15)	70 (42)
Daily prayers	29 (44)	55 (63)
Belief in God	61 (74)	80 (98)
Belief in after-life	57·5 (37)	80 (73)
Belief in divinity of Christ	56 (64)	—

Source: British figures from Wright and Cox (1967); US figures from Bealer and Willets (1967). Comparable adult figures in brackets, from Table 2.17.

We turn now to the level of religious activity and beliefs of teenagers, as found in recent studies. It is clear from Table 4.2 that teenagers in both countries have a much higher level of church attendance than the adult population, even allowing for some exaggeration in the responses. However, there is a lower level of belief. One reason is that a lot of young people go to church for non-religious reasons, such as belonging to the youth club or the choir (Wright and Cox, 1967). In the USA adolescents, it has been suggested, are unwilling to accept the religion of their family without question, but do not want to risk social rejection by making their doubts public (Bealer and Willets, 1967).

There is no doubt that many young people are considerably concerned about religious matters, more than superficial observations of teenagers suggest. Loukes (1961) studied British 14-year-olds, and found them very concerned about religion and other goals and values; they seemed to be trying to make sense of religious propositions.

The teenagers' high level of churchgoing is not sustained, and several investigators have found a decline in religious activity during the late teens. Horton (1940) found that this took place during the last years of high school in America, and before going to college. Moreton (1944) found a similar decline in England over the period 15–19. Furthermore, there is no evidence of any increased attendance at any point during the period from 10 to 18.

We are now faced with a curious paradox: while the studies of conversion show a peak of activity at 15–16, the cross-sectional studies show an increasing doubt over the earlier part of the period, and a decrease of attendance later on. The explanation is probably that this period of life is one of heightened decision about values, identity and religious beliefs. The longitudinal studies of 'conversion' only tell us about those who decide to become religious. It would be expected that those who become irreligious make their decision at about the same time. Since the two sets of decisions take place in opposite directions simultaneously, both are concealed in the cross-sectional averages.

This two-way flow, together with an overall change in beliefs, is also found for students (p. 34f).

Young adulthood: 18–30 years

A number of studies carried out in 1947–55 showed a sharp decline in religious activity between 18 and 30, followed by a continuous increase from 30 onwards (Fichter, 1954; Gorer, 1955; Cauter and Downham, 1954). This pattern has come to be known as the 'traditional theory'. A number of later studies however have found very little change in religious activity with age (Orbach, 1961; Lazerwitz, 1961a). This pattern has come to be known as the 'stability theory'. Unfortunately all these findings are cross-sectional, i.e. obtained at the same point in time, and so could be explained historically. For example, the results may reflect the effects of the depression, World War II, and the revival of 1945–60, on different age-groups.

There have been some longitudinal studies. Nelson (1956) found an increase in positive religious attitude in a group of 836 persons, tested firstly during college in 1936 and then in 1950. Bender (1958) and Kelly (1955) retested students after 16- and 20-year intervals respectively, and found increases in the Vernon-Allport religious value. They both recognize these results are probably due to the revival of religious activity in the USA at the time of the follow-up. Shand (1969) reported no major changes in religious beliefs in a group of subjects tested in college in 1942 and tested again in 1964. Wingrove and Alston (1971) report a cohort analysis of different generations, and find that different models apply to each cohort, though all groups were most active between 1950 and 1960. These studies suggest that the effects of age are less important than are historical trends.

However, between 18 and 30 there is little doubt that there is a decline in religious activity. Most surveys, including those giving evidence of 'stability', used only adults. An example of a survey including adolescents is that by Fichter (1954). He divided 8,363 Catholic parishioners into ten-year age cohorts, and found that the youngest and the oldest groups (10–19 and 60+) were the most active in church attendance, and the middle group (age 30–9) was lowest in church activity. Table 4.3 presents some of Fichter's findings.

TABLE 4.3   *Religious participation among Catholics at three stages in life*

Age	Easter rites	Sunday mass
	%	%
10–19	92·1	92·8
30–9	63·4	69·3
60+	86·6	90·9

Source: Fichter (1954).

Gorer (1955) found that English weekly church attendance fell from 28 per cent at 16 to 16 per cent at 30, while reported daily prayer fell from 44 per cent to 32 per cent. In a more recent British study it was found that weekly church attendance fell from 25 per cent at 16–24 to 18 per cent at 25–34 (Social Surveys, 1964). Bahr (1970) interviewed 600 American males from varied walks of life, and plotted their degree of regular church attendance at different ages in the past. He found a drop from about 60 per cent at 15 to 38 per cent at 30. We have just seen that church attendance is far higher for adolescents than adults (p. 64); in a period of slow religious decline it follows that adolescents must reduce their rate of attendance as they become older. It is not known how other aspects of religious activity change between 18 and 30, but it seems likely that they too will move towards the adult norms, which in this case means a small increase of belief.

Middle age: 30–60 years

Several models have been proposed to describe changes in religious behaviour and beliefs during this period. A number of studies support the 'traditional' model, according to which there is a decline in religious activity from 15 to 30, followed by a continuous increase. Others support the 'stability' model, according to which there are no changes with age at all. A third model is that of 'disengagement', according to which there is a continuous decline of religious activity with increasing age. Which is correct?

The strongest evidence for an increase in activity between 30 and 60 comes from studies carried out between 1947 and 1953 (e.g. Gorer, 1955; Fichter, 1954). More recent surveys have found little change (e.g. Orbach, 1961; Lazerwitz, 1961a). This suggests that the increase found in the earlier studies may have been due to historical, generational factors rather than to ageing. Stark (1968) compared orthodox beliefs (in a personal God, divinity of Christ, miracles, the Devil) in different age-groups. While the older respondents held more orthodox beliefs, the only real difference was between those older or younger than 50, and Stark concludes that the more orthodox beliefs were a result of the older people establishing their beliefs before World War II.

There is stronger evidence for an increase with age in prayer (Gorer, 1955), religious values (Bender, 1968; Kelly, 1955), perception of the importance of religion (Cameron, 1969) and interest in religion (Marshall and Oden, 1962), rather than in frequency of church attendance. Some of these studies were follow-up studies, and it is possible that increased interest reflected the revival of 1950–60. If there is any increase between 30 and 60, due to age, it is fairly small, and affects attitudes more than behaviour. Some studies have found a peak of church attendance at 50–60.

Ordinary 'conversions' are rare after 30; but members of Pentecostal and other sects may undergo a second 'conversion' ('baptism of the Holy Spirit') (Wilson, 1970). In addition 'mystical conversions' also occur during this period (Thouless, 1923). By a mystical conversion is meant the occasion on which an already religious person begins to have emotional religious experiences of a stronger and more continuous nature, and which may lead to his taking up a contemplative life. Bucke (1901) describes forty-three such cases, including

67

some of the famous historical saints and mystics. Almost all had their mystical conversion in the thirties, often about the age of 33.

Middle-aged people come to play a more important role in the organizational side of church life: as sidesmen, churchwardens, committee members, and other officials.

Old age: 60 years onwards

The 'traditional', 'stability' and 'disengagement' models have all been proposed to describe this period. The picture is now fairly clear, though different for different aspects of religious activity.

Church attendance The over-60s go to church less as they get older, as a number of studies of older people have shown (Moberg, 1965). The reduction in activities is sometimes explained by physical disabilities which are more frequent with age. Even those who remain active past the age of sixty usually retire from leadership positions in the church (Havinghurst and Albrecht, 1953); and many who continue in their sixties reduce their attendance after the age of seventy-five. These changes can be explained simply by the physical effects of old age, which sometimes result in debilitating disabilities, and always in reducing energy (Hunter and Maurice, 1953).

Kingsbury (1937) found reasons given for going to church changed with age. After 30 the number saying 'habit', 'to encourage family attendance', 'to keep alive the spirit of Christ' and 'for reassurance of immortality' increased rapidly—the last two to 80 per cent at 50 plus. Other reasons given fell off with age: such as 'to formulate a philosophy of life', to 'gain new friends', and 'to hear literature and music'. Old people are much more likely to listen to radio or television services: 60 per cent of those in their nineties against 21·5 per cent of those in their sixties (see Table 4.4).

Private prayer Both earlier studies (e.g. Gorer, 1955) and more recent ones (e.g. Stark, 1968) have found a large increase in private prayer with age. In the Gorer study the percentage reporting daily prayer showed a regular increase from 32 per cent at 30 to 72 per cent at 70. Stark found similar figures, with an age-trend for each denomination.

Attitudes Various measures of attitudes towards the church or religion show changes with age. In Cavan's study (Table 4.5) there was a sharp increase in female attitudes towards religion, and a smaller shift for males. In a number of surveys of old people 50–70 per cent claim that religion has come to mean more to them, or has become more important (Moberg, 1965). An increasing proportion of old people regard themselves as religious persons (Barron, 1961).

Beliefs Several studies have found that older people are more certain in their belief in God and more often think of him as a loving father, but the differences are small (Moberg, 1965). Belief in an after-life on the other hand shows a clear and continuous increase with age. This is shown in Table 4.4; it can be seen that 100 per cent of those over 90 in this study were certain of an after-life. Older people are also more likely to believe in automatic heaven, without problems of judgment (Gorer, 1955). Stark (1968) found that liberal Protestants increased from 38 per cent at an earlier age who were certain that there is a life after death to 70 per cent at 70, while moderate Protestants increased from 56 per cent to 87 per cent, conservative Protestants from 87 per cent to 100 per cent, with Catholics fairly steady at 80 per cent.

TABLE 4.4   *Religious attitudes and activities during the later years*

Attitude or activity	Percentage of age group with given religious attitude							
	60–4	65–9	70–4	75–9	80–4	85–9	90–4	95–9
Men								
Favourable attitudes toward religion	38	41	42	39	53	55	50	
Certain of an after-life	71	64	69	67	72	81	100	100
Attend religious services once a week or oftener	45	41	46	45	50	45	17	
Listen to church services regularly on radio	16	21	19	26	33	37	20	50
Read Bible at least once a week	25	29	33	41	48	45	33	25
Women								
Favourable attitudes towards religion	51	56	57	64	69	81	93	100
Certain of an after-life	83	78	86	77	91	90	100	100
Attend religious services once a week or oftener	60	53	52	53	56	33	50	
Listen to church services regularly on radio	22	27	37	30	46	59	69	100
Read Bible at least once a week	50	60	64	62	61	76	58	100

Source: Cavan *et al.* (1949).

The heightened religion of age is very different from the heightened religion of adolescence. In adolescence there is a great intellectual perplexity and doubt coupled with emotional turmoil: young people suddenly change their whole orientation one way or the other. In old age, when both intellect and emotions are dimmed, there is no worry about the niceties of theology, nor is there any emotional excitement about religious matters.

Summary

We can now decide which of the three models applies at different stages of the life cycle, for different aspects of religious activity, and set out our conclusions in tabular form, as in Table 4.5.

TABLE 4.5 *Ageing models*

	Church attendance	*Attitudes*	*Beliefs*
18–30	traditional (i.e. decline)	stability	stability
30–60	stability (but small peak at 50–60)	traditional (i.e. increase)	stability
60+	disengagement (but watch television)	traditional (i.e. increase)	traditional (i.e. increase)

5 Sex differences

The differences between men and women in their religious behaviour and beliefs are considerable. Furthermore, since many social surveys report the results for the two sexes separately, there is a lot of evidence available. This is therefore one of the most important of the statistical comparisons to be made in this book. We shall first consider the extent of the difference, using various criteria for religious activity, and go on to compare different denominations for the proportions of male and female members.

Sex differences on different criteria

The percentages of men and women who engage in various kinds of religious behaviour are given in the tables. It is obvious that women are more religious on every criterion. It is possible to derive various indices of how much more religious they are. The index which we shall use is the ratio of the percentage of women to the percentage of men who engage in the activity in question. The main difficulty with this index is that it is smaller when both percentages are large. Since Americans are rather more religious on most criteria than British people, it is not possible to compare British and American sex ratios, and so they will be treated separately.

Church membership This is a useful criterion, which will be made the basis for denominational comparisons later. The percentages ratio for American church members can be calculated in two ways. In the 1936 Census of Religious Bodies (*Census* 1936) the total membership of men and women is given as 20·13 million and 25·65 million respectively. This gives a percentage ratio of 1·32 after making allowances for the fact that there were 0·7 per cent more men in the population (*Census* 1940). However, if we compare the

71

percentages of people claiming to be church members in social surveys, a ratio of about 1·10 is obtained (cf. Rosten, 1955, p. 239). This is partly an artefact resulting from the higher percentages of claimed members, but it must also be the case that a lot of men claim to be members who are not.

British church records do not report males and females separately. However, several surveys have asked people what their religious denomination is, if any; the findings are set out in Table 5.1.

TABLE 5.1   *Sex differences in church membership*

	Great Britain	males	females	sex ratio
		%	%	
Gorer (1955)	British adults (claim affil.)	75	75	1·00
BIPO (1950)	British adults (claim affil.)	89	94	1·05
	USA	*males*	*females*	*sex ratio*
Census of Religious Bodies, 1936	US population	20·13m	25·65m	1·32

Church attendance   Typical results of British and American surveys are given in Table 5.2. As argued above, the difference between the British and American indices is simply an artefact: if the percentages of English men and women who go to church at least once every three months are compared we get 44 and 55 per cent, giving an index of 1·25 which is the same as the American figure (Odham, 1947). There has been a historical shift in the British sex ratio. A

TABLE 5.2   *Sex differences in church attendance*

	Great Britain	males	females	sex ratio
		%	%	
BIPO (1948)	British adults (weekly)	12	18	1·50
Odham (1947)	British adults (3 months' attendance)	44	55	1·25
	USA	*males*	*females*	*sex ratio*
Gallup Poll (1972)	US adults	45	55	1·22

preponderance of women in English churches was first noted in the 1890s.

Prayer   The sex ratio is higher than for any other aspect of religious behaviour, as is shown in Table 5.3.

TABLE 5.3   *Sex difference in reported daily private prayer*

	Great Britain	*males*	*females*	*sex ratio*
		%	%	
Gorer (1955)	English adults	31	58	1·87
Social Surveys (1964)	Adults in ITV area	33	53	1·56
	USA	*males*	*females*	*sex ratio*
Allport *et al.* (1948)	Harvard and Radcliffe students	22	35	1·59
Ross (1950)	YMCA members	37·8	64·2	1·70

Beliefs   A number of studies have found that women are more 'conservative' in their religious beliefs (Fagan and Breed, 1970). However, as Table 5.4 shows, where large percentages of the population hold a belief (e.g. belief in God), the sex ratio is fairly small.

TABLE 5.4   *Sex differences in religious beliefs*

		males	*females*	*sex ratio*
Believe in God				
	Great Britain			
Social Surveys (1964)	British adults (personal God)	30	45	1·50
	British adults (spirit or life force)	33	33	1·00
	USA			
Gallup Poll (1968)	US adults	96	98	1·02
Believe in an after-life				
	Great Britain			
Odham (1947)	English adults	39	56	1·44
	USA			
Gallup Poll (1960)	US adults	68	78	1·15
Believe Jesus Christ was the Son of God				
	Great Britain			
Social Surveys (1964)	British adults	46	71	1·54

Cox (1967) and Wright and Cox (1967) found that girls are more likely to describe God as loving, comforting and forgiving, while boys tend to view him as a supreme power, a driving force and a planner or controller. The difference in descriptions in this case seems to fit male and female ideals and motivations.

Mystical experiences Back and Bourque (1970) report that in three Gallup Polls dealing with intense religious experiences, such experiences tended to be reported more often by women than by men. In a smaller study of American students (Bourque and Back, 1968), respondents were asked to report both aesthetic experiences (e.g. feeling very sad or happy in response to music or art) and religious experiences (e.g. feeling the presence of God). There were negligible differences between males and females on aesthetic experiences, but women reported more religious experiences. This finding goes against the view that relates the greater religiosity of women to their higher level of 'emotionality'.

The highest rates of religious experience were reported by black members of Baptist and similar churches, where the proportion of females is high. Alland (1962), in an observational study of 'possession' in a small Negro sect, found that females were more likely than males to enter religious 'trance' states during services.

TABLE 5.5   *Sex differences in mystical experiences*

	USA	males	females	sex ratio
		%	%	
Back and Bourque (1970) average of 3 national surveys	US adults	29·5	35·4	1·20

Differences in attitude Attitudes towards the church and towards religion also vary between the sexes. The Thurstone–Chave scale of attitudes towards the church was used by Newcomb and Svehla (1937), who found women consistently more favourable; the difference was greatest for working-class subjects and for young people. Several studies found that women had higher religious value scores on the Allport–Vernon Study of Values (Clark, 1950; Spoerl, 1952). As a result, female norms for the revised version of this measure, the Allport-Vernon-Lindzey Study of Values, are much higher on the religious value scale. Women also score higher on the aesthetic and social values. Reporting on repeated measurements of attitudes of students towards the church between 1930 and 1967,

Jones (1970) found consistently more favourable attitudes on the part of women. The figures presented in Tables 5.1 to 5.5 show that the sex ratio is consistently higher in Britain than in the USA. This may be because the higher US percentages produce higher pressures towards conformity, which have the effect of reducing sex differences, as Katz and Allport (1931) suggested.

The sex ratio is consistently greater for saying daily prayers than for church attendance or membership. The latter are again more under the influence of social pressures, while prayers are a private matter and reflect more spontaneous religious concern. This suggests that the larger sex ratios should be taken more seriously than the smaller ones. On the other hand the sex ratio for mystical experience is fairly low (1·20:1).

Sex differences in different denominations

In most denominations and religious groups, there are differences in the proportion of men and women members, with women usually outnumbering men. Table 5.6 shows the ratios of men to women in

TABLE 5.6 *The ratio of women to men in the American denominations* $(p < 0.01)$

Eastern Orthodox	0·75–0·99
Roman Catholics	1·09
Lutherans	1·04–1·23
Mennonites	1·14–1·16
Friends	1·25
Episcopalians	1·37
Presbyterians	1·34–1·44
Unitarians	1·40
Methodists	1·33–1·47
Baptists	1·35–1·50
Congregationalists	1·55
Negro Baptists	1·55
Negro Methodists	1·64–1·71
Assembly of God	1·71
Adventists	1·52–2·00
Church of the Nazarene	1·75
Pentecostalists	1·71–2·09
Christian Scientists	3·19

Calculated from *Census* 1936. This shows the ratio of women to men among the members. When different figures are shown for separate branches of a denomination, the range of ratios for the main branches is given.

American sects and denominations in the 1936 census. Three main groups of churches can be distinguished. Firstly, there are the Eastern Orthodox church, the Catholics, the Lutheran and the Mennonite churches with up to 15 per cent more women than men, but with more men than women in some cases. Secondly, there are the major Protestant bodies, which have between 25 and 55 per cent more women. Thirdly, the Pentecostal church and similar minor Protestant sects have over 55 per cent more women. The above classification can be summarized by saying that the proportion of women is higher the further one moves towards small sects. The minor Protestant sects have the highest ratio; Table 5.6 shows that in America there are over 55 per cent more women members. The highest ratio of all is found for the Christian Scientists, who have more than three women to each male member.

When we study other aspects of religious activity, essentially the same picture appears, with similar differences between denominations. Sex differences in weekly attendance are shown in Table 5.7.

TABLE 5.7   *Sex ratios for British denominations for reported weekly attendance*

	weekly attendance
Church of England	1·63
Roman Catholic	1·19
Nonconformist	1·48

Source: Jones (1934).

Rowntree and Lavers (1951) counted attendance in York and found 57 per cent more women in nonconformist churches, 48 per cent more in the Church of England and 23 per cent more in the Roman Catholic churches.

The ratio for Catholics can be analysed in greater detail on the basis of figures obtained by Fichter (1952) for three Catholic parishes, involving 8,363 people. The differences are greatest for confession, especially for older people, where the ratio is 1·93. For the obligatory functions of Easter duties and mass, which over 80 per cent attended, the sex differences were slight. This supports Katz and Allport's suggestion (1931) that the sex ratio is smaller the greater the institutional pressure to conform. It fits in also with the greater sex differences found on private prayer compared with attendance at church services.

Wilson (1961) in his study of English small sects found a ratio of

2–3 : 1 for attendance at the Elim Foursquare Gospel; 2–4 : 1 for the Christian Scientists; but only about 1·25 : 1 for the Christadelphians: Wilson accounts for the small ratio for this sect by the lack of emotional release at the services. In Billy Graham's campaign at Glasgow, the ratio for converts was 1·8 : 1 (Colquhoun, 1955).

Explanation

In explaining the observed sex differences in religious activities and beliefs, we shall make use of hypotheses derived from two sources. They are based partly on the specific functions that religion may fulfil for women, and partly from general physiological or psychological sex differences.

(1) If the function of religion is to relieve guilt feelings, and if women have more guilt feelings than men, women should be more religious (p. 196). In fact women do have more guilt feelings; furthermore the proportion of women rises as we move from Catholicism towards extreme Protestantism, as would be expected from the emphasis on sin and salvation in the latter groups; data on suicide and crime also support the theory (p. 142f).

(2) If God is a projected father figure, as Freud suggests, and if children prefer the opposite-sex parent, it follows that girls should be more concerned with a deity presented as a fatherly male (p. 183f). This theory too can explain denominational differences: Catholicism offers a mother-figure in the Virgin Mary, so that this faith should be as attractive to men as to women, whereas Protestantism should not be.

(3) Several basic psychological differences between the sexes seem to be related to qualities that lead to greater religiosity. Gray (1971) pointed to two sex differences which seem to appear in all primates, and suggested that they are biologically determined: females are found to be less aggressive and more fearful than males. Garai and Scheinfeld (1968), in a review of the literature on sex differences, reported that females were found to be more submissive and passive, more anxious and more dependent. Garai (1970) reported that women were found to have more worries and distress. These psychological findings can be easily related to the elements of 'fear and trembling' in the experience of the religious person.

(4) These basic sex differences are probably increased by differences in the upbringing of boys and girls. In a cross-cultural study of sex differences in socialization, Barry, Bacon and Child (1957) found that nearly all cultures put emphasis on training girls for nurturance, obedience and responsibility, while boys were trained for self-reliance and independence. D'Andrade (1967), summarizing

77

cross-cultural data on sex differences in behaviour, states that males in most cultures are less nurturant and less expressive emotionally than females. Religion in most cultures has strong emotional and nurturant components, and we would expect most females to respond to them.

(5) McGuire (1969) reported on the greater influenceability of women. Studies of conformity, suggestibility and persuasibility all point to a clear sex difference, with women scoring higher in every case. The greater conformity of women is reflected in many studies of social attitudes and intolerance. Findings reported by Hutt (1972) suggest that the greater conformity of women may be related to the closer interaction they have with parents in early childhood. Garai and Scheinfeld (1968) report that girls have closer contact with their mothers, and are encouraged early to develop responsiveness and compliance. In peer groups girls are observed to be more affiliative and to develop pro-social aggression, i.e. aggression in the service of social norms. Similarly, McClelland et al. (1953) found that women were more interested in 'affiliative achievement', thus being more dependent on approval from others (cf. Douvan and Adelson, 1966). From the above women emerge as 'oversocialized' compared with boys, affiliative, and conforming. These traits should lead to more activity in religious groups and a stronger adherence to their norms.

(6) The deprivation-compensation theory of religious behaviour, which will be analysed later (Chapter 11), seems to apply rather well to women. It can be argued that women are more deprived than men in many respects. Bourque and Back (1968) argued that the higher frequency of reported religious experiences among women is a reaction to the greater level of frustration they face in society. Campbell and Fukuyama (1970) constructed a measure of deprivation, which included being female, and found that on measures of traditional beliefs, for example, women scored higher, together with other deprived groups such as older people, the less educated, and the poor. We argue later that small sects also fit in well with the deprivation-compensation model; women comprise the majority of their members. Sex differences in religiosity may be related to the sex difference in fantasy behaviour found by May (1966, 1969). He found that in the sequence of a fantasy story, women show a movement from negative emotion and experiences to more positive emotions and experience, while men show the opposite pattern. This finding agrees with the explanation of women's religiosity as a reaction to relative deprivation.

From a general view of women as being deprived compared to men we can look at specific areas of deprivation. Several writers have suggested that women are especially deprived in the area of sexual behaviour, since they have not hitherto been allowed to express their sexual drives as freely as men. It is possible that some religious activity on the part of women is a substitute for sexual impulses or their distorted expression. The erotic nature of religious ecstasy among women and the connection between religion and preoccupation with sexual taboos would tend to support this view (see the discussion on p. 198f).

(7) Luckman (1967) suggested that there is a general negative relationship between work involvement and religiosity in modern societies. On the basis of European statistics, he reported that non-working women, the young, and the old, who are not involved in work activities, are all higher on religiosity. Working women, who are more similar to men than housewives, were found to be less religious.

6   Personality and religion

To what extent do religious people, or members of different denominations, have distinctive kinds of personality? And if there are differences, which causes which? It may be that people with certain kinds of personality are more likely to adopt particular beliefs and practices, as some psychological theories of religion postulate. Or the teachings and practices of churches may affect the personalities of those belonging to them; this is one index of the power of religion to affect people's lives. Or it may be the case that both religious behaviour and aspects of personality are influenced by common factors, such as methods of child-rearing.

Since large proportions of the population are involved in religious behaviour and beliefs, we should not expect to find very large differences in personality between different groups. And it is important to hold constant other sources of variation in personality, such as social class. It may also be found that personality-religion links are found only for particular sub-groups of the population (Argyle and Delin, 1965). A further problem is that, during recent years, the whole concept of personality traits has come under attack, with the discovery that behaviour varies greatly between different situations, and that trait measures fail to predict actual behaviour very well (Mischel, 1968). This is leading to a search for invariant aspects of personality, which correlate with behaviour in a range of situations. The research reported here shows which aspects of personality are related to a sphere quite remote from their original area of application: religious behaviour and beliefs.

A number of carefully conducted studies with large numbers of subjects have investigated the correlations between religious beliefs or behaviour and familiar personality traits. In most of these studies very little relationship was found between religion and personality. Brown (1962), for example, using 203 subjects found that religious

80

beliefs correlated 0·03 with neuroticism, 0·07 with extraversion (both non-significant). Siegman (1963), on the other hand, found that religiosity correlated with extraversion for Protestants, and with introversion for Jews; however, this study used rather small numbers of subjects, and the correlations were very small for some of the samples of students used. Brown and Lowe (1951) tested 887 students on the Minnesota Multiphasic Personality Inventory (MMPI), and found less than the chance number of differences between different religious groups. It appears that relations between religiosity and general personality traits are weak. In this chapter we shall explore X possible links between religion and more specialized aspects of personality.

Child-rearing differences

Are there any special characteristics or effects of growing up in a religious family, regardless of denomination, and are there any discernible differences in child-rearing practices among religious groups, which might explain personality differences in adult members? Some evidence on the effects of growing up in a religious family was discussed in the section on religion in childhood (Chapter 4). Findings on differences among denominations are available for three areas: authoritarian relationships, the use of physical punishment, and training for independence.

Catholic children tend more often to see one parent or the other (more often the father) as the dominant one. Protestant children are more likely to see their parents as equal partners (Hess and Torney, 1962). The clear division of authority may be related to later perceptions of authority figures and institutions. Similar authoritarian effects may be expected to result from the 'coalition with God' technique (Nunn, 1964), in which parents use religious references to buttress their discipline over their children. Nunn described parents who tended to use this technique as ineffective and authoritarian, and found that they also tended to use physical punishment. Elder (1965) found that Catholic parents in the USA are more autocratic in their relationship with their children, and this finding was explained as stemming from the autocratic theology and structure of the Catholic church.

Miller and Swanson (1958) found that Catholic parents were more likely to use physical punishment and material rewards, while Protestant parents were more likely to use scolding or restriction of privileges as punishment, and praise as a reward for good behaviour. Lenski (1963) found that Catholic mothers tended to advocate physical punishment more than Protestant mothers. Physical punishment, which is more prevalent in Catholic families, is supposed to be part of the background of the authoritarian personality (Adorno *et al.*, 1950), but physical punishment is also more prevalent among lower-class parents (Bronfenbrenner, 1958). Part at least of the denominational differences in authoritarian attitudes to children and the use of physical punishment is due to class differences.

The degree of encouragement given by parents to children's independent actions differs in different denominations. Lenski (1963) reported that in answer to the question of whether a 12-year-old should decide for himself his participation in religious activities, 7 per cent of the Catholic respondents, 21 per cent of the Protestant respondents, and 32 per cent of the Jewish respondents replied affirmatively. In this and other studies it was found that Catholics were more concerned with obedience than with independence (Miller and Swanson, 1958). The finding that Jewish parents encourage more independent thinking and intellectual autonomy was also obtained by Psathas (1957).

Differences in the age at which parents expect their children to show independence and mastery were studied in the USA by Rosen and McClelland, and the findings are summarized in Table 6.1.

TABLE 6.1   *Differences in the average age at which independence and mastery are expected by parents*

Source of data	Religious groups					Significance of diff. Prot. v. Cath.
				Catholic		
	Protestant	Jewish	French Canadian	Italian	Irish	
Rosen (1959)	N = 122 6·87	N = 57 6·83	N = 62 7·99	N = 74 8·03		<0·01
McClelland *et al.* (1955)	N = 42 6·64	N = 45 6·59		N = 35 8·42	N = 33 7·66	<0·01

The Protestant ethic and achievement motivation

Weber's theory (1904), later elaborated in psychological terms by McClelland (1961), suggests an interesting link between religion and personality. Weber observed that Protestantism coincided with the rise of capitalism in a number of countries, and that Protestants seemed to work harder, save more money, and do better economically.

The Protestant ethic

Weber's explanation was that certain Protestant ideas encouraged capitalistic activities. The reformers taught that men would be individually judged, and would be judged on the basis of their whole life's work, of which their 'calling' was the most important part; on the other hand, money should not be spent on oneself. This led to a life of hard work, self-discipline, asceticism and concern with achievement; it also led to the accumulation of money which could not be spent on luxury, but which could be put into one's own business. Calvin taught predestination, and here the link with capitalism is more obscure: it was thought that the elect could be recognized by certain outward signs, which included self-denial and devotion to duty, and it was also believed that God caused the elect to prosper.

McClelland offered a social-psychological explanation for the link between Protestantism and capitalism. This is shown in Figure 3. The theory is that Protestant ideas and values produce (1) a certain way of bringing up children, which (2) leads to the children acquiring strong achievement motivation, and (3) high achievers become entrepreneurs and create an expansion of business.

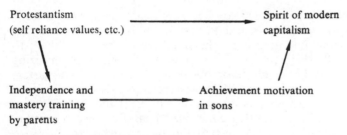

FIGURE 3   *The Weber hypothesis*

Source: McClelland (1961).

Historical accounts of the early entrepreneurs who started the Industrial Revolution show that they had exactly this kind of personality; they were also Protestants. Do Catholics and Protestants today differ in achievement motivation, attitudes to work, and economic success, as the theory predicts?

Achievement motivation

Earlier studies, using rather small samples, found that Protestants and Jews scored higher in n.Ach than Catholics, in the USA (McClelland, 1955; Rosen, 1959), and that this was related to differences in the age at which independence training was given (Table 6.1). McClelland (1961) showed that Catholic–Protestant differences in achievement motivation can be accounted for by social-class factors within the same society, and by the traditionalism factor across societies. Veroff *et al.* (1962) studied a national sample of 1,620 Americans, and arrived at a rather different conclusion. Overall the Catholic males had higher n.Ach, though Protestants scored higher in the group that lived in the north-east and had larger incomes (like the subjects in the earlier studies). Catholic males had higher n.Ach when they had low incomes and large families, which was not the case with Protestants. The authors conclude that Catholic n.Ach is aroused by immediate material needs and that generalized abstract strivings may be stronger in Protestants. Carney and McKeachie (1962) in a study of college students found that Jewish students scored the highest on n.Ach.

The conclusion is that in the USA at the present time there is no clear difference in achievement motivation between Catholics and Protestants, but that Jews are stronger in this form of motivation than either.

Attitudes to work

Lenski (1963) found that Catholics were negative in their attitude toward work, while Jews and Protestants were positive. Catholics attached more importance to the family, and this was likely to interfere with their success in an industrial society emphasizing social mobility. The emphasis on obedience in Catholic child-rearing, as opposed to the Jewish and Protestant emphasis on early independence, was also seen as interfering with Catholic integration in the economy. Greeley (1963) challenged Lenski's conclusions, and suggested that Catholic–Protestant differences in attitudes toward work, achievement and mobility are likely to change as they are assimilated into American society. In Greeley's sample of American university graduates Catholics were just as achievement-oriented as the others, and even more interested in economic success. Schuman (1971) also failed to replicate Lenski's results, and found no difference between Catholics and Protestants in attitudes to work, spending or consumption. It is very likely that there has been a change in the attitudes and positions of American Catholics, especially in urban areas. Broom and Glenn (1966) reported minimal differences in attitude towards work between Catholics and Protestants in large urban areas.

Occupational success, socio-economic status

Results supporting the hypothesis that Protestants would be in more advanced positions in their jobs than Catholics were reported by Jackson and Crockett (1964), and others. Jackson, Fox and Crockett (1970) analysed a US national survey made in 1957, and reported that

Protestants were more likely than Catholics to be upward mobile and Catholics were more likely to be downward mobile. Glenn and Hyland (1967) showed that there was a gradual equalization of occupational status between Protestants and Catholics in the USA. While Protestants still have a very slight edge over Catholics in the highest income group, there is an overrepresentation of Protestants in the lowest income categories. They found that between 1943 and 1964 Catholics have been gaining in occupational level, educational level, and income. The findings were mainly attributed to urbanization and the assimilation of Catholic immigrants.

The narrowing of the gap in occupation and status between Catholics and Protestants in the USA since 1930 is reflected in Table 6.2. A more specific prediction from the Protestant-ethic

TABLE 6.2   *The trend in Protestant-Catholic occupational differentials*

| | | Indices of dissimilarity between Prot. and Cath. | |
| | | *With farmers* | *Without farmers* |
Source	*Date*		
A	*c.*1930	31·3	15·6
B	1954	17	9
A	1957	17·3	11·0
C	1957	11·0	7·2
D	1962	11	7
E	1964	8·6	4·4

Key to sources:
A—Jackson, Fox, and Crockett, 1970.
B—Lipset and Bendix, 1959.
C—Goldstein, 1969.
D—Crespi, 1963.
E—Glenn and Hyland, 1967.
Comparisons are restricted to employed white adult males. The first line represents the fathers of respondents interviewed in 1957. Source: Mueller (1971).

hypothesis is that independent businessmen are more likely to come from Protestant backgrounds. Lenski (1963) reports that in the USA 33 per cent of Jews are self-employed, compared with 10 per cent of Protestants and 8 per cent of Catholics.

It looks as if early training of children for independence, high level of achievement motivation, positive attitudes towards work, occupational success, and a preference to be self-employed, associated with the 'Protestant ethic', are now found most among Jews in the USA. It has been suggested that this behaviour may be due to desire for money and status rather than to internalized strivings as described by the Protestant ethic. While Protestants differed from Catholics until quite recently, the gap has narrowed or closed during the last twenty years.

Educational achievement

Differences in the level of education obtained by members of various religious groups have been investigated in the USA. Most studies deal with two kinds of comparisons: one between the achievements of Catholics and Protestants (related to the Protestant ethic issues discussed above), and the other between Jews and all other groups.

Lenski (1963) found in the USA that 63 per cent of Jews complete high school compared with 49 per cent of Protestants and 43 per cent of Catholics, but Elder (1965) found that American Catholics are more likely to reach secondary school than American Protestants when regional and social class differences are eliminated. Thus Catholic-Protestant differences in educational achievement can be attributed to initial social class and other differences, though these may have been partly due to the effects of religion at a previous period. Greeley (1963) suggested that differences in educational aspirations and career choices between Catholics and Protestants are decreasing. Differences in the aspirations of high school students for higher education were found by Rhodes and Nam (1970), and are presented in Table 6.3.

TABLE 6.3 *White high school students in the USA who expect to enrol in college, by religious affiliation, 1965*

Religion	Percentage planning college
All cases	53
Baptist	42
Small Protestant groups	48
Roman Catholic	55
Large Protestant groups	58
Jewish	86
Others	59
No affiliation	58

Source: Rhodes and Nam (1970).

Even when all other variables such as occupation of parents, IQ, and income, are held constant, the relationship between religion and educational plans still holds. Rhodes and Nam (1970) interpreted the results as supporting the view that the values promoted by some religious denominations lead to higher educational aspirations. We may hypothesize that more fundamentalist and authoritarian denominations are less supportive of free inquiry. (See the following section on academic and scientific achievement.)

With all other variables such as father's occupation and education held constant, Protestants were found to be slightly more likely than Catholics to become college graduates, and more likely to persist in college once they got there (Fox and Jackson, 1973).

These observed differences in the educational aspirations of religious groups are important, since educational achievements in turn affect other factors, such as socio-economic status (Featherman, 1971). Educational level also affects a variety of attitude patterns, such as authoritarianism and ethno-centrism. Given the effects of education (see Chapter 3) on religion and other attitudes, the differences in educational aspirations may account for the greater traditionalism of some groups, or help to maintain it.

Academic and scientific achievement

Religious groups are not equally represented among members of different occupational groups. This is especially notable in the case of academics and scientists, where certain groups are over-represented, while other groups are severely under-represented. Another notable finding is the significant minority of scientists who declare themselves to be followers of no religion at all.

Knapp and Goodrich (1951) show the high percentage of successful scientists coming from American liberal arts colleges, and the very small number from Roman Catholic universities; they suggest that Protestant ideology is more in line with scientific activity. Fry (1933) also studied the professional fields in which members of each denomination became eminent. Some of these results are not surprising: for example, there are no Christian Science doctors or Quaker soldiers. Others are less obvious: there are many Catholic artists, actors and politicians, few social scientists; Unitarians produce a lot of natural scientists and social workers, but not many soldiers or politicians; Episcopalians produce a large number of soldiers, architects and engineers, but few natural scientists and agriculturists. Table 6.4 shows the differences in religious preferences between American scientists, their parents, and the general population.

Two conclusions can be drawn from Table 6.4. First, there is a wide gap between the rates of religious affiliation in the US population in general, and that of American scientists. Second, American scientists are not equally recruited from different religious groups. The Catholic group is under-represented, and the Jewish group

TABLE 6.4 *Religious affiliation of American scientists (1954), their parents and US population (1957)*

Religious affiliation	% of scientists	% of their parents	% of US population
Protestant	23	53	66·3
Catholic	<1	5	26·2
Jewish	9	23	3·0
None	45	8	2·1
Other and no affiliation	23	5	1·9

Source: Bello (1954).

over-represented among the families that these scientists came from. Steinberg (1973) showed that the religious composition of faculty members in American colleges and universities is markedly different from that of the general population, in the same way.

Leuba (1934) showed that religious beliefs among scientists tended to decrease with their eminence. He found that 48 per cent of those classified as 'lesser' scientists believed in God, compared with 32 per cent of the 'greater' scientists. The corresponding figures for belief in immortality were 59 and 37 per cent, and the same relation for each kind of scientist taken separately. Clark (1955) also found that eminence, as measured by appearance in *Who's Who*, is associated with religious scepticism and religious non-affiliation. Roe (1956) studied a group of 64 eminent scientists, including 22 psychologists and anthropologists. Most of them came from Protestant backgrounds, none was a Catholic, and a few were Jews. Out of the whole group, only three were active in any church, and the rest were 'indifferent' to religion. Heist *et al.* (1961) compared productive and non-productive university teachers and found that the highly productive ones were lowest on the religious scale of the Allport-Vernon-Lindzey Study of Values.

Differences among scientists in various disciplines have been found, those in the natural sciences being more religious then those in the social sciences (Lehman and Witty, 1931; Lehman and Shriver, 1968). Table 6.5 (opposite) sets out the distribution of religious preference among one group of American social scientists. The data presented in Table 6.5 allow us to draw the following conclusions. It seems clear that the religious preferences of American sociologists differ sharply from those of the population in general. Of special significance is the percentage of those who have no religious preference (35·7). The over-representation of Jews and the under-representation of Catholics seems to be a function of initial choice,

TABLE 6.5   *Religious preference of mother, own late adolescent, and current (1967) religious preferences, for 429 American sociologists*

Preference	Protestant	Catholic	Jewish	None	Other and unknown
	%	%	%	%	%
Mother's	60·4	8·4	18·9	5·4	7·0
Late adolescent	49·4	7·7	15·2	20·3	7·4
Current	37·5	6·5	12·8	35·7	7·5
US population (1957)	66·3	26·2	3·0	2·1	1·9

Source: Glenn and Weiner (1969).

and not of later 'desertion' or apostasy. The reported data on religious preferences of these sociologists in their late adolescence show that the apostasy process is not a function of training in the social sciences alone: 20·3 per cent reported no religious preference in late adolescence, probably before any exposure to social science training. Thus, early religious apostasy seems to be a factor in recruiting future social scientists (cf. Zelan, 1968).

Within the medical profession there is an interesting pattern of denominational preferences, as Kosa (1969) found (see Table 6.6). Psychologists, who show a number of unconventional attitudes, are also generally low on measures of religiosity. Both Leuba (1934) and Struening and Spilka (1952) reported that among scientists and academicians psychologists are the least religious of all groups. Leuba (1934) studied the religious beliefs of 50 'distinguished psychologists' and 57 'lesser psychologists'. They were compared

TABLE 6.6   *Selection of medical speciality by religious affiliation*

Per cent of students most interested in working in:	Protestant (1,080)	Catholic (435)	Jewish (765)	None (166)
	%	%	%	%
General practice	51	41	20	23
Surgery	16	23	22	20
Internal medicine	19	22	37	28
Psychiatry	5	4	11	25
Obstetrics-gynaecology	9	10	10	4

The highest percentage in each line is underlined. Source: Kosa (1969).

with natural scientists, sociologists and historians. The proportion of believers in God among the distinguished psychologists was the lowest of all groups studied (13·2 per cent). The percentage of believers for the 'lesser' psychologists was 32·1, and for the whole group it was 24·2. Henry, Sims and Spray (1971) found that out of 1,387 American clinical psychologists, 50 per cent came from Jewish families, but only 30 per cent described themselves as currently Jewish. Only 20 per cent of the clinical psychologists described themselves as Protestant, 8 per cent as Catholic, and 42 per cent were unaffiliated.

Finally Leuba (1934) found that he could not report the religious beliefs of philosophers, since they apparently could not understand the questions or agree with any of the alternative answers offered.

What has to be explained in the relationship between scientific achievement and religion can be divided into two parts. The first, treating religious affiliation as an independent variable, is that there is a relationship between religious background (i.e. religion of the scientist's family) and scientific achievement. The second is the marked lack of religiosity among scientists who have achieved their eminence. What has been suggested as a general explanation is that there is an incompatibility between a religious world view and the scientific or scholarly approach to the world.

It has been shown that sectarian schools in the US, which are dominated by religious organizations, have a lower quality of students, faculty, and educational programmes (e.g. Hassenger, 1967). A study by Lehman (1972) showed that faculty members committed to a scholarly orientation were less involved in traditional religious activities than faculty members who were less scholarly. In a study of 2,842 graduate students in the USA, Stark (1963) found that church attendance was negatively associated with self-identification as an intellectual, and positive attitudes towards creativity, occupational freedom, and professional ambition. Thus, those who were more conforming religiously appeared to place less value on scientific and intellectual achievement.

How does this theory of the basic contradiction between the scholarly orientation and religion apply to the over-representation of certain groups, such as Jews, among eminent scientists? Since all studies show that members of liberal religious groups are over-represented among eminent scientists, we can assume that coming from a religiously liberal or secularized family minimizes the difficulty in transferring from the religious orientation to the scholarly orientation, if such a transfer is necessary at all. Most eminent Jewish scientists came from liberal families, and have gone through a process of growing secularization as they achieved their eminence. At the same time, it is possible that traditional Jewish values have supported the application of the scholarly ethos to other areas of knowledge and encouraged creativity.

One of the most striking denominational differences is in the production of scientists. Catholics produce about one-sixth as many as do Jews or Protestants (Lenski, 1963), perhaps the biggest difference between these groups. What is the explanation of the low scientific activity of Catholics? Conflict between science and religion, attitudes to authority and other values, and the absence of a scholarly tradition would seem to be among the contributing factors.

Conflict between science and religion   Since the days of Galileo, there has been some conflict between the Catholic church and science. Protestantism, apart from trouble over evolution, has been able to live with science more easily. Lenski (1963) reports that 32 per cent of Catholic graduates saw a serious conflict between science and church teachings compared with 17 per cent for Protestant graduates.

Attitudes to authority and other values   We have seen that Catholic parents place more value on obedience than independence in their children (p. 82). Catholics score higher on authoritarianism (p. 94f). The Catholic church is a hierarchical organization, where beliefs are handed down from the top. It seems likely that people who are taught to accept traditional ideas from those in authority and have learnt that innovation, independence, and new ideas are not welcome, will be less likely to become the innovators of new scientific ideas or research. Kosa (1969), in a study of 2,630 American medical students, found differences in values and career choices related to religious affiliation. Table 6.7 shows the differences in value choices and Table 6.6 shows the differences in career choices. It can be seen that Catholic medical students do not prefer to deal with problems requiring exact analysis, independent action, working long hard hours, using high-level abilities, contributing to knowledge, or having prestige among colleagues, all of which characterize the life of scientists. Jews and the non-religious show the opposite pattern.

Absence of scholarly tradition   Greeley (1967) thinks that the lack of scientific activity on the part of Catholics can be explained by the absence of scholarly tradition, able young Catholics entering the religious life, and economic factors. He found that graduates of Catholic colleges in the 1960s in the USA did not have anti-scientific attitudes. Wagner, Fisher and Doyle (1959) found no differences between Catholic and other students in preference for scientific and technical courses. Perhaps the Catholics are catching up, and differences in scientific achievement will eventually disappear.

91

TABLE 6.7 *Preference for medical values by religious affiliation*

Per cent of students to whom it is important to:	Protestant (1,080)	Catholic (435)	Jewish (765)	None (166)
	%	%	%	%
Deal with problems requiring exact analysis	23	21	29	<u>32</u>
Have the greatest scope for independent actions	48	47	60	<u>62</u>
Have working hours that are not extremely long	8	7	11	<u>16</u>
Reach a yearly income of $15,000	19	20	30	<u>26</u>
Use high-level abilities	40	36	<u>52</u>	46
Be in a position to contribute to knowledge	28	25	<u>39</u>	31
Have prestige among colleagues	35	28	<u>44</u>	23
Develop warm personal relations with patients	59	52	<u>60</u>	57
Have no serious consequences resulting from mistakes	36	<u>40</u>	35	24
Be certain of the desired results	53	<u>57</u>	54	36
Spend time with physiological rather than functional illness	17	<u>22</u>	12	15
Be able to rely on experienced persons	<u>32</u>	31	26	25

The highest percentage in each line is underlined. Source: Kosa (1969).

Other factors It is also important to consider the influence of other factors such as social class and educational opportunities. Datta (1967) showed that while Jewish teenagers produced more creative science projects than either Catholics or Protestants, the differences were markedly reduced for subjects from large cities. Thus, interpreting differences in scientific achievement only in terms of religious group values can be misleading.

Physical v. social sciences

Another finding which goes against the common-sense view and calls for an explanation is the greater degree of religiosity among physical scientists, as compared with social scientists, especially psychologists. These differences among fields of study appear even among undergraduate students, as the following studies show. Bereiter and

Freedman (1962) found that social science majors take a more liberal and less conventional stand on most issues, while students in the applied fields are more conservative in their attitudes. We would predict then that students in the social sciences will be less religious than those in applied fields, and this prediction seems to be borne out by empirical surveys.

Jones (1970) found that among American university freshmen, those majoring in natural sciences were the most favourable towards the church, while those majoring in psychology were the least favourable.

One factor may be that of self-selection in terms of unconventionality. Social scientists are members of young, 'unconventional' disciplines and tend to deviate from many social norms, The mere fact of choosing human society or human behaviour as the subject of study suggests a curiosity about basic social beliefs and conventions, and a readiness to reject them. Studying cultures and societies leads to relativism regarding one's own society. Among physical scientists a compartmentalization of scientific attitudes and religious attitudes is easier. Social scientists, who examine beliefs critically, may find it harder to compartmentalize their scientific attitudes.

Intelligence and creativity

A number of early American studies found negative correlations between intelligence and measures of religious conservatism and religious attitudes (e.g. Howells, 1928; Symington, 1935; Brown and Lowe, 1951). Symington divided his subjects into those from liberal and conservative homes. It is interesting that the correlation was higher for those from a liberal background ($-0 \cdot 42$ to $-0 \cdot 55$) than for subjects from a conservative background ($-0 \cdot 13$ to $-0 \cdot 29$). He suggests that those from liberal homes had been free to use their brains to discard orthodox ideas. These negative correlations are higher for measures of religious conservatism ($-0 \cdot 15$ to $-0 \cdot 55$) than for religious attitudes ($-0 \cdot 19$ to $0 \cdot 19$). The explanation of these results is probably that university education brings about a critical and sceptical attitude to traditional and non-rational ideas (p. 37).

Kosa and Schommer (1961) reported that among Catholic students knowledge of religious doctrine was positively correlated with scholastic achievement. The problem is that knowledge of religious doctrine in a religious environment is in itself a 'scholastic achievement'.

Denominational differences in intelligence are also found. Jews and Episcopalians come out high on average, Baptists and Catholics low (Fry, 1933; Pratt, 1937; Rummell, 1934). The most likely explanation of these denominational differences is in terms of the social class differences between denominations (p. 166f). These in turn are partly due to the fact that particular sets of beliefs and practices have more appeal to one class than another. A further factor is family size: Catholics, Mormons and others have larger families (p. 159f), and large family size may be a source of lower intelligence, since the children receive less attention from their parents. A further factor is that a proportion of intelligent Catholics become priests and have no children.

Studies comparing IQ scores in religious groups have become rare, but Levinson (1963) reported that Jews still did better than non-Jews on IQ tests. Jewish superiority was most pronounced on the verbal part of the test. Rhodes and Nam (1970) arranged categories of religious identification according to their degree of fundamentalism and anti-intellectualism, with Baptists highest and Jews lowest. When the religious groups were ranked according to their distance from fundamentalism, there was a positive significant correlation of $0 \cdot 17$ with IQ. Belonging to the Jewish or major Protestant group was associated with a higher IQ, compared with Catholics, small Protestant groups, and Baptists.

In denominational groups matched for social background, differences have been found in creativity which are probably due to religious factors. Marino (1971) found that Catholic schoolchildren (aged 13–14) scored well below Protestant children in Wisconsin, and Belfast. In Eire there was a significant difference on one measure (originality on the uses of objects test) but not on other measures. In Scotland there were no differences. Marino concludes that in Scotland the effects of school teaching override any differences due to background. It is important to distinguish between the effects of religion and of associated cultural variables; in the USA it is found that Irish Catholics are more successful educationally than Polish Catholics.

Bender (1968) compared church attenders to non-attenders on various psychological measures, and found that non-attenders were more creative in terms of activity in the arts and sciences. The explanation of these results may be similar to that for Catholics not becoming scientists: authoritarian training does not encourage innovation.

Authoritarianism and dogmatism

Authoritarianism

We should first establish which aspects of religion are correlated with authoritarianism. The measures which have been reported to correlate most strongly are orthodoxy of beliefs (e.g. Brown, 1962;

Gregory, 1957; Putney and Middleton, 1961), and fundamentalism (Rhodes, 1960). The findings by Brown (1962) regarding denominational differences in authoritarianism and humanitarianism appear in Table 6.8.

TABLE 6.8 *Scores on authoritarianism and humanitarianism in a group of 203 Australian students by denomination*

Denomination	Authoritarian	Humanitarian
Church of England	45·1	53·7
Roman Catholic	43·6	77·7
Other denominations	42·0	55·1
Methodists	40·0	56·2
No religion	34·0	58·3

Source: Brown (1962).

The findings are instructive in several respects. They show the existence of denominational differences in authoritarianism. They show the inverse relationship between authoritarianism and humanitarianism, and that those with no religion score lowest on authoritarianism. The only significant difference among the scores was between those with no religion and those with religious affiliation, on authoritarianism. The finding that non-believers score lowest on authoritarianism was also reported by Rokeach (1960), among others. What has to be explained is the fact that religious people tend to score higher than non-religious people, and that Catholics and fundamentalists tend to score higher than other religious groups. However, the concept and measurement of authoritarianism has been criticized in several ways, and these criticisms affect the interpretation of the above findings.

Acquiescence response set The most widely used measure of authoritarianism, the F scale, is arranged so that the 'yes' answers are all scored as authoritarian. The scale is therefore measuring acquiescence as well, which however is itself correlated with authoritarianism. The conclusion of a long series of experiments is that 'acquiescence has been a factor in standard F-scale scores but not the major factor' (Brown, 1965, p. 514). A similar British scale, measuring conservatism, which was counterbalanced for yes-no direction, yielded a very high score for Gideons, the people who put Bibles in hotel rooms (Wilson and Patterson, 1968). While it is possible that the findings are due to the greater acquiescence or suggestibility of religious people, this is probably only part of the explanation.

The dynamic basis of authoritarianism There is a good deal of further empirical support for the original findings by Adorno *et al.* (1950), that authoritarianism consists of a number of correlated variables: ethno-centrism, idealization of self and of parents, and having rigid conservative attitudes (Brown, 1965). According to the original theory, it is due to a set of personality mechanisms (displacement, projection, etc.) forming a defensive and constricted personality, all ultimately derived from rigid and authoritarian childhood discipline. It may be asked why should the components of authoritarianism correlate together, if there is no unified system underneath (Sanford, 1973). On the other hand, the evidence for the dynamic processes is weak, and the components may cohere because they are the norms of uneducated, low-status people (Brown, 1965). If the dynamic processes do operate, on the other hand, they open the door to explaining the findings in terms of psychological processes like projection and rationalization.

Authoritarianism as a world-view Adorno *et al.* (1950) and a number of later investigators have found that authoritarianism is lower in better-educated people. The correlation with years of education is between $-0 \cdot 50$ and $-0 \cdot 60$ (Christie and Jahoda, 1954). It has been suggested that authoritarianism is simply the pattern of attitudes shared by uneducated people. A further development of this view is that authoritarianism does not reflect personality dynamics, but rather a narrow perspective and the view that the social world is fixed and unchangeable, so that authority should be obeyed (Gabennesch, 1972). If this is so, then the results can be explained in terms of several factors which contribute to the narrower world-view in groups which score high on authoritarianism. Lower educational level and lower socio-economic status undoubtedly contribute to a narrow perspective. The specific religious factor of orthodoxy and fundamentalism can then be an additional determinant. The resulting perspective, whereby the world is perceived in terms of authority relationships, may be reflected in the F-scale scores.

Dogmatism

Rokeach (1960) devised a dogmatism scale, which contained some of the components of authoritarianism, but stressed intolerance, and was independent of right-wing ideology. In this and a number of subsequent studies it was found that Catholics emerged as more dogmatic than other religious groups, and than the non-religious, though the differences are quite small (Kilpatrick *et al.*, 1970). Rokeach (1960) reports differences between groups of students approximately equated for parental income (and own education), so that the effect is probably not due to class or education. However, in studies carried out in the American South it was found that Protestants had higher scores than Catholics and non-religious people (Kilpatrick *et al.*, 1970; Seaman *et al.*, 1971). It is suggested by Seamen *et al.* that dogmatism is socially rewarded inside certain religious groups, and is a cognitive style not related to personality dynamics. Feather (1964) found that pro-religious subjects tended to judge false pro-religious arguments as valid, while corresponding distortion was not found for anti-religious subjects.

Suggestibility

As several investigations have now shown, suggestibility is not a single trait, but is composed of a number of relatively independent elements. Eysenck (1947) experimented with a variety of different test situations and concluded that there were at least three types. (1) Primary (or psychomotor) suggestibility, in which people carry out a motor movement, upon repeated suggestion by the experimenter but without conscious participation by the agent. (2) Secondary suggestibility, in which people will perceive or remember the thing suggested. (3) Prestige and social suggestion, in which people change their opinion after being told that a 'prestige' leader or group holds a different one.

There is evidence on primary suggestibility from a variety of religious groups, in every case showing that religious people are more suggestible. Howells (1928) gave a series of psychomotor tests to fifty extreme radicals and the same number of conservatives. Five tests of psychomotor suggestibility all showed the conservatives to be the more suggestible. Sinclair (1928) obtained similar results comparing fifty students who did have marked mystical experiences with fifty at the other extreme.

Primary suggestibility seems to be particularly strong amongst members of revivalist and evangelical bodies. As reported in another section (p. 41), many people at early revivals showed signs of twitching and jerking before finally collapsing; this is primary suggestibility and may be a particular trait of revivalist audiences. Some of them are sent to hospital in states of religious excitement, a form of hysteria Coe. (1916) studied 100 people who had been converted, and found that those who had been converted 'suddenly', i.e. at revivals, produced motor automatisms more frequently under hypnosis. Brown and Lowe (1951) tested a large number of students on the MMPI and found that a group of Bible students—extreme Protestants—scored high on hysteria. Janet (1907) and others thought

97

that hysterics were particularly prone to primary suggestibility. Eysenck (1947) found that while neurotics in general were thus suggestible, hysterics were no more so than other neurotics; however, he agrees that the impersonal suggestions which were used might have been less effective for hysterics than face-to-face suggestions.

While there is a little experimental evidence on secondary suggestibility, there is evidence on the effects of placebo treatment. Lasagna *et al.* (1954) reported that in a hospitalized sample receiving placebo for pain relief, those who responded to the placebo reported a greater regularity of church attendance, and were described as 'pillars of the church'. Gelfand *et al.* (1965) found a correlation of 0·53 between placebo pain relief and religiosity. Duke (1964) studied both reactions to placebo for insomnia and reactions to tests of secondary suggestibility in relation to church attendance. Reported church attendance correlated +0·31 with the effectiveness of the placebo, and positive correlations were obtained with the suggestibility measures. Liberman (1962) suggested that the positive relationship of placebo responsivity and religiosity stems from personality factors of conformity and low critical ability, which are likely to characterize religious people.

Social suggestibility is also greater in religious people. Symington (1935) studied 612 people using a comprehensive test of orthodoxy of belief. There was clear evidence from the questionnaire answers that the conservatives were more dependent on group opinion; for example, liberals said they disliked being told what to do, and gave evidence of facing facts squarely before forming an opinion. Later studies have confirmed this finding. Fisher (1964) found a positive correlation between the Bass Social Acquiescence Scale (Bass, 1956), and three measures of religiosity: the Allport-Vernon-Lindzey Study of Values religious scale, self-ratings of religiosity, and frequency of church attendance. All three measures were related to high scores on acquiescence for both males and females, though more strongly for females. Gibbons and De Jarnette (1972) found that, in a group of 185 American students, those scoring high on the Harvard Group Scale of Hypnotic Susceptibility reported significantly more religious experiences. The results were interpreted as meaning that religious experiences are in many cases a response to suggestion.

Other studies suggest why religious people are more affected by social influence. Graff and Ladd (1971), in a questionnaire measure of 152 male students, found that the more religious students were more dependent on others, less inner-directed and less self-accepting. Ranck (1961) found religious people more dependent and submissive. Several studies of Catholic theological students and novices show them to be submissive and to have inferiority feelings on various personality tests or self-ratings (e.g. McCarthy, 1942).

Why are religious people more suggestible? One possibility is that the churches teach humility, obedience and respect for authority. Another is that those with a suggestible personality are more likely to accept church teaching. Primary suggestibility is linked with hysteria, and has a definite genetic basis; probably the personality comes first, and reacts to certain religious influences, like revivals, in a characteristic way. Social suggestibility is probably more a product of social learning, and could well be partly learnt from the church.

Methods of handling anger

The Protestant concern with sin, and the relatively high rate of suicide, suggests the hypothesis that Protestants are intro-punitive, i.e. direct anger inwards. The Catholic proscription of suicide and their high crime rate suggest that Catholics may be extra-punitive, i.e. direct anger outwards. King and Funkenstein (1957), using physiological measures, found that religious conservatives had the extra-punitive cardiovascular response. Brown (1965), using the Rosenzweig Picture-Frustration test with Australian students, found that Catholics were more extra-punitive than Protestants, and Protestant females more intro-punitive than Catholic females. Protestant males were more intro-punitive. Argyle and Delin (1965), in a study of 700 schoolchildren, found that guilt feelings (which can be equated conceptually with inner-directed anger) correlated with church attendance $0 \cdot 30$, for Protestant females only. Bateman and Jensen (1958) with 33 Protestant males found that religious background correlated $0 \cdot 66$ with intro-punitiveness, $-0 \cdot 33$ with extra-punitiveness on the Rosenzweig test; present religious belief showed much lower correlations in the same direction.

Not all studies have confirmed these findings, but there does seem to be a body of evidence showing that Protestants have stronger guilt feelings, and direct their anger inwards. The explanation may be that Protestant teaching encourages feelings of guilt, and discourages outward aggression. Or people with strong guilt feelings may be attracted by the Protestant emphasis on forgiveness and salvation. Some studies of conversion found that converts had strong guilt feelings before being converted (Starbuck, 1899).

Conclusion

We saw at the beginning of this chapter that religious beliefs and behaviour have little correlation with familiar personality traits.

99

How should we interpret the findings for those further aspects of individual differences that have now been discussed? Some of them are primarily differences between Catholics and Protestants or Jews, in the USA, in child-rearing, occupational status, educational achievement, intelligence, authoritarianism and dogmatism. All of these differences can probably be explained by class differences between the three religious groups.

Other differences are more likely to be due to the teaching of different churches: the low creativity and scientific achievement of Catholics, the stronger guilt feelings of Protestants. The educational and occupational success of Jews has probably little to do with religion, but reflects motivations common in Jewish culture.

There are, however, two results which may be due to religion meeting the needs of a certain kind of person, so that personality mechanisms may sustain religious activity. There is a fairly strong correlation between religiosity and suggestibility; while churches may encourage acquiescence, it is also probable that suggestible people will like firm guidance about beliefs and behaviour, and will be more affected by evangelists. Secondly, the guilt and intropunitiveness of Protestants may be due to the church's teaching; but they may also arise because guilty people are attracted by the doctrines of salvation and forgiveness (p. 195f), especially in the case of sects or British nonconformist churches.

7 Social and political attitudes

Possible relationships and causal effects between religious affiliation and beliefs, on the one hand, and social and political views on the other hand, will be explored in this chapter. It might be said that we are dealing with the connections of several sets of beliefs or identifications, which most people possess at the same time. Political and social attitudes reflect a person's beliefs regarding the social order, the divisions of power and positions around him. They reflect the way he regards those in power, those more or less fortunate than himself, and those whom he considers different or peculiar because of race, nationality or tradition. The findings in this area have implications both in terms of the social consequences of religious behaviour, theoretically speaking, and in terms of everyday social behaviour in the social and political domain.

Religious affiliation and party preference

Patterns of religious group voting in USA have been observed to persist over the last five decades and more (e.g. Campbell *et al.*, 1960). The tendency is for Protestants to prefer the Republicans, and for Catholics and Jews to prefer the Democrats. Centres (1949) reported a correlation of $0 \cdot 36$ between Protestantism and Republican voting. Lenski (1963) found the probability of voting Republican in various religions varied as follows (from highest to lowest): white Protestants, white Catholics, Negro Protestants, Jews. Erskine (1960) reported that in 32 out of 33 comparisons Catholics exceeded Protestants in the percentage voting for the Democrats. This is partly due to class differences, since Catholics have a higher working-class composition in both countries. However, a number of American studies show that Protestants are still more Republican with social class held constant (cf. Lipset, 1963, p. 1140). Table 7.1 shows this for Lazarsfeld's 1944 study of Erie County.

TABLE 7.1   *Denomination, voting and social class, Erie County, 1944;*
percentage of the denomination voting Republican

Social class	Protestant	Catholic
	%	%
Av+	76	29
Av	66	25
Av−	54	23
Very poor	43	14

Source: Lazarsfeld *et al.* (1944).

Catholic loyalty to the Democratic party in US national elections
is by no means unswerving. Even when Catholics are more likely
to consider themselves Democrats, they are ready to vote for
a Republican nominee for president, as happened in the Eisenhower
elections and the 1972 elections. In 1956 only 51 per cent of Catholics
voted Democrat (Gallup, 1972). Catholic support for the first
Catholic president, John F. Kennedy, in 1960, was by no means
unanimous, as only 61 per cent of the Catholics voted for him
(White, 1961).

The association between religious affiliation and political party
preference exists in Great Britain, where Catholics are more likely
to vote for the Labour Party than Anglicans and nonconformists
(Alford, 1963). Table 7.2 shows the relationship between church
affiliation and political preference and party preference in Great
Britain in 1963, and it is clear that the association between Catholicism
and support for the Labour Party is still quite powerful. Both this
fact, and the association between Methodism and Labour voting,

TABLE 7.2   *Religious denomination and political party preference*
in Great Britain, 1963; percentages of those affiliated

1963	Conservative	Labour	Liberal	Other/none
Church of England	41	44	10	5
Church of Scotland	39	48	6	7
Methodist	23	55	19	3
Other nonconformists	37	36	20	7
Roman Catholic	24	62	8	6
No religion	31	52	8	9

Source: Butler and Stokes (1969).

are to be expected on historical and social grounds. The relationship between Conservatism and Church of England affiliation is changing with time as shown in Figure 4, which relates this association to date of birth.

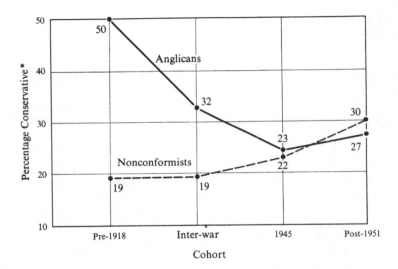

FIGURE 4 *Conservative strength among working-class Anglicans and nonconformists by cohort*

* of partisan self-images aligned with the Conservative, Labour, and Liberal parties.
Source: Butler and Stokes (1969).

In a survey of religious affiliation and voting in Dundee, Scotland, Bochel and Denver (1970) found a clear connection between denomination and party preference; religious affiliation was strictly defined, and other variables held constant. Some of the findings are shown in Table 7.3.

Explanation

Voting patterns of religious groups are partly due to socio-economic factors (Allinsmith and Allinsmith, 1948), and there are signs that these patterns of voting are gradually changing. Most studies of voting in relation to membership of religious group suggest that minority religious groups tend to support liberal political movements. This relationship is not based on any specific content of religious

103

TABLE 7.3 *Voting in Dundee in the 1966 General Election, by religious denomination*

Denomination Party	None	Church of Scotland	Roman Catholic	Other
	%	%	%	%
Conservative	21	59	7·5	52
Labour	79	41	93	48
	N = 124	N = 230	N = 69	N = 48

Source: Bochel and Denver (1970)

beliefs or behaviour, but rather on the minority position of certain groups. This explanation applies particularly to Catholics, in both Great Britain and the USA.

In explaining the relationship between membership of religious groups and voting, Janowitz and Segal (1967) claimed that it was the minority status of Catholics in the USA that created their liberal politics. Another factor is the more recent immigration of most Catholics. Alford (1963) points to the fact that Roman Catholics in both Great Britain and the USA tend to vote for the major Left party. This tendency can be explained by the fact that some of the Roman Catholics in both countries were historically an immigrant, low-status minority. This connection with the Left may be expected to disappear as Roman Catholics climb up the social ladder. Such change may have been in evidence in the USA 1972 presidential elections. Still, such special issues as parochial education or birth control may cause a continuation of the distinct Roman Catholic voting patterns.

Domhoff (1967) suggested that the Republican party in the USA has been the instrument of the Protestant industrialists and bankers who came to power in the last part of the nineteenth century, while the Democratic party has been controlled by a much varied group of Protestant, Catholic and Jewish industrialists and bankers. Thus, Republicanism has been identified with Protestantism, and Democratic leanings have become identified with a more heterogeneous group. The persistence of religious group voting patterns has been explained by Anderson (1968) as a result not of any ideological differences, but of continuing tradition in religious sub-groups. He found that persons who were more involved in their religious community were more likely to follow the particular group pattern in voting, except in the case of Catholics, where preference for the Democrats was strong regardless of community involvement.

While most researchers do not consider religious beliefs to be causal agents, but rather correlates, of specific political positions, casual relationships have also been suggested. Johnson (1962) suggested 'that religious factors by themselves do significantly account for an important part of the political propensities of individuals who are involved in denominations that are part of . . . Ascetic Protestantism' (p. 36). Johnson suggested that fundamentalists are more likely to vote Republican (despite their low status), and modernists are more likely to vote Democrat (despite their higher socio-economic status). This proposition has been tested several times (e.g. Johnson, 1966), but has not always been supported (Summers *et al.*, 1970). Even if correct, this thesis would apply only to a relatively small group.

Parenti (1967) suggested that there are consistent relationships between religious culture, based on beliefs and traditions regarding attitudes towards this world and man's responsibility in it, and political positions of religious groups. Such a relationship leads to conservatism in the case of Catholicism, because of the emphasis on an unchanging dogma and individual sin.

Religiosity and party preference

Glock and Stark (1965) showed that among Protestants in the USA Democrats are less likely to attend church than Republicans, and suggest that for Protestants even the mild form of dissatisfaction with the *status quo* offered by the Democrats is associated with estrangement from religious institutions. Anderson (1966) found a similar correlation among Protestants between church attendance and a preference for the Republicans. Hadden (1963) found that for college students there was a positive correlation between being Republican and scoring high on religious conservatism, which were both seen as part of a general conservatism factor. Bender (1968) found that in a group of middle-aged, college-educated, upper-middle-class men, those who attended church tended more often to vote Republican.

There is a clear relationship between political party preference and reported church attendance in Great Britain, as Table 7.4 shows. Supporters of the Labour Party are much less likely to report church attendance, compared to independent voters and those supporting the Conservative Party. The notion that religious conservatism will be related to a conservative political ideology has been confirmed in several studies. Putney and Middleton (1961) found that students subscribing to orthodox religious beliefs also held conservative economic and political attitudes. The correlation between religious conservatism and political conservatism was also found by Baer and Mosele (1971), and others. Supporters of

105

Goldwater, the Republican candidate in the USA in 1964, were found to score higher on two measures of religiosity than supporters of Johnson in the same election (Goldberg and Stark, 1965). Among Catholics, however, more liberal political attitudes are not always correlated with liberal religious attitudes, but there may be a social class factor involved. Among Protestant clergymen, a positive relationship between theological conservatism and political conservatism was found by Johnson (1966) and Hadden (1969).

TABLE 7.4   *Party preferences and church attendance in Great Britain, 1957*

Party	Percentage attending at least 'now and again'
Conservative	62 (546)
Labour	36 (631)
Other and don't know	50 (373)

Source: Stark (1964).

The connection between conservative religious beliefs and anti-communist attitudes in America has been noted by several investigators (e.g. Lipset, 1963). Stouffer (1955) found that the most feared aspect of communism to the general American population was its atheistic and anti-Christian character. Kosa and Nunn (1964) found religiosity was positively related to expressed intolerance of communism both among Negroes and whites. Hoge (1971 a and b) found positive correlations between anticommunism and religious orthodoxy in several groups of American students. The tie between Protestant (and sometimes Catholic – see Gargan, 1961) fundamentalism and extreme right-wing politics in the USA has been widely noted (e.g. Lipset, 1964). Orum (1970) showed that fundamentalist Protestants accounted for much of the support given to George C. Wallace in the 1968 US elections. The support for Wallace was strongest among Baptists and weakest among Episcopalians, but religious fundamentalism was related to support for him regardless of religious affiliation.

Among American religious groups, Jews have been found to be more liberal on almost every political issue. Allinsmith and Allinsmith (1948) found Jews to be consistently liberal on all social and political issues, regardless of their socio-economic position. Attitudes of Catholics and Protestants were more related to their socio-economic status. Thus, Catholics and fundamentalist Protestants, coming from lower socio-economic backgrounds, favoured welfare programmes, but were conservative on political issues. Upper class Protestants were more liberal on political issues, compared with all Catholic and Protestant groups. Blau (1953) found that Jews supported the notion of co-operation rather than power in international relations, more than Catholics or Protestants.

While some studies did not find a connection between religious orthodoxy and political attitudes (Lenski, 1963), no empirical study has ever found a relation between doctrinal orthodoxy and political liberalism or radicalism. The correlation between rejection of religious beliefs and radical political views has been demonstrated in several studies (e.g. Demerath, 1969). Spray and Marx (1969) showed that the degree of political radicalism was directly related to the degree of irreligiosity. Self-identified atheists were more radical than self-identified agnostics.

Attitudes towards war

Attitudes towards war in general and to particular wars have been studied in relation to religious affiliation and religiosity. Droba (1932) found that in a group of 1,000 American students the Lutherans and the Catholics were most militaristic. He suggested that more conservative churches are more supportive of war (cf. Fuse, 1968).

In a survey of 1,062 American students, Connors, Leonard and Burnham (1968) found that Catholic students showed most acceptance of modern war, and that students with no religious affiliation were most opposed to it. Students from non-religious colleges showed more opposition to war than students at Catholic colleges. As might be expected, students from Quaker colleges were most opposed. Quakers and those without religious affiliation were most likely to participate in demonstrations against war. Catholic students were most likely to be pro-war demonstrators. The relationship between church attendance and opposition to war was curvilinear, with those who rarely go and those who go frequently more opposed than those who go regularly.

Hamilton (1968) showed that in both 1952 and 1964, when the USA was involved in foreign wars, Protestants were most supportive of strong military actions, Catholics were less supportive, and Jews were the least supportive. In both cases, those having no religious affiliations were most opposed to military measures. A survey of American students on attitudes towards the Vietnam War in 1966, before the war became a major political issue, revealed that students in general were quite similar to the general public in their views (Tygart, 1971). Table 7.5 shows the attitudes by religious affiliation, and it is clear that non-believers are the most 'dove-ish', while Protestants and Catholics are the more 'hawkish', with Jewish respondents also on the side of the doves. Regularity of church attendance and the importance given by respondents to their religion were both unrelated to war attitudes.

TABLE 7.5 *Vietnam War policy preferences by religious affiliation among American students, 1966 (N=1,066), in percentages*

Position Religion	Complete withdrawal	Some withdrawal	Present level	Increase	All out
Total	11	16	14	25	29
Catholic	7	12	12	21	49
Protestant	5	10	18	31	36
Jewish	13	22	15	30	20
None	22	25	13	18	22

Source: Tygart (1971).

Among participants in a demonstration against the Vietnam War, 61 per cent reported no religious affiliation (Parrott, 1970), and among American students in the 1960s, participation in protest demonstrations against the war was positively correlated with having no religious affiliation or coming from a Jewish family. It was negatively correlated with the practice of praying (Astin, 1968).

Minority groups

The relationship between religiosity and political attitudes in minority groups has been studied in the case of the American Negro group. The church has often been described as a mechanism for social control of the Negro minority (Dollard, 1949; Myrdal, 1944). Religiosity has been explained as a sublimation of Negro frustrations, and religious teachings as an effective means of keeping Negroes away from any realistic action to change their conditions (Alland, 1962). A psychiatric interpretation of black religion was offered by Grier and Cobbs (1971). They described religion as a basic element of black culture and black life, but also as originating in slavery and causing psychological bondage. The black religionist, according to Grier and Cobbs, is conservative and passive. He prays for social change, rather than working for it. For blacks, yielding to God's will means in most cases yielding to the white man. The other-worldly orientation directs the faithful away from material concerns and immediate change.

A nationwide survey of Negroes in the USA in 1964 (Marx, 1967) showed that religiosity, on the whole, tended to be negatively related to political militancy and positively related to acceptance of the *status quo*. Nevertheless, the kind of religious orientation did make a difference. Those with a temporal (this-worldly) religious orientation tended to show more militancy.

Tables 7.6 and 7.7 show some of the findings of the Marx surveys. The first of these tables shows that there is a relationship between denominations in the degree of militancy. Members of cults and fundamentalist, all-black denominations are less likely to be militant. Members of predominantly white denominations are more likely to be militant. Table 7.7 shows that militancy increased with the decreased subjective importance of religion.

TABLE 7.6 *Proportion militant by denomination among US Negroes, 1964, in percentages*

Denomination	Militant
Episcopalian	46 (24)
United Church of Christ	42 (12)
Presbyterian	40 (25)
Catholic	40 (109)
Methodist	34 (142)
Baptist	32 (658)
Sects and cults	20 (106)

25 respondents are not shown in this table because they did not specify a denomination, or belonged to a non-Christian religious group, or other small Christian group.
Source: Marx (1967).

TABLE 7.7 *Militancy by subjective importance assigned to religion among US Negroes, 1964, in percentages*

Importance	Militant
Extremely important	29 (688)
Somewhat important	39 (195)
Fairly important	48 (96)
Not too important	56 (18)
Not at all important	62 (13)

Sects are excluded here. Source: Marx (1967).

An extensive survey of attitudes in one Negro community was conducted in the Watts area of Los Angeles following the 1965 riots (McConahay, 1970). It showed that most Negroes had extremely positive attitudes towards the church and religious leaders. There was a negative relationship between education and political awareness on the one hand, and religiosity on the other hand. Alston *et al.* (1972) replicated in 1969 the study by Marx (1967) and found a weaker association between religiosity and lack of militant attitudes among blacks. Among older blacks the more religious were less militant in 1969, just as they were in 1964. Among younger blacks the more religious were slightly more militant. Alston *et al.* (1972) suggested that the reason for the difference may lie in cultural and political changes.

Influence of clergy

Do the clergy influence the political attitudes of their parishioners? A number of studies show that in the USA the clergy have on average more liberal views than their parishioners (Glock *et al.*, 1967). Their views vary with the church they belong to, and their theological position; fundamentalists are much more likely to be Republicans than are liberal churchmen (Johnson, 1966; Hadden, 1969). There is little relation between the political outlook in a parish (as a result of social class, etc.), and the views of the clergy; if anything there is an inverse relationship, because more prosperous parishes get clergy from the better universities and theological centres, which are liberal and progressive in outlook (Hadden, 1969). The great majority of parishioners think that the church should concern itself with political and social affairs, but prefer that the clergy should do this by prayer and moral instruction, rather than by supporting political candidates (Glock *et al.*, 1967). In fact about 14 per cent of American clergy support political candidates from the pulpits. Glock *et al.* showed that there is very little correlation between the political views of clergy and those of parishioners, and suggests that belonging to a church has little influence on political attitudes.

Summary

On the basis of the findings presented above, it seems clear that religion serves a conservative function in the political life of both the USA and Great Britain. Hennessey (1965) stated that the net effect of religion in American public life is conservative, and that religion is an important factor in the maintenance of conservative values and the political *status quo*. Hamilton (1942), who had analysed the content of sermons in the USA between 1929 and 1940, found an increase in the amount of 'social pessimism', i.e. discouragement of social reform. Hennessey notices two sources of conservative religious influences in the USA: the Protestant influence can be identified with visions of rugged individualism and minimal government welfare programmes, while the Catholic influence is expressed through the disregard for civil rights of minorities and dissenters.

Hoge (1971 a and b) suggested higher levels of religious activity and religious commitment in the late 1940s and the early 1950s in the USA were related to a loss of interest in politics. We can assume then a negative relationship between religious commitment and concern about social change. The general relationship between political positions and religiosity has been expressed by Glock and Stark (1965) as follows: 'The churches offer to make things better in the next world, while leftist parties offer change in this world' (p. 195). Stark (1964) stated that both religion and radicalism function as solutions to status deprivations, and the choice of one precludes the other. Thus, the effect of religious involvement will be to neutralize radicalism. It has been suggested that religion, especially in the form of salvationist sects, has served in the USA as an alternative to political radicalism (Lipset, 1964).

Many observers have noted the connection between the prevalence of sectarian religious groups and the paucity of radical political groups in the USA, which has been formulated as follows: 'As sects have continued to emerge here, radicalism has been anaemic and without appreciable lower-class support' (Glock and Stark, 1965, p. 216). Sectarian activity is regarded as incompatible with, and exclusive of, radical politics, and can be viewed as an alternative expression to lower-class frustrations (Elinson, 1965). Bourque and Back (1968), in a study of religious experiences and their correlates, found that those reporting such experiences scored lower on political and economic interests, as measured by the Allport-Vernon-Lindzey Study of Values.

Wilson (1966) reported that sects in modern society tend either to support or to ignore as irrelevant the political arrangements in the wider society, while established churches tend to legitimate political authority and act as instruments of social control. The neo-Pentecostal groups of the 1970s in the USA show the familiar sectarian tendency to be either conservative or else indifferent to politics. A neo-Pentecostal leader is quoted as saying: 'The charismatic experience has completely changed my church politics and my national politics. I began to understand why it is that the Scriptures enjoin us to be submissive to those in authority over us. Now I'm totally in support of those in authority who minister order to the nation' (*Newsweek*, 1973, p. 85A).

The political position of the Jewish group cannot be explained on socio-economic grounds alone. For Jews have been found to

111

support the idea of the welfare state more than any other group, and to oppose racial integration less than other whites (Lenski, 1963). Fuchs (1956) described American Jews as economic liberals regardless of their own socio-economic position, and as internationalists in foreign policy matters. He suggested that Jewish liberalism stems from the tradition of intellectualism, charity and non-asceticism in the Jewish sub-culture. Hennessey (1965) mentions Jewish minority consciousness and their history of oppression as possible sources of present-day liberalism.

Lenski (1963) explained Jewish liberalism in terms of status inconsistency. While Jews as a group scored high on all measures of socio-economic achievement, they were still socially excluded by other groups. This created a persistence of the 'underdog' feeling, with sensitivity to social injustices, despite the objective reality of high socio-economic status. Thus Jewish liberalism can be explained not only on historical grounds but also by their contemporary situation in American society. Cohn (1957) explained Jewish liberalism on political and social issues as a result of historical, political and socio-economic forces, and pointed out that most Jews are notably irreligious. American Jews score lowest on all measures of religious activity and beliefs, compared with all other groups, and thus it is difficult to correlate many of their characteristics with religious factors.

Ethno-centrism and racial prejudice

The basic finding that church members are more prejudiced than non-members has been widely confirmed in American studies. A recent British study by Bagley (1970; see Table 7.9) found a similar relationship in a survey of 1,400 adults. Prejudice also varies with

TABLE 7.8   *Prejudice in relation to frequency of church attendance*

frequency per month	N	prejudice score
0	261	14·7
1	143	25·0
2	103	26·0
3	84	23·8
4	157	22·0
5–7	94	19·9
8–10	26	16·3
11+	21	11·7

Source: Struening (1963).

112

frequency of attendance. A number of studies have found a curvi-linear relationship, i.e. that those who go to church, but infre-quently, are most prejudiced. The findings of an American study are shown in Table 7.8. A similar result was obtained in the 1970 study by Bagley, with denomination, age, occupation and education held constant.

Denominational differences in racial prejudice and ethno-centrism are not so clear. Adorno *et al.* (1950) found that Catholics were most prejudiced, followed by Protestants. A number of other studies have found Catholics slightly more prejudiced or ethno-centric than Protestants, and both more prejudiced than Jews, in the USA (Burnham, Connors and Lennard, 1969; Allport and Kramer, 1946), even with class held constant (Triandis and Triandis, 1960). Members of conservative Jewish and strict Protestant groups, like Baptists and small sects, are also very ethno-centric (Triandis and Triandis, 1960). Bagley (1970) found that in England and Wales members of the Church of England were most prejudiced (Table 7.9) – perhaps because of the high proportion of people with high 'extrinsic' religiosity (see p. 114).

TABLE 7.9 *Hostile perception of immigrants in relation to denomination in England and Wales*

Church of England	Roman Catholic	Nonconformist	Non-Christian	No religion
76·3%	62·0%	26·1%	52·0%	56·2%

Age, occupation, education, and church attendance are held constant.
Source: Bagley (1970).

Another problem is that the results vary with the object of prejudice. There is very little difference between denominations in American studies on anti-Semitism, but there are clearer differences in anti-Negro prejudice. This kind of prejudice is much stronger in working class people, and is one source of Catholic prejudice. Successive Gallup Polls show that Catholic anti-Semitism declined between 1939–62, and is now less than among Protestants (Stember, *et al.* 1966). Mutual images of Protestants, Catholics, and Jews in one American city are presented in Table 7.10 (p. 114). From it we can see that Protestants were most critical of others, but the least criticized. Jews were the least critical, and the most criticized.

We have seen that frequent church attenders have a low level of prejudice, while infrequent attenders have a high level. This led Allport (1966) to propose a distinction between 'intrinsic' and

TABLE 7.10 *Percentage expressing favourable image of various socio-religious groups with respect to tolerance, business fairness, and power, by socio-religious group*

	Percentage expressing favourable image regarding:									
	Religious tolerance			Business fairness			Power			
Group passing judgment	of Prots.	of Caths.	of Jews	of Prots.	of Caths.	of Jews	of Prots.	of Caths.	of Jews	Mean
White Protestants	—	30	49	—	71	47	—	49	56	50
Negro Protestants	—	44	49	—	64	39	—	63	44	51
White Catholics	60	—	54	78	—	45	68	—	58	61
Jews	65	31	—	62	68	—	73	65	—	61
Mean	63	35	51	70	68	44	71	59	53	56

Responses were defined as favourable if the out-group was rated as equal with, or better than, the in-group in tolerance and fairness, and if the out-group was said not to be trying to get (or not having) too much power. Source: Lenski (1963).

'extrinsic' religious attitudes. 'The distinction helps us to separate churchgoers whose communal type of membership supports and serves other (non-religious) ends from those for whom religion is an end in itself—a final, not instrumental, good'.

A number of research workers constructed scales to measure these two attitudes. For example, Feagin (1964) used 21 items derived from Allport's papers, and gave them to 286 Baptists; factor analysis yielded two clear factors. He found that his extrinsic factor correlated $0 \cdot 35$ with anti-Negro attitudes, while the intrinsic factor correlated $-0 \cdot 01$. Examples of the intrinsic items are: 'My religious beliefs are what really lie behind my whole approach to life'; and 'The prayers I say when I am alone carry as much meaning and personal emotion as those said by me during services'. Examples of extrinsic items are: 'One reason for my being a church member is that such memberships help to establish a person on the community'; and 'What religion offers most is comfort when some misfortune strikes'. Similar findings were obtained by Allen and Spilka (1967) and others. These studies found that intrinsic as compared with extrinsic religious people are less prejudiced, go to church more often, say more private prayers, are more sure of their beliefs, feel their lives are meaningful, and trust other people; extrinsically religious people on the other hand see religion as a means to ends, such as living a happy and peaceful life.

The extrinsic-intrinsic differentiation can explain the positive correlation between church attendance and prejudice, if we assume that most church members are extrinsic in their religious orientation, and that they account for most of the correlation found. Allport and Ross (1967) found that 35 per cent of 309 church members could be classed as intrinsic, the remainder being extrinsic or mixed. The concept of intrinsic-extrinsic orientation has been criticized by Hunt and King (1971). They suggested that these concepts have not been operationally defined, and may not be opposites. They also suggested that the differences found in studies using the concepts may be due to general personality variables.

The limitations of the intrinsic-extrinsic dimension in religiosity were shown by the Strickland and Weddell (1972) study, which found that this dimension can have different meanings according to denomination. It was found that members of the Unitarian church, a highly liberal denomination, were both extrinsic in their orientation, according to the scale because of their liberal beliefs, and less prejudiced than Baptists, who were more intrinsic and more prejudiced. Unitarians, who are more liberal in their beliefs, are likely to appear extrinsic, while Baptists are more intrinsic and also more prejudiced. The extrinsic-intrinsic typology seems to be a psychological formulation of the old view which regarded 'true believers' as being in the minority. This view seems to be as valid as it has ever been, but it does not explain the attitudes of the non-devout majority.

It also does not explain the other side of the prejudice-religion coin: why is it that those who have no religious affiliation have consistently been found to be less prejudiced, more open-minded, and more tolerant towards minority groups? It seems that the positive correlation between irreligiosity and tolerance should be explained as well.

Explanation

Why are religious people, apart from the most devout, more prejudiced? Explanations suggested are of two kinds. (1) That religion in some way causes prejudice. (2) That some third factor, or factors, are the cause of both.

1. *Religion as a cause of prejudice*   Two main theories of this type have been put forward. The first is that the religious group by its very nature fosters strong out-group hostility. Claims of exclusive access to divine truth and the strong emotional involvement in the group create hostility toward those who do not share in the group's beliefs. This hostility could be directed to all those who are perceived as outsiders. Freud (1922) suggested that 'a religion, even if it calls itself the religion of love, must be hard and unloving to those who do not belong to it . . . . cruelty and intolerance towards those who do not belong to it are natural to every religion' (p. 51). This group psychology aspect of religious affiliation was also suggested by Allport (1966). Williams (1956) points to the dual role of religion as unifying the community of believers around a consensus of values, while at the same time making in-group and out-group distinctions

115

which contribute to social divisions. This aspect of religion is most obvious in the case of the small sects, who do draw a sharp line between those who are saved and those who are not.

The second theory is that in some cases churches have beliefs or traditions which imply that some social group is inferior. Glock and Stark (1966) maintain that about a quarter of anti-Semitism in American Christians is due to church teaching about the Jews. They found that the statement 'Jews can never be forgiven for crucifying Christ' was agreed with by 86 per cent of Southern Baptists, 60 per cent of Protestants and 46 per cent of Catholics. For 'Being Jewish could prevent salvation' the result was: Southern Baptists 53 per cent, Sects 55 per cent, Lutherans 54 per cent, Protestants 25 per cent, and Catholics 12 per cent. A series of similar questions established that members of strict Protestant groups, who accepted orthodox beliefs, tended to be anti-Semitic. This study has been criticized on the grounds that the measure of orthodoxy used contained anti-Semitic items, which would account for some of the relationship found between orthodoxy and anti-Semitism. It has also been suggested that what relationship there may be is not causal, but the result of common factors such as authoritarianism or dogmatism (Dittes, 1971b).

Another example of the connection between religious teachings and ethnic prejudice is that of the Latter Day Saints (Mormon) Church, which does not admit Negroes to priesthood, though some rank in the priesthood is almost universal among white members. This rule is based on specific teaching about the history and destiny of the Negroes; those with the most orthodox beliefs are also most anti-Negro (Brewer, 1970). Smith (1972) pointed to the direct support given by Southern churches in the USA to slavery and racism as one factor which affected both social conditions and social attitudes.

2. *Religion and prejudice the product of common causes* One theory put forward is that conformity to norms may be the common factor which produces both. Adorno *et al.* (1950) suggested that the acceptance of religion by the individual is related to the factors of conformity, conventionalism, authoritarian submission and thinking in in-group out-group terms. Thus the religious individual tends to be more conventional and group-orientated in his thinking, and prejudice is one natural expression of these tendencies.

Orpen (1972) and Orpen and Van der Schyff (1972) showed that where prejudice is the norm (as it is in South Africa) acquiring the prejudice is simply a matter of conforming to the prevailing norms, and there is no need to assume any special psychological mechanisms to explain it. Ehrlich (1973) suggested that the correlation between religiosity and prejudice stems from the greater conformity of religious people to social norms. Since prejudices are reflections of social distance norms and actual differences in status and power, religious people can be said to follow these norms more closely, as part of their general conformity and conservatism. There is no need to consider any special religious factors here; the basic factor is generally conformity, which leads to both religiosity and prejudice. Individual differences in holding prejudicial attitudes are explained on the basis of individual differences in conformity.

Another version of this theory is that the churches encourage conformity and uncritical acceptance. This theory predicts that religious people will be most prejudiced when they belong to an official or majority church, and when a majority of the population are prejudiced. This could apply in parts of the USA; in Britain the non-attending (i.e. extrinsic) members of the Church of England are the most prejudiced.

A second group of theories postulates common personality mechanisms behind religion and prejudice. Intolerance of ambiguity is one of these: it is found in prejudiced people, and has also been found to be true of religious people (Allen and Spilka, 1967). A more general theory which includes this and other personality mechanisms, such as projection, is that of authoritarianism, which is discussed elsewhere (p. 94f). However, as we have seen, personality has a rather weak relationship with religiosity, except for those most involved (who are not prejudiced). It seems unlikely therefore that common personality mechanisms will explain the relation between religion and prejudice.

Do the clergy have any influence over their parishioners in this sphere? As in the case of other political attitudes, the clergy are rather more liberal than their flocks, on average (Glock et al., 1967). But, if the churches are working against prejudice, why are church-goers more prejudiced, while non-churchgoers (who are not exposed to church influences) are less prejudiced? Perhaps the explanation is that 'Love thy neighbour' depends on who is defined as your neighbour. Many sermons do not deal with specific social relations, but rather with relations between believers and the supernatural. And even if the churches were preaching day and night against prejudice, other forces in society, which are more powerful than the churches, are working in the opposite direction.

Sometimes the church does have some effect. Nelsen and Yokley (1970) found that familiarity with the (liberal) pronouncements of Presbyterian church leaders correlated 0·42 with liberal views on civil rights of 3,000 elders; there was also a correlation of 0·38 between reporting being influenced by statements made by church leaders, and participation in civil-rights activities.

Friedrichs (1971) studied a housing estate before and after efforts by the local clergy to counteract racial prejudice among church-goers. There was an increase in tolerance among those who had attended more services (see Table 7.11).

TABLE 7.11   *Changes in racial tolerance and frequency of church attendance*

Religious services attended over previous year (as estimated by subjects)	Percent 'Tolerant' (N in parentheses)		
	1959	*1965*	*Contrast*
None	50 (12)	50 —(4)	0
1–10	51 (21)	29 (7)	−22
11–30	44 (16)	57 (14)	+13
31–60	38 (37)	80 (20)	+42
61 or more	64 (25)	65 (29)	+01

Source: Friedrichs (1971).

Many American clergy have been active or even prominent in the Negro cause. In Britain the churches have been extremely active in the field of race relations, as surveys of the subject testify (Patterson, 1969), but no hard data are available on the consequences, and parishioners have not always been as welcoming to immigrants as their clergy have.

Attitudes to social issues

Many studies have been carried out on the relationship between church membership or attendance and attitudes to civil rights, compassion for deviates and the underprivileged, and concern about social issues in general.

Civil rights   Eckhardt (1970) reports a survey of 1,325 students at nine liberal arts colleges. They were categorized from their replies on civil rights militancy and on various aspects of religiosity (see Table 7.12). The more religious on all criteria were less militant. Jews and those with no religion were most militant, Catholics least. Salisbury (1962) found that religious orthodoxy was positively correlated with social conservatism on such issues as racial segregation and the rights of women.

Hadden (1963) reported that, in a group of American students, those whose parents were less religious, and who themselves were not members of religious groups, were more likely to oppose racial segregation. De Jong and Faulkner (1967), in a survey at a large state university, found religious students rather more in favour of full integration than other students, Protestants more than Catholics. But most religious students did not feel that the church or clergy should take an active part in bringing integration about; Lutherans were most in favour, Catholics least. It is not clear how these different results can be reconciled; part of the answer is probably that religious people are not in favour of violent social action, while they may be in favour of integration.

TABLE 7.12 *Proportion militantly supporting civil rights on each dimension of religiosity*

	% Militant per position of religiosity			
Dimension	High	Moderate	Low	N
	%	%	%	
Church attendance	28 (384)	33 (234)	41 (694)	1324
Subjective importance	26 (608)	28 (292)	43 (525)	1325
Belief in God	21 (586)	41 (631)	53 (118)	1325

Figures in parenthesis indicate the base number of respondents for each type.
Source: Eckhard (1970).

A survey of 2,945 white Americans in 1968 (Campbell, 1971) revealed that there were few differences in racial attitudes between Protestants and Catholics, but Jews and those with no religion showed the most liberal pattern of attitudes. The results are presented in Table 7.13.

TABLE 7.13 *Racial attitudes according to religion in percentages among 2,945 respondents*

Racial Attitudes	Catholic	Protestant	Jewish	No religion
Favour interracial contact	54	56	72	68
Perceive much discrimination	56	51	74	75
Sympathetic to black protest	33	36	51	57
Favour civil rights legislation	46	44	67	63
Favour federal aid to cities	58	46	83	56
Prefer improvement of Negro conditions	53	50	68	61
Condone counter-rioting	6	5	1	9

Source: Campbell (1971).

Compassion   Cline and Richards (1965) carried out a factor analysis, using questionnaire, projection tests and interview data. Factor analysis yielded an extrinsic religiosity factor, and a 'good Samaritan' factor which was quite independent of the first. Rokeach (1969) carried out a survey of 1,400 adults; while the overall results suggest that regular church attenders are less compassionate, this is mainly in their attitude towards Negroes (see also p. 112f) and to student protest. Concerning the poor, church attenders were less in favour of passing laws to help them, and more likely to agree that poverty is caused by lack of effort; however on nine out of eleven issues there were no differences in compassion towards the poor. Hartnett and Peterson (1968) studied 1,500 freshmen at 37 varied American colleges. A 'liberalism' factor was extracted, consisting of support for a welfare state, organized labour, and social change towards greater equality. The non-religious and Jews scored highest, Protestants lowest. These results are partly due to class differences: Protestants are of a higher social class and more opposed to left-wing measures. We conclude that while there is no evidence that religious people are more compassionate, there is little evidence that they are any less so, apart from their racial attitudes.

Tolerance of deviates   A number of studies have investigated attitudes to deviates of various kinds. The results are clear: religious people, and especially Catholics, are less tolerant, Jews and the irreligious are most tolerant. Kirkpatrick (1949) found that people who scored high on his 'religionism' factor had more punitive attitudes towards criminals, homosexuals, unmarried mothers and conscientious objectors, though the relationship was very weak. Similar findings have been obtained for tolerance of sexual deviation (p. 155f). Stouffer (1955) found that churchgoers were more intolerant of political dissent than non-churchgoers: 'There would appear to be something about people who go to church regularly that makes fewer of them, as compared with non-churchgoers, willing to accord civil rights to nonconformists who might be Communists, suspected Communists, or merely Socialists' (p. 142). The Jewish subjects were more tolerant than the others. Rooney and Gibbons (1966) found that Catholics were less tolerant of 'victimless' offences, such as homosexuality and drug addiction, compared with Protestants and Jews.

Positive social behaviour

Honesty and resisting temptation were studied by Hartshorne and May (1928) in a large number of Chicago children, using a variety of tests of cheating; there was no difference between regular church attenders and others. Franzblau (1934) found no relationship between acceptance of traditional religious beliefs and co-operativeness or readiness to confess undesirable behaviour. Among American college students several studies found no connection between religiosity and cheating (Goldsen *et al.*, 1960; Garfield *et al.*, 1967). There is no information about cheating in Britain.

Faulkner and De Jong (1968) reported that among Catholics those who were more religious reported more cheating. This may mean either that those who are more religious cheat more, or that they are more honest in reporting it. The reverse is however more common. Crandall and Gozali (1969), for example, found that children from Catholic schools in the USA and Lutheran schools in Norway tried to present themselves in a favourable light. Though religious people are no more honest than other people, they are motivated to appear so.

Altruism and helping were slightly more common for church members in the Hartshorne and May research (1928), and Protestants scored higher than Catholics. Friedrichs (1959) also found that a measure of altruism was positively related to church attendance. Clark and Warner (1955) correlated church attendance and the reputations for kindness and honesty of 72 individuals. The correlations were 0·41 for kindness and 0·64 for honesty. Forbes, TeVault and Gromoll (1971) used the 'lost letter' technique, in which unmailed letters are left in public places to assess willingness of church members to help strangers. They left unstamped letters near 25 churches in an American city. By counting the number of letters which arrived at their destination they found that members of theologically conservative churches were less willing to make sacrifices for total strangers. These investigators also observed that persons attending conservative church services tend to lock their cars more often than those attending liberal churches. This was interpreted as an indication of suspiciousness. Cline and Richards (1965), in a factor-analytic study, found no connection between their 'good Samaritan' attitude and religious belief. Friedrichs (1959), on the other hand, found a small tendency for reported charitable behaviour to correlate with belief in God.

Darley and Batson (1973) produced an interesting simulation of the parable of the Good Samaritan, using 40 students at a theological college. While passing from one part of the experiment to another each subject came across a groaning man sitting slumped in a doorway. Some subjects were in a hurry, one of the experimental conditions: these were less likely to stop and help. Some subjects were on their way to give a talk on the Good Samaritan: they were no more likely to stop. Measures of religiosity had no correlation with helping; however for those who *did* stop, those high

121

on intrinsic religiosity gave extra help, though in a rather rigid way. But as the experimenters point out, the subjects were after all helping the experimenters, and were in some conflict over whom to help.

Bock and Warren (1972) used Milgram's procedure in which subjects were instructed to give 'electrical shocks' to a 'victim' who supposedly made errors on a learning task. It was hypothesized that persons with mid-range religiosity scores would be the least obedient to such destructive commands, but the exact opposite was found. Those with moderate religious beliefs administered significantly more punishment than either the religious or the non-religious extreme groups.

So far as *Moral attitudes* are concerned, a number of studies have shown that people who express strong commitment to Christian belief and who attend church fairly frequently have more stringent and exacting moral beliefs than non-believers; they judge more actions wrong, judge them more wrong, and are less ready to recognize extenuating circumstances (Wright, 1971, p. 183). Examples of studies in this area are Wright and Cox (1967) and Gorer (1955). We shall examine attitudes to sexual behaviour in detail later (p. 155f).

Boehm (1962) found that children in Catholic parochial schools scored higher at an earlier age than state school children on a test of recognizing the distinction between intention and results of an action, as a basis for moral judgment. Boehm (1963) found that children in Jewish parochial schools showed more empathy with an injured peer than any other group of children from state schools or Catholic parochial schools. These findings were interpreted as showing definite variations in the content of conscience created by particular religious training. Other studies found that children in parochial schools are less mature than other children (MacRae, 1954), or that there are no differences which might be attributed to religious upbringing (Whiteman and Cosier, 1964).

However, studies of moral ideology show that religion plays an important part in the system of moral judgments for many people. In the ITA survey (1970) respondents were asked 'How do you think a parson knows what is right and what is wrong?', to which 43 per cent answered 'Conscience, inner self, or God'; this answer was given by 40 per cent of religious people, and 33 per cent of non-religious people. For many people morals are felt to be sanctioned by religion. Wright and Cox (1967) found that a lot of young people gave religious reasons for refraining from proscribed sexual behaviour.

As far as moral behaviour is concerned, religion appears to have little effect. This is partly since there are many other factors besides

122

the influence of religious teachings which affect moral or altruistic behaviour (Wright, 1971); and religion may be influential only in cases where particular prescriptions or proscriptions are central to a certain faith. This may be the case with sexual behaviour, and the relevant evidence will be discussed in Chapter 9.

8 Religion and personal adjustment

When we consider the broad question of the relationship between religion and personal adjustment, several hypotheses need to be considered. The first, presented by supporters and promoters of religion, proposes that religious faith contributes to individual wellbeing, happiness, and 'peace of mind'. The second suggests that religion itself is an expression of psychopathology, that religiosity is a reflection of psychopathology, or at least that religion contributes to personal maladjustment. A third possibility is that emotionally disturbed people turn to religion to help them with their problems.

Physical health

This topic is included here because of the close connection found between mental and physical health (Hinkle and Wolff, 1957). Comstock and Partridge (1972) and others have studied the incidence of various diseases in relation to church attendance, using matched samples drawn from census returns. The main results are shown in Table 8.1. Other studies have shown that church attenders also have lower rates of chronic bronchitis and fatal one-car accidents. No correlation with church attendance has been found for cancer of the colon; conflicting results have been obtained for cancer of the rectum; for Catholic males cirrhosis of the liver did not vary with frequency of church attendance, nor did the amount of drinking.

There are several possible explanations. The results for some individual diseases can be accounted for; less drinking produces less alcoholism, and perhaps less fat and so less heart disease. However, the very broad range of effects noticed suggests that the phenomenon may be more general. As Comstock and Partridge suggest, peace of mind and release of tensions could affect pulse and blood pressure, and so could the effects of a supporting group. Most of the ailments studied particularly affect the elderly, and the effects of religion on psychological health are strongest for this group (p. 129f).

TABLE 8.1 *Disease and church attendance*

	Once or more per week	*Less than once per week*	*Infre-quent attenders*
Arteriosclerotic heart disease females, death in 5 years per 1,000	8·52	18·12	2·1*
males, deaths per year, per 1,000 (smoking, social status and water hardness held constant)	4·9	8·7	
Lung emphysema deaths in 3 years per 1,000	0·74	1·70	2·3
Cirrhosis of the liver deaths in 3 years per 1,000	0·21	0·82	3·9
Tuberculosis new cases in 5 years per 100,000	57	84	138
Trichomoniasis females incidence%	12·4		17·8
Cancer of the cervix females incidence %	0·64		1·88

* Unreliable, since numbers small. Source: Comstock and Partridge (1972).

One religious group which is heavily involved with issues of physical health, though mainly by denying them, is the Christian Scientists (Wardwell, 1965; Nudelman and Nudelman, 1972). Wilson (1961) reports that Christian Science congregations include a large number of crippled and deformed persons. In conformity with Christian Science beliefs members ignore these defects, and make only the most perfunctory inquiries about each other's health. Despite the fact that Christian Scientists try to minimize contacts with physical medicine, and consult physicians much less frequently than the general population, their average life-span does not seem to be affected (Wilson, 1956). It is important to note that despite their reluctance to use medical techniques, Christian Scientists do benefit from public health measures. Another possible cause of Christian Science longevity is the lower use of alcohol and tobacco, which would lower the incidence of diseases such as lung cancer, emphysema, or cirrhosis of the liver. Many other sects have emphasized religious healing (Weatherhead, 1951), and this is particularly common in underdeveloped countries where orthodox medicine is not available.

There is a certain amount of evidence that faith healing has some effect, at any rate for psychosomatic ailments (Frank, 1961). About 3 per cent of the many thousands of visitors to Lourdes are cured or partly cured (McComb, 1928).

If Christian Scientists can be said to deal with health problems by denial, Jews may be said to be just the opposite, dealing with health problems by preoccupation. Mechanic (1953) found that Jewish students in the USA were more likely to engage in illness behaviour (e.g. taking medicines and visiting a physician) compared with Protestants and Catholics. The relationship was found for religious affiliation, but not for religiosity. The findings support the theory of traditional Jewish concern with health and illness. Any possible religious, rather than social and historical, roots of such a tradition are hard to trace, especially since we are dealing with secularized Jews.

Measures of adequacy and neuroticism

In this section we shall review a variety of studies dealing with general adequacy and functioning in individuals. Measurement problems in this area are considerable because of the limitations of the instruments used in assessing personal adequacy and it is difficult to interpret the results.

There have been several studies of American students, using questionnaire measures of adjustment. These have usually found the more religious students report themselves to be more anxious, to have lower self-esteem, and feel less adequate (Dittes, 1969). Funk (1956) found a correlation of $0 \cdot 29$ between scores on the Taylor anxiety scale, and a measure for orthodoxy of belief, using 255 students of elementary psychology aged 17–19. Dreger (1952) selected the thirty most orthodox and the thirty most liberal out of 490 members of different Californian churches. The orthodox scored higher on ego-defensiveness and dependency measured by various projective tests. A number of studies have found that self-esteem is lower in religious students (for example Cowen, 1954). Rokeach (1960) observed that religious believers, as compared with non-believers, complained more often of tension and fitful sleep. They were also more anxious. No difference in adjustment has been found between students with liberal and conservative beliefs (Becker, 1971).

Graff and Ladd (1971) using a questionnaire measure of self-actualization, the Personal Orientation Inventory, arrived at the conclusion that religion was inversely related to self-actualization. Less religious subjects were found to be more self-accepting, less dependent, and more spontaneous, compared with more religious subjects. Maslow (1962) reported that in a group of persons whom he considered self-actualized and psychologically healthy, there was only one person who was religious in the conventional sense.

This type of inner conflict appears to give rise to a defensive style of behaviour. MMPI data reported by Mayo, Puryear and Richek (1969) show that religious males tend to be more defensive, trying to present a more socially desirable picture of themselves. Religious females were as defensive as non-religious ones.

TABLE 8.2 *Mental health impairment in relation to religiosity of home**

| | Parental religion | | |
	very important	somewhat important	not important
Jewish parents	15·3	18·5	20·5
Protestants—upper class	16·8	19·3	16·2
Protestants—middle and lower	27·8	17·3	37·5
Catholic	26·9	21·7	36·1

* Percentage impaired.
Source: Srole *et al.* (1962)

Another group of studies consists of social surveys of the adult population, in which a number of questions were asked related to mental health. Stark (1971) found that those who belonged to churches had a distinctly lower rate of psychiatric impairment. On the other hand Gurin, Veroff and Field (1960) found very little relationship. Srole *et al.* (1962), in the Midtown Manhattan Study, found there was a higher rate of impairment for those from non-religious homes, in the case of middle- and lower-class Protestants, and for Catholics and Jews, but not for those of upper-class Protestant origins (see Table 8.2). It was also observed that those who had shifted from religious origins to 'no religion' had a higher rate of psychological impairment, though those who shifted to a different religious group had a lower rate of impairment.

Stark (1971) compared 100 outpatients at a mental health clinic in California, with matched controls. The rate of church attendance and membership was much lower for the patients (see Table 8.3).

127

TABLE 8.3 *Differences in religious commitment between a sample of persons diagnosed as mentally ill and a matched control group*

	Mentally ill* (N = 100)	Matched controls† (N = 100)	Level of significance
Per cent who claim no religious affiliation‡	16	3	$p < 0.01$
Per cent who say religion is 'not important at all' to them	16	4	$p < 0.01$
Per cent who do not belong to a church congregation	54	40	$p < 0.05$
Per cent who attend church:			
Once a month or more	47	57	
At least several times a year	24	32	
Once a year or less	8	6	
Never	21	5	$p < 0.01$

* In treatment at an outpatient clinic; 71 had a record of previous hospitalization.
† Randomly selected (stratified) from the same community, matched on sex, marital status, education, and age.
‡ While others claimed to be Protestant, Catholic, Jewish, or other, these responded none.
Source: Stark (1971).

The results of the studies by Stark (1971) and by Srole *et al.* (1962) can be interpreted in terms of what psychiatric impairment involves for individual functioning, and the relationship of psychiatric impairment to social participation. It is quite clear that psychiatrically impaired individuals, especially those who are labelled 'mental patients', are likely to deviate from social norms in many areas; this is how they get the label. Since some religious participation is normative in American culture, it is no wonder that those who deviate from normal behaviour should deviate in this area as well. The data in Table 8.3 could be interpreted as showing that 'mental patients' are unconventional, as might be expected.

Since public religious activities are social activities, and involve social interaction, they demand a certain level of interpersonal skills and personal adequacy. We should predict that persons who are lacking in social skills would be less likely to participate in social groups. This is indeed the case. Lindenthal *et al.* (1970) found that psychologically impaired persons were less likely to go to church, and less likely to belong to other social organizations. On the other hand, they were much more likely to pray in private.

Another aspect of formal religious participation, by its social nature, is that the participating individual is offered support and companionship, which in turn may enhance his level of social functioning.

TABLE 8.4 *Scores on an index of adjustment, and church membership*

	Church leaders	Other church members	Non-church members
Married	15	15	12
Widowed	15	11	7
Single	12	8	5
65–70	18	14	10
71–79	15	12	7
80+	13	8	6
Fully employed	18	18	17
Partly employed	16	16	13
Fully retired	15	12	7
Health (self-rated)			
Excellent	17	14	13
Good	15	14	11
Fair	17	6	8
More active in religious organizations than in fifties	16	13	9
Less active	14	11	7

Source: Moberg and Taves (1965).

There is one section of the population for whom there is a clear relation between religion and adjustment: the elderly. In one of the most extensive studies of this group, Moberg and Taves (1965) carried out a survey of 5,000 people of 60 and over, using a series of questions dealing with 'happiness, enjoyment, or satisfaction with or from health, friendships, employment status, religion, feelings of usefulness, family, and general orientation towards, or happiness in, the later years of life' (see Table 8.4). Church leaders and members were significantly better adjusted, within nearly all sub-groups analysed. While religion made a difference within most sub-groups, the difference was greatest for the widowed and single, those in homes, the fully retired, and those in poor health. There was no significant difference for those still in full employment. This suggests that it is either the social support, or the provision of something to do, that has the therapeutic effect.

A number of other studies have obtained similar results. For example, Acuff and Gorman (1967) reported that retired professors who were active religiously showed a better degree of adjustment and less demoralization following retirement, as compared with a control group. The studies reviewed earlier, however, suggest that the direction of causation should be reversed; a certain level of personal functioning is necessary for participation in religious activities (Lindenthal et al., 1970).

The findings can be summed up in two generalizations: that religiosity is related to personal inadequacy in students, according to psychological tests and inventories; and that participation in public religious activities is positively related to personal adjustment in the adult population, especially among the elderly. Since both generalizations are correlational, they are difficult to interpret.

The connection between personal inadequacy and religious orthodoxy may be seen as resulting from the former leading to the latter. It is possible that those uncertain of themselves find support in the certainty of faith, or would like to find support there. Jones (1951) suggested that a feeling of inadequacy in the face of external and internal difficulties should lead to religiosity, especially in connection with feelings of guilt (see Chapter 11).

The positive relationship between personal adjustment and formal religious participation can be explained by two factors: first, some degree of personal functioning is a prerequisite for any social participation; and second the group itself becomes a source of support for the individual, providing companionship, belonging, and identity. This is especially crucial for older people.

Mental disorder and religious affiliation

In this section we shall use statistics of treatment and diagnosis, showing the different rates of certain disorders for religious denominations. The most extensive British study of this problem is Slater's analysis (1947) of the religious denominations of non-commissioned servicemen admitted to the Sutton Emergency Hospital in England during World War II. Out of the 13,556 admitted, 9,354 were placed in the neuro-psychiatric wards, and 4,202 in the general wards. The men placed in the general ward can be regarded as representative of the Army as a whole and used as a control. The percentages of each denomination placed in the neuro-psychiatric wards are given in Table 8.5. The results were explained as reflecting tendencies to breakdowns among various religious groups. Both members of the Salvation Army and Jews were found to be much more likely to have a breakdown than members of other groups.

TABLE 8.5   *The percentages of neuro-psychiatric cases of different denominations at the Sutton Emergency Hospital*

Church of England	61
Roman Catholic	72
Methodist	74
Salvation Army	85
Jews	92
Total	69

Source: Slater (1947).

Two American studies confirm the higher rate of neurosis among Jews. Roberts and Myers (1954) carried out an analysis of all patients under treatment in New Haven, Connecticut, on 1 December 1950: 24 per cent of the neurotic patients were Jewish, although Jews only comprised 9·5 per cent of the total population. Dayton (1940) analysed the 89,910 first admissions in Massachusetts, between 1917 and 1933: 9·54 per cent of the neurotic cases were Jewish, compared with 3·91 per cent in the total population.

Denominational differences have been found in the predominant types of psychosis. The most extensive study is Dayton's (1940), referred to above. He found that Catholics had a rate for alcoholic psychosis which was 40 per cent above average, as well as a slightly higher rate for schizophrenia (8·5 per cent above). Protestants were 39 per cent above average for senile psychosis, 34 per cent above for cerebral arteriosclerosis. Jews, as stated previously, scored 144 per cent above average for neurosis, and 69 per cent above average for manic depression.

Meadow and Bronson (1969) found that in a group of Mexican Americans, those who had converted to Protestantism, compared with those who had remained Catholic, reported fewer pathological responses on a psychiatric screening instrument. The finding was explained on the basis of two factors. The first is the greater level of support provided by Protestant churches in this particular environment. The second is the content of religious doctrines, which in the case of these Protestant sects emphasized individual responsibility and impulse control.

A survey of hospitalization for psychiatric reasons by Kleiner,

Tuckman and Lavell (1959) found that Catholics in Philadelphia showed a higher incidence of schizophrenia, while Protestants showed more organically caused syndromes. This in turn was related to the age of admission, which was lower for Catholics. The findings were interpreted as a result of status differences, with Catholics regarded as having lower status, which had been found to be tied to a higher incidence of functional psychoses. Further support for this explanation was given by the fact that the highest incidence of psychosis occurred among those who were both Negro and Catholic and thus had two lower status identifications.

Srole *et al.* (1962) in the study reported earlier found a positive relationship between parental emphasis on religious training and personal functioning for Catholics and Protestants, but not for Jews. They reported that more Jews were undergoing private treatment, compared with non-Jews, while non-Jews were over-represented in public mental hospitals. This finding can be explained by the greater likelihood of Jews to seek treatment, and also the lower incidence of severe psychiatric impairment among them. Using a rating of psychiatric impairment, Srole *et al.* concluded that while Jews were less likely to be at the lower end of the scale (i.e. functioning well) they were also least likely to be at the upper end of the scale. Malzberg (1962), in a study of first admissions to mental hospitals in New York State between 1949 and 1951, found that Jews had a lower rate of admissions for organic psychoses, compared with Catholics and Protestants. Jews also had much higher rates for manic-depressive psychosis and for psychoneuroses.

Burgess and Wagner (1971) compared rates of admissions to mental hospitals for different denominations, and found significantly higher proportions of Roman Catholics and Baptists, compared with their rates in the population. Methodists and Lutherans had proportions smaller than their proportions in the population, while the rates for Episcopalians and Jews were similar to their proportions of the population. These findings can be interpreted as being related to the social class status of the respective denominations, as proposed by Lazerwitz (1964) and reproduced in Chapter 10, p. 166f. We see that the lower classes are over-represented, the middle group is under-represented, while those at the top are proportionately represented. We cannot assume, as Burgess and Wagner (1971) did, that any particular religious factors are at work here.

Explanation

One important factor which affects the representation of various religious groups in psychiatric treatment statistics is the differential readiness of members of different groups to seek treatment. In many cases a patient or client seeking psychotherapeutic help is self-selected, especially when this patient is also covering the expenses involved. This factor applies mainly to outpatients, and not to hospitialized ones, who are mostly involuntary.

The available data show a clear over-representation of Jews among those who seek psychotherapy or psychoanalysis (Weintraub and Aronson, 1968; Hamburg, 1967). Jews constitute almost half of those who seek psychoanalysis in the USA, while Catholics constitute around 10 per cent, and are, therefore, under-represented. Myers and Roberts (1958) found that Jews are more inclined to seek out psychotherapy compared with either Protestants or Catholics. Fischer and Cohen (1972) found that Jewish students were more favourable in their attitudes toward seeking professional psychological help, compared with Catholics and Protestants. The large number of Jews among those who seek psychoanalysis or psychotherapy is paralleled by the number of Jews among those practising psychoanalysis and psychotherapy (Henry, Sims and Spray, 1971). One possible result of the readiness of Jews to seek outpatient treatment is their lower likelihood to be totally impaired in terms of social functioning (Srole et al., 1962).

Some of the differences in rates of psychiatric hospitalization reported in this section can be explained on the basis of social class differences among religious groups (see Chapter 10). The working classes have higher rates of alcoholic psychosis and schizophrenia, the upper and middle classes have higher rates for manic depression and neurosis (Rose, 1956). Hollingshead and Redlich (1958) found that the diagnosed prevalence of psychiatric disorders was significantly related to the individual's social class. The neuroses were concentrated at the higher levels and the psychoses at the lower levels of the class structure. The rate of schizophrenia in the lowest of five social strata was eight times that of the highest two strata. The type of treatment received by a diagnosed patient was also related to his social class. Members of the lower classes were more likely to be hospitalized, receive organic treatment, and remain hospitalized for longer periods. Outpatient treatment and psychotherapy were concentrated in the upper and middle classes.

Jaco (1960) reported that in cases of first admissions with a diagnosis of schizophrenia there was a negative relationship with social class. There was a higher incidence of psychosis in the lower socio-economic group. The neurosis rate for American Jews can partly be accounted for by class differences: there are more Jews in the upper and middle classes. Finally, it may be membership of a minority group rather than anything intrinsic to the religion that is responsible.

Whether or not rates and types of psychiatric illness are related

133

in some way to the beliefs, practices, or organizations of different religious bodies has yet to be shown.

Religious ideas and psychiatric disorders

The occurrence of religious ideas and religious claims among psychotic patients is often mentioned in psychiatric textbooks (e.g. Henderson and Gillespie, 1956; Slater and Roth, 1969). The best known cases are those in which patients claim to be famous religious or mythological figures, or when they adopt religious postures, such as crucifixion (Rokeach, 1964; Boisen, 1955). Sometimes religious delusions lead to cases of extreme self-mutilation (Kushner, 1967).

There are several studies of increase in the number of mental patients suffering from religious excitement or exaltation at the time of revival movements. Stone (1934) carried out an interesting analysis of admissions to the New Hampshire State Hospital for three months in 1842–3, during the height of the Millerite Second Adventist movement in New England. Out of 100 admissions, 24 were judged to have religious excitement as a result of attending Miller's meetings. Of the 24, 18 were diagnosed manic, 3 depressive, and 2 catatonic.

Farr and Howe (1932) give an analysis of hospital records for a number of American states for the year 1848. Religious excitement is given as the diagnosis in $14 \cdot 7$ to $0 \cdot 8$ per cent of cases, the median State percentage being 7 per cent. Stone (1934) reports that at the Salpetrière in Paris before the Revolution the percentage of patients with this diagnosis was 20–25 per cent, but this had almost disappeared by 1828. Similarly during the Welsh revival of 1905 there was an increase of the hospital cases suffering from religious exaltation from 1 to 6 per cent. At the same time the number of cases due to alcoholism fell from 16 to 12 per cent, while police records fell from 10,686 to 5,673 per year in the county of Glamorgan.

Several studies have reported on the prevalence of religious ideas among mental patients and their connection with particular disorders. Farr and Howe (1932) examined 500 consecutive cases, out of which 68 (that is $13 \cdot 5$ per cent) were judged to have a definite religious content; 64 per cent of the patients with religious symptoms were diagnosed as manic or depressive, compared with 50 per cent for the whole 500 studied. These authors also report a previous analysis by Strecker, who found religious ideas most frequently associated with the affective psychoses—in 28 out of 100 such cases studied. Kaufman (1939) has developed Freud's thesis that the ideas of psychotics are simply individual religions, while ordinary religious ideas are the result of more widely shared psychological mechanisms. The same beliefs would not lead to a diagnosis of psychosis if it appeared that the patient was a member of a religious group holding these ideas (Oates, 1957).

Among psychotic patients, Oates (1949) reported that religious concerns and conflicts were present in almost half the cases, and religious content of psychotic delusions was present in 20·5 per cent. It should be noted that this study was done in the southern USA, where patients in a state hospital are more likely to come from fundamentalist backgrounds and from the lower class. Lowe (1953, 1954, 1955), after studying a group of psychotic patients, concluded that the specific content of their delusions was often taken from the dogma of their respective religions, while the formation of the psychosis was a result of social conditions. Religious content can be found in neurotic and psychotic disturbances of all kinds, according to Mailloux and Ancona (1960). They report finding religious content in obsessive-compulsive, phobic, depressive, and paranoid disturbances.

The Group for the Advancement of Psychiatry (1968) stated that religion is more likely to play a part in depression and schizophrenia. Brightwell (1962) found that religious delusions were found most frequently among paranoid schizophrenics coming from lower-class backgrounds. Two studies report on the special connection between religiosity and affective (manic-depressive) disorders. Daly and Cochrane (1968), in a study of affective disorders in Britain, found that a high degree of religiosity was quite common among female middle-aged hospitalized patients. Manic-depressive patients were found to have a higher incidence of religious experiences, described as 'conversion' or 'salvation', compared with a control group (Gallenmore, Wilson and Rhoads, 1969). Among the patients 52 per cent reported such experiences, while among the controls only 20 per cent did. Both groups came from fairly religious families, and most were Baptists and Methodists. The results were interpreted in terms of the general emotional reactivity of these patients.

From the studies summarized above it seems that religious ideas are more likely to be connected with cases of affective disorders and cases of paranoid schizophrenia. The appearance of such religious content can be explained on the basis of differential learning and exposure to certain religious ideas. After comparing the content of schizophrenic ideas over the past two centuries, Klaf and Hamilton (1961) came to the conclusion that religious content in psychotic delusions is merely a result of cultural factors. Patients in the mid-nineteenth century were more likely to express religious concerns, since religion was more influential as a social force at that time. Religious delusions today are more common among members of the lower classes, where fundamental beliefs and intense religiosity are common, as opposed to the more formal religion of the middle class.

Mental disorder in religious leaders and clergy

Cases of gross psychopathology in religious leaders have been reported and analysed in great detail (Lombroso, 1891; Clark, 1958). Such analyses are of great interest in understanding individual personalities, but are of little value in explaining the religious movements which were started by some of these disturbed individuals. There are a number of instances of individuals who were accepted locally as the Messiah for a short time: there were over twenty messianic movements among the North American Indians at the end of the last century (Barber, 1941), and there have been at least six English Messiahs who attracted some following (Matthews, 1936). Biographical details of the English Messiahs are provided by Matthews, who concludes that three were suffering from paranoid schizophrenia, and one each from paranoia, hysteria and mania.

Other writers have attempted clinical diagnoses of more eminent religious leaders on the basis of what evidence is available. William James said, 'you will in point of fact hardly find a religious leader of any kind in whose life there is no record of automatisms . . . . Saint Paul had his visions, his ecstasies, his gift of tongues, small as was the importance he attached to the latter. The whole array of Christian saints and heresiarchs, including the greatest, the Barnards, the Loyolas, the Luthers, the Foxes, the Wesleys, had their visions, rapt conditions, guiding impressions and "openings"' (1902, p. 467.)

The view that many of the well-known medieval mystics, like St Theresa, had marked symptoms of hysteria, has been expressed by many psychologists, as well as by writers like Evelyn Underhill (1911). Father Thurston (1951) says that most of those who have received the stigmata have been women of hysterical personality. Other well-known religious men may have been epileptic: this was certainly the case with Dostoievsky, and may have been with St Paul; it is at any rate one explanation of his experiences on the road to Damascus (Weatherhead, 1951). Boisen gives a case-study of a Pentecostalist leader who was an epileptic (1955).

There have been many, rather speculative, interpretations of religious personalities in the past. Joan of Arc has been diagnosed as Lesbian, transvestite; schizophrenic, paranoid, creative psychopath, hysteric and epileptic. Kenyon (1971) discusses these theories but concludes that she was basically normal, 'a simple, pious girl, immature, suggestible, and she overidentified with [the] saints', but probably had very strong eidetic imagery (p. 842).

James (1902) describes a number of people such as Bunyan, Tolstoy and St Augustine who showed marked signs of melancholia, and how some of these managed to throw off their despair and preoccupation with evil by conversion. Ludwig Christian Haeusser was twice diagnosed as a manic-depressive at the Hamburg University Clinic, but obtained 40,000 votes for his politico-religious party whose aim was to make Haeusser World President (Weygandt, 1926).

What exactly is the difference between people diagnosed as psychotic who have religious ideas (see p. 134 f.), and those religious leaders who appear to have symptoms of mental disorder? The most obvious practical distinction between those in the first group and those in the second is that the latter were widely accepted as leaders whereas the others were not. The religious difference, presumably, is that those in the second group were genuine, the others bogus, although it is clear that there has been some difficulty in drawing the distinction in a number of instances. What is the psychological difference between the two groups? There must be some empirical difference which determines the different fates of the two groups. The Messiahs mentioned above can be contrasted with the 'Three Christs of Ypslianti', described by Rokeach (1964), who were all inmates of a mental hospital. What is the difference between the two groups?

This need not be a difference in personality structure, it could be a sociological or historical difference. Leaders are accepted only if the times are ripe, and those who were revered as mystics in the Middle Ages might be hospitalized today. It is probable that there is a personality difference as well: successful leaders of any kind have to be more in touch with other people, and to be more skilful organizers than are most psychotics. Another difference is presumably that the successful religious leader develops ideas which have some universal appeal; they meet the needs or solve the problems of many people besides himself.

There has been a certain amount of research into mental disorder in ordinands and clergy. Roe (1956) reported a high degree of neuroticism in the USA among people choosing the clergy as a vocation. The report was based on studies with both practising clergy and seminary students. A series of studies consistently found that Catholic priests and members of religious orders emerged more neurotic, withdrawn, and perfectionist than other students or other control groups, while their training seemed to make them worse, according to Dunn's review of his literature (1965). Other studies found that they were also more depressed and felt more inferior, were more awkward and ill at ease in social situations, and lacking confidence about social relationships. Dittes (1971a) has put forward the theory that the clergy are 'little adults', i.e. that they try to reconstruct a set of relationships similar to those of childhood, based on strong dependency ties. Some confirmation for this theory was obtained by Potvin and Suziedelis (1969) who carried out a comparison of 20 per cent of all Catholic ordinands in the USA and 1,000 controls. The ordinands described their parents in more positive terms, were more often the firstborn, and the favourite child, their mothers were strict and their fathers lacking in influence.

However, Stark (1971) points out that such studies did not hold constant factors like age, social class, intelligence or regional origins. It is difficult to know whether neurotic tendencies among Catholic clergy are due to the strains and deprivations of the role, or whether people of neurotic dispositions are drawn towards it.

Moore (1936) found that the incidence of hospitalized mental illness was lower for Catholic priests, monks and nuns, though cloistered nuns had a higher rate than those active in the outside world. Pearson and Ferguson (1953) diagnosed twelve hospitalized nuns as being predominantly paranoid, and claim that the religious life had postponed breakdown by providing a partial adjustment. A later study by Kelley (1958) found that the rate of hospitalization for nuns was much lower than for women in general, and that it was higher for cloistered nuns, though the gap between cloistered and active nuns was less than in the earlier study. There was a higher rate of schizophrenia, but a lower rate of chronic brain disorders, which are mainly caused by alcohol and syphilis. These studies suggest that pre-psychotic women may be attracted towards the cloistered life, but that being a nun reduces the chance of becoming a mental patient.

Intense religious experiences and mental disorders

Intense religious experiences, such as mystical experience, conversion, or glossolalia ('speaking in tongues') have often been regarded as symptoms or results of mental disorders. While personal observations and judgments on this topic are common, systematic data are hard to come by. We shall attempt to look at evidence related to glossolalia, conversion and mystical experiences.

Psychopathological explanation of religious experiences, which link them to specific psychiatric disturbances, are hard to accept when these experiences become common in a certain sect or sub-culture. The objection was expressed by Alland (1962), when he stated: 'A culture or sub-culture composed of either hysterics or schizophrenics would be difficult to imagine' (p. 209). This is especially unlikely in view of the fact that sect members are well adjusted in all other respects, and the overall effect of sect member-ship is in the direction of greater adjustment to the wider society.

Boisen (1939) was among the first to reject psychopathological explanations of intense religious experiences, and to concentrate on social factors instead. Hine (1969) reported that Pentecostal glossolalics in the USA appeared to be well integrated and productive members of society, and that members of snake-handling groups appear to be otherwise as normal as members of more conventional churches.

Speaking with tongues   This is one of the distinguishing features of Pentecostalism, which as we have seen is a rapidly growing sect in both the USA and Britain (p. 25). It is also found in non-Christian sects in primitive societies (Goodman, 1972). It has been suggested that religious experiences connected with Pentecostal sects are a reflection of lower-class neuroses (Kiev, 1964). This can be viewed as another version of the deprivation-compensation view of religious behaviour (see Chapters 10 and 11). However, clinical studies have found no differences in the mental health of Pentecostals and others (Samarin, 1972).

It is fairly clear that glossolalics are not speaking in foreign languages, though Biblical names and syllables from foreign langu-ages known to the speaker may be included. Indeed they are not using language at all, since there is no grammar and the sounds have no meaning in the usual sense. The message communicated is a non-verbal one, conveying emotional excitement and religious enthusiasm. The sounds do follow a pattern: there is a regular rhythm, with variations on a few repeated syllables, starting with consonants, e.g.:

kelalaiyanano, kelalaiyenayeno, etc. (Samarin, *op. cit.* p. 252).

Goodman (1972) suggests that glossolalia is a speech automatism in which extreme emotional arousal produces a state of dissociation: cortical control of speech is withdrawn, and the speech centres are activated by almost rhythmic discharges from sub-cortical centres. She observes that speaking in tongues is often accompanied by rhythmic bodily movements, such as trembling, shaking and jumping. There must be some cortical influence, to account for the intro-duction of, for example, Biblical sounds.

One can understand how this pattern of behaviour can communi-cate intensity of feeling, and comes to be interpreted as religious devotion. However, it is still difficult to explain why it became associated with religion in the first place.

Conversion   Discussion of conversion experiences is likely to suffer from a certain semantic confusion. As we pointed out in Chapter 3, the proper use of the term 'conversion', should be kept to cases where there is a change from one belief system to another. However, most users of the term 'conversion' in the literature refer to cases where there is no dramatic change from one system to another, but a sudden recommitment to a familiar belief system. This recommitment experience, nevertheless, may be intense and dramatic, and accompanied by profound psychological changes. Still, the psychological process involved in 'conversion' may be different from the one involved in real conversion. Roberts (1965) made the distinction between conversion to a different faith and 'conversion' experiences which involved the same faith, and found that 'conversion' cases show more neuroticism. Christensen (1965) concluded that sudden 'conversion' experiences in adolescence were temporary acute hallucinatory episodes in persons with previous fundamentalist religious training. Allison (1967) reported that a 'conversion' experience among divinity students was related to a better capacity to integrate crisis experiences, and was not related to psychopathology. Spellman, Baskett and Byrne (1971) found that subjects reporting a 'conversion' experience, i.e. religious recommitment, also reported more anxiety on the Taylor manifest anxiety scale (see p. 60f for further discussion of conversion). On the other hand Srole *et al.* (1962), as reported above, found that those people who had switched to another religion had better mental health than others; this supports the view that such shifts can be regarded as attempts at integration and growth.

Mystical experience Little reliable information beyond case studies is available for determining the role of psychopathological factors in mystical experiences. Various case studies seem to indicate that many individuals reporting mystical experience in previous times were quite disturbed by contemporary standards. The section on mental disorders in religious leaders and clergy contains references to some of the best-known cases of mystical experiences. Dittes (1971b) considers that mystical experiences can be interpreted as a loss of control by the ego, and an abandonment to group influences. Such weakening of the self can be brought about by fatigue and fasting, or by drugs (p. 46f), but presumably some personalities are more disposed towards it.

We may conclude that psychopathology may play a part in the individual dynamics of those involved in individual religious experiences. In a group setting, however, these actions take on a different meaning, and can be regarded as acts of commitment to the group (Hine, 1969). Religious sects and groups which encourage intense religious experiences often contribute to the overall adjustment of their members *vis-à-vis* society by providing a supporting environment and resocializing their members.

Adjustment to life crises

Times of life crisis, either universal (birth, death, war) or unexpected and personal, have always been the times in which religion has been called upon to provide emotional support in the face of uncertainty. There may be a religious reaction to personal problems and difficulties. Shaw (1970) described it as the 'theological model' of behaviour. The question is: does the use of this model help adjustment? It may affect help-seeking behaviour, and we may hypothesize that belief in the theological model of personal problems will decrease the likelihood of seeking professional help. Belief in the divine causation of human problems may also affect the way individuals react to crises in their lives.

The support and solace offered by religion in the face of crises and difficulties in a person's life are often suggested as examples of the utility and advantage of religious beliefs. The effects of religion as a source of support have been tested in several studies. Nunn, Kosa and Alpert (1968) found that religious explanations for the causes of illness were only marginally helpful in adjustment to life crises. Some positive function of religion in supporting family stability in a situation of 'cultural shock' was noted by Babchuk, Crockett and Ballweg (1967).

Information on religious reactions to crisis situation was collected by Lindenthal *et al.* (1970). Respondents were asked if they had experienced any of sixty-two crises, involving pain, change of status, etc. These experiences led to reduced church attendance, especially for previously regular attenders, and the more seriously impaired. However, the greater the impairment, the more often they prayed for help, especially for problems which were catastrophic, or connected with health, family or job. In a British survey it was found that in times of trouble people were more likely to see a doctor, except for two particular kinds of trouble: marital difficulties and death (that of relatives, or fear of one's own) (ITA, 1970). Evidently most people do not turn to the church, though they do resort to prayer, when emotionally disturbed.

Biersdorf and Johnson (1966) found that religion offered three kinds of help to disabled persons. One was the ability to accept physical disability; another was the ability to suffer pain. The third kind of support contributed to the ability to endure the process of rehabilitation. The findings regarding the effects of religion in adjusting to life crises are rather limited, but we may have reason to suspect that religion is probably used as a source of support less often than in the past. The theological model of human suffering (Shaw, 1970) is likely to be used still among those whose religiosity includes a high degree of psychological commitment, and whose deprivations are sometimes severe, e.g. sect members.

Suicidal behaviour

The subject of the relationship between religious behaviour and suicide has been a focus of interest and speculation ever since Durkheim's *Suicide* (1897). In this section we shall review the relevant studies using both general suicide rates and psychological data on individuals who have attempted suicide.

Studies using suicide rates

Durkheim (1897) found that suicide rates were higher for Protestants than for either Catholics or Jews. Using the Durkheim data and additional findings, Halbwachs (1930) reported that the suicide rate for Protestants was two to three times the rate for Roman Catholics. Durkheim's explanation was that the Protestant church does not provide the same degree of social integration as Catholicism or Judaism.

Suicide rates for religious denominations in the USA are hard to obtain, since religion is not normally entered on death certificates. Several early studies, reported by Dublin (1933), showed that the same denominational differences that had been observed in Europe existed in the USA. Dublin reported that in the USA Jews have the lowest suicide rates, and Protestants have the highest rates. European statistics before 1914, and US statistics later, show Jews as having the lowest rate of suicide among major religious groups. More recent studies show that the absolute suicide rate for European Jews has risen considerably. Most of the rise has been noted during the first quarter of the century (Dublin, 1933; Cavan, 1928).

When whole nations are compared, there is still a tendency for Catholic countries to have lower rates. Kramer *et al.* (1972) suggested that differences in suicide rates among European countries still follow the Durkheim thesis. If we look at the data in Table 8.6 more systematically, and perform a simple statistical test, it becomes clear that in 1960 there was no longer any relationship between the dominant religion and suicide rates in European countries. In order to test this, we used the data provided by Kramer *et al.* (1972) for 18 European nations (the United Kingdom was divided into England, Wales, Scotland and Northern Ireland). The suicide rates in all these countries were divided in a 2×2 table on the basis of the predominant religion in the country ('mixed' religion countries, such as Belgium, were not included) and the suicide rate. A suicide rate of 10·0 per 100,000 or above was defined as high, and a suicide rate below that as low. From inspecting the table it becomes clear that the cases are almost equally distributed.

TABLE 8.6 *Suicide rates and dominant religion in eighteen European nations, 1960*

	Low	High
Protestant	Iceland, Netherlands, Norway, Scotland 4	Denmark, Finland, England, Wales, Sweden 5
Catholic	Eire, Italy, Poland, Portugal, Spain 5	Austria, Czechoslovakia, France, Hungary 4

High: above 10·0 per 100,000.
Data from Kramer *et al.* (1972).

This test suggests that the possible influence of religion is only one among many factors, and that economic, social and political conditions also play important roles in determining suicide rates. Whitt, Gordon and Hofley (1972) found that increasing industrialization is related to an increase in suicide rates and a decrease in homicide rates, regardless of religion.

Official suicide rates reflect only reported suicides, while many suicides go unreported or are included in other categories of death causes, such as accidents. Thus lower suicide rates in some countries may mean inefficient reporting techniques or the deliberate concealment of suicide cases, as a result of strong social or religious norms against it. A significant finding reported by Comstock and Partridge (1972) relates church attendance in the USA to suicide rates. In a six-year study of one county, suicide rates per 1,000 were determined for frequent church attenders (once a week or more), irregular attenders (less than once a week) and infrequent attenders. The suicide rates for the three groups was 0·45, 0·95, and 2·1, respectively. This result lends support to the view of religious activity as supporting individual integration. On the other hand it is possible that reduced church attendance is simply a reflection of deteriorating personal integration, as was found by Lindenthal *et al.* (1970).

Studies of suicidal patients

Clinical studies of actual suicidal patients test the hypothesis that religious beliefs act as a deterrent to suicidal behaviour. This

143

hypothesis can be seen as partially derived from Durkheim's (1897) analysis, and partially derived from the content of religious attitudes towards the act of suicide. These attitudes, which presumably would affect individual actions, are quite clear: all Western religions denounce suicide as an act of faithlessness. In Catholicism it is a mortal sin, depriving the soul of the chance of receiving eternal grace. These strong religious prohibitions are presumed to have an influence on the individual, and would lead us to predict a negative correlation between religiosity and suicidal behaviour.

Stengel (1964) pointed out that Catholics, Orthodox Jews and Moslems who live in predominantly Protestant countries have a lower suicide rate compared with the majority group. He suggested that the decisive factor was the degree of religiosity, rather than the specific religious faith. Epps (1957) reported on the religious affiliation of 100 women charged with attempted suicide and imprisoned for this offence in England: 58 reported membership of the Church of England, 29 were Roman Catholic, 3 Lutheran, 2 Jewish, and the rest belonged to sects or were unaffiliated. However, most of those reporting a religious affiliation reported a lack of interest in religion. The overall impression was that religion was totally unimportant in their lives. Middleton et al. (1961) surveyed 219 cases of attempted suicide and reported an unexpectedly high percentage of Roman Catholics, twice as high as their percentage among general admissions.

Another study by Balfour and Hamilton (1963) found that, among 180 cases of attempted suicide, Protestant and Catholic representation was proportional to their percentage in the population. Similar findings were reported by Whitlock and Schapira (1967), who found that Catholics were slightly over-represented among attempted suicides. Morphew (1968) studied 50 cases of self-poisoning admitted to a British hospital during a three-month period. He determined for each case the religious affiliation, level of religious activity and belief, and level of punitiveness based on questionnaire items selected from the MMPI. The degree of religiosity in the group did not differ from that of the general population; Roman Catholics were somewhat over-represented, but nominal religious affiliation for Protestants did not seem to reflect any kind of religious commitment. There were no significant differences in punitiveness between Catholics and Protestants. Morphew's conclusion is that both personality and social factors outweigh religious attitudes in the genesis of suicidal behaviour.

Kranitz et al. (1968) tested the hypothesis that within the same religious denomination there would be differences in the degree of religiosity between 20 suicidal patients and matched non-suicidal controls, but there were no significant differences. The evidence did not suggest that religiosity was an important factor affecting individual suicidal behaviour. Hole (1971) reported the results of a clinical study which indicated that religion had an inhibiting effect on suicidal behaviour only in a limited number of cases. Such an effect was observed only in cases where religion was judged of more than average importance for the individual.

Summary

The statistical studies show that Protestants no longer have a higher suicide rate than Catholics; there is some evidence that religious people are less likely to commit suicide. All the clinical studies reviewed above conclude that neither affiliation nor degree of religious involvement seems related in any significant way to suicide attempts.

Drinking and alcoholism

The connection between religious affiliation and religiosity as independent variables and drinking and alcoholism as dependent variables has been the object of much research. The observed differences in alcoholism rates among religious groups are one reason for the interest in this question. Another reason is historical. Alcohol is second only to sex in being a target for prohibitions and denunciations from religious sources. We can speculate that the action of alcohol as a chemical agent which weakens cortical inhibitions has been the cause of its becoming a central target for preachers who described it as an instrument of the Devil.

Religious and ethnic affiliation studies in the USA have always found differences between two extreme groups: Jews had the lowest alcoholism rate, while Irish Catholics had the highest (Skolnick, 1958; Malzberg, 1962). Milt (1967) in a survey of cultural and religious differences in alcohol use in USA found that in general Protestants are more likely to be heavy drinkers, though this may be explained by their higher socio-economic status. Within the Roman Catholic population there are ethnic differences, with Italian Americans scoring high on alcohol consumption but low on alcoholism, and Irish Americans having a high rate of both. Jews have a high rate of alcohol use, but a low rate of alcoholism.

Despite the low rate of alcoholism, the percentage of total abstainers among Jews is remarkably low, and has been reported as 1 per cent (Snyder, 1958) or 4 per cent (Knupfer and Room, 1967). Wechsler *et al.* (1970) used the breathalyser to determine blood-alcohol levels in 8,461 people admitted to the emergency service

145

of a Boston hospital. Level of alcohol use, as measured by this technique, was significantly related to religio-ethnic affiliation. Positive indications of alcohol were lowest for the Jewish and Italian Catholic groups. They were highest for Catholics, and then Protestants.

Several explanations have been proposed to explain the differences between religious groups in drinking problems. Straus and Bacon (1953) first noticed the connection between the general orientation of a religious group towards drinking and the existence of drinking problems among its members. They made the observation that the incidence of alcohol use was greater in the religious groups which are more permissive about drink (i.e. Jews and Catholics), but when those who belong to stricter groups (Baptists, Mormons) use alcohol, they are more likely to develop drinking problems.

Skolnick (1958) also suggested that it was the attitude toward drinking, as formulated in the religious traditions of the group, that was most important in determining drinking behaviour and producing problems. In a comparative study of Jews, Methodists and Episcopalians, Skolnick found that Episcopalians, whose religious tradition tolerates drinking but does not encourage it, contributed the highest number of heavy drinkers; Methodists, whose religious tradition forbids drinking, had a lower number; and Jews, whose tradition incorporates drinking into the religious rituals within the home, had the lowest. Snyder (1958) suggested two factors in Jewish tradition which determined the unique pattern of alcohol use among the Jews. The first is the controlled use of alcohol in religious ceremonies, which teaches Jews how to drink; and the second is the strong condemnation of drunkenness, which is seen as un-Jewish, and teaches Jews how not to drink.

The suggestion that the patterns of alcohol use among the Irish was determined by culture, and not religious affiliation, was made by Knupfer and Room (1967). They found that religious affiliation did not make a significant difference in drinking patterns among Irish men. The reported frequency of drunkenness was similar for Irish Protestant men married to Protestant wives, Irish Catholic men married to Catholic wives, and Irish Catholic men married to Protestant wives. The absence of similar drinking patterns among other Catholic groups tends to support the view that the high rate of alcoholism among the Irish is a matter of ethnic-cultural tradition and history. Whether such patterns will continue into the future is unclear, but there are signs of diminishing differences, at least among Catholics and Protestants. A 1969 poll of 1,030 American students (Gallup, 1972), focusing on Catholic-Protestant differences, showed no differences between the two groups in the reported use of alcohol, marijuana, barbiturates, and LSD.

The relationship of drinking habits to individual religiosity has been studied less often than their relationship to religious affiliation. We may assume a restraining influence of religiosity on drinking, as part of religion's impact on impulsive behaviour. Religious prohibitions are often given as reasons for abstinence from alcohol (e.g. Straus and Bacon, 1953). Moberg (1969) found a correlation between religious conservatism, as defined by the person himself, and negative attitudes towards drinking. Cahalan, Cisin and Crossley (1969), in a study of drinking patterns in the USA, found that among frequent churchgoers only 10 per cent were heavy drinkers, compared with 22 per cent among those who never went to church. The relationship was found for Protestant men and women, and for Catholic women, but not for Catholic men. Carman (1971) found significant negative correlations between the level of religious involvement and the level of alcohol consumption and the frequency of drunkenness and related social problems. Negative correlations between religious activity and drinking among college students were found by Straus and Bacon (1953), and by others.

Parental religiosity as a background factor among alcoholics has been reported in several studies. Walters (1957) reported a high degree of religiosity in the families of alcoholics, compared with a control group. The alcoholics were also more likely to hold their childhood religious beliefs. Wittman (1939) reported that parents of alcoholics were above average in religiosity and religious conservatism. Pascal and Jenkins (1960) in a study of incarcerated alcoholics found that their parents were likely to be less active religiously, thus deviating from the group norm in southern USA.

One explanation for the greater rate of alcoholics among those coming from strictly religious (and often abstaining) families is the 'rebellion' hypothesis (Straus and Bacon, 1953). It is possible that these individuals are reacting to strict religious and parental prohibitions by going in the opposite direction. Skolnick (1958) similarly stated that 'the abstinence orientation to drinking seems prone to encourage problem drinking in those who reject the norm of total abstinence' (p. 466). Without using the psychological explanation of rebellion against parental authority, Skolnick suggests that the abstinence norm permits only two options, total abstinence and heavy drinking. Thus, the absolute demands of abstinence are likely to lead to problem drinking behaviour, whereas open acceptance of alcohol use, and its early occurrence (e.g. among Jews) are likely to result in lower rates of problem drinking.

On the basis of the reported findings, it seems that religious attitudes towards alcohol use do play a role in the formation of drinking patterns and in the creation of drinking problems. As will be seen in the sections on sexual behaviour and sexual attitudes

147

below, religious prohibitions show some impact in controlling impulsive behaviour in general.

Crime and delinquency

Most studies looking at the relationship between religion and illegal behaviour usually start with a hypothesis stating the presumed connection between religion and ethical behaviour. The problems of measurement and definition in this area are quite serious. The basic problem with most studies of crime and delinquency is that they use recorded crimes, arrests, convictions, and prison populations, and define as criminals or delinquents those found guilty by the courts. Using such statistics enables us to measure 'visible' areas of criminal activities, but we must assume that there are additional acts of 'hidden criminality', which go unreported (Sellin and Wolfgang, 1958).

TABLE 8.7 *Delinquency and denomination in the British Army, in percentages*

	Delinquents	Normal Army
	%	%
Church of England	71	70
Nonconformist	8	19
Roman Catholic	20	10
Jews	1	1

Source: Trenaman (1952).

Historically, studies of the relationship between crime rates and religious affiliation started in Europe (Bonger, 1943) where the religious background of offenders was routinely recorded in official statistics. Many of the old European findings are quite consistent with more recent studies. European studies usually found that Catholics have the highest rate, Jews and non-religious people the lowest (Lombroso, 1911; Gillin, 1945). Von Hentig (1948), defining religious affiliation more strictly, showed that Catholics and Protestants are over-represented in criminal statistics, while Jews and those unaffiliated are under-represented. According to the Von Hentig findings, being unaffiliated with any religious organization is the best predictor of law-abiding behaviour. Comparing delinquency for different denominations in the British Army, Trenaman (1952) found considerable differences, as shown in Table 8.7.

If delinquents are analysed by type of crime, interesting denominational differences appear. Table 8.8 shows the results of such an analysis of crimes in the Netherlands for the years 1910–15 and 1919. It will be noticed that Catholics have a high rate of crimes of violence, Protestants of sexual offences, and Jews of fraud.

TABLE 8.8 *Percentages of those sentenced for various crimes belonging to different religious groups*

	Protestant	Catholic	Jew	No church
Theft	52·4	43·9	1·3	1·8
Aggravated theft	58·2	37·4	1·5	2·2
Embezzlement	56·3	37·8	2·5	2·6
Swindling	53·8	38·1	4·6	2·6
Receiving stolen goods	51·5	41·1	4·9	1·9
Offences against public decency	48·7	46·9	1·9	1·7
Minor sexual offences	72·7	24·1	1·4	1·7
Rape	59·7	39·0	0·0	0·0
Sexual offences by school teachers	59·8	38·1	0·5	1·6
Rebellion against authority	52·1	43·9	1·2	2·4
Disturbance of domestic peace	58·2	38·1	0·8	2·6
Assault	56·3	40·1	1·3	2·0
Serious assault	48·2	49·3	0·6	1·5
Manslaughter and murder	58·3	38·3	0·4	2·0
Percentage of the population aged 20 and over	54·4	35·0	1·8	7·3

Source: Bonger (1943).

Recent American studies still show the same trend for denominational differences, though studies report varying results depending on the definition of affiliation and type of offence (e.g. Goldscheider and Simpson, 1967; Rhodes and Reiss, 1970). However, the higher rate for Catholics and the lower rate for Jews are at least partly due to class differences. One of the few studies in which class and other variables were held constant is that by the Gluecks (1950) in which 500 delinquents were compared with a carefully matched control group of 500 non-delinquents (see Table 8.9). The delinquents, but not their parents, included a higher percentage of Catholics; they were more likely to have parents of different faiths, and were less often Protestants than the control group.

Studies which tried to relate delinquent behaviour and church membership or church attendance show various results, depending on the sample used (Neumeyer, 1961). Studies of institutionalized and recidivist offenders tend to report a lower proportion of church

149

membership and religious activity than in other groups of offenders. This may be due to a social class bias, since middle class offenders are usually treated by police or mental health clinics, and so institutionalized offenders would show the lower church membership rates typical of the lower class.

TABLE 8.9 *The denominations of delinquents, non-delinquents, and their parents*

| | Delinquents | | Non-delinquents | |
	Boys	Parents	Boys	Parents
	%	%	%	%
Roman Catholic	81·2	67·6	71·6	65·4
Greek Catholic		1·9		2·6
Protestant	15·8	12·3	23·6	20·3
Jew	2·0	1·2	2·0	2·2
Mixed Catholic/Protestant		15·0		8·5
Other religions	1·0	2·0	2·8	1·0

Source: Glueck and Glueck (1950).

Glueck and Glueck (1950) found that of the delinquent group 39 per cent went to church weekly, compared with 67 per cent of the controls. Healy and Bronner (1923) obtained the corresponding figures of 44 per cent for the delinquents, 61 per cent for the controls. Ferguson (1952) found that 14·9 per cent of a group of 670 young people in Glasgow who were not church attenders had been convicted between the ages of 8 and 18, compared with 8·9 per cent for 633 regular attenders. Church attendance was found to be unrelated to delinquency in more recent surveys of adolescents in Great Britain (McDonald, 1969).

Differences in religious attitudes and beliefs between delinquents and non-delinquents are small or absent altogether (for example Middleton and Fay, 1941; Conger and Miller, 1966). Middleton and Fay found that delinquent girls expressed more favourable attitudes towards Sunday observance and Bible teachings. School and Becker (1964) found no significant differences between delinquent and non-delinquent Protestant boys in terms of religious attitudes and beliefs. Middleton and Putney (1962) found no connection between acceptance or non-acceptance of religious beliefs and antisocial behaviour. Only one study, by Allen and Sandhu (1967), reported a significant difference in religiosity between delinquents and non-delinquent boys, with the delinquents showing less religious feeling.

Gannon (1967) studied the effect of a training programme in

150

religious morality given to Catholic inmates in a youth reformatory. An increase in religious attitudes, which did occur, was not accompanied by a change in moral attitudes. Hirschi and Stark (1969) measured the connection between religiosity, measured by beliefs and church attendance, and delinquency, measured by self-reports of illegal acts. They found that church attendance leads to the acceptance of certain religious beliefs, but that these are unrelated to actual illegal behaviour. It was found that those students who believed in the Devil and an after-life were just as likely to commit illegal acts as students who did not hold these beliefs. Regular church attenders were as likely to commit illegal acts as those who never attended.

9   Sex and marriage

Sexual activity

Surveys of sexual activity have been carried out in both countries,
notably by Kinsey in the USA and by Chesser for English women.
These are the main sources of information for this section, since
these surveys were both extensive and rigorous. Kinsey and his
collaborators interviewed 5,300 men (1948) and 5,940 women (1953).
Although the samples were unduly weighted with middle-class
people and with Jews, they included widely varying sections of the
population, and great efforts were made to avoid volunteers by
interviewing 100 per cent of each group contacted. The interviews
show test-retest and inter-interviewer consistency, and various
ingenious crosschecks were carried out. However, in an effort to
induce frankness, the questions were phrased in a way that might
be expected to produce exaggeration in the answers. There is, of
course, no final check on the validity of such interview material.
There has subsequently been a series of further studies in Britain
and America.

In these surveys sexual activity is reported for those who belong
to different churches, or to no church at all, and for those who go to
church with different frequencies. Kinsey distinguished the 'devout',
by which he meant 'regular attendance and/or active participation
in church activities'.

It is possible that some of the results to be reported are due
to the fact that religious people are less willing to report forms of
sexual behaviour disapproved of by their church. However, the
differences found are very large, and are unlikely to be due to this
alone. In addition Kinsey, for example, took great trouble to obtain
full and frank replies, while some other surveys were anonymous.
The index of sexual activity is either orgasms per week—the medians

for each group being compared—or alternatively the percentage of each group who report the activity in question at all.

Total sexual outlet, in terms of median orgasms per week, was lower for the devout in all groups studied by Kinsey, male and female, married and single. The median frequency for the devout was about two-thirds that of the others, the percentage of devout people experiencing orgasm was less, and the age of onset later. Comparing denominations, Jews were least active, followed by Catholics and Protestants, not only for total output but for most kinds of sexual activity.

Premarital intercourse (PMI) is reported by fewer religious people in all studies. Kinsey found that PMI was reported by about half as many of the devout as by other respondents, both for males (1948) and females (1953). He also found small denominational differences, Orthodox Jews being least active. In a more recent American study Kantner and Zelnik (1972) interviewed a national sample of 4,240 unmarried girls aged 15 to 19. The percentage of different groups who had had intercourse are given in Table 9.1. In all denominations there is a strong connection between church attendance and a low rate of PMI. There are also denominational differences, Mormons, Jews and Catholics having the lowest rates.

TABLE 9.1   *Percentage reporting* PMI *by denomination and frequency of church attendance*

| | | | Denomination | | | |
| | | | Catho- | Fundamen- | Other | |
Attendance	Mormons	Jews	lic	talist	Prot.	None
less than 3 times per month	10·4	16·2	32·1	38·6	37·3	47·0
3–4 times per month		27·2	19·2	34·4	26·1	
4 or more times per month	9·1	8·9	9·3	14·2	17·7	
All	8·4	16·8	21·1	25·7	30·1	46·4

Source: Kantner and Zelnik (1972).

In Britain, Schofield (1965) found a correlation of $-0·21$ between church attendance and PMI, in a survey of 1,873 young people aged 15 to 19. Nominal membership is sufficient to reduce the rate of PMI from 77 per cent to 63 per cent, and the rate of pre-engagement intercourse from 62 per cent to 47 per cent (Gorer, 1971). Nonconformists have the lowest rate. The level of PMI has risen sharply in Britain between 1960 and 1970, and there seems

153

to be a new 'moral' rule to the effect that 'sex is all right if accompanied by love'. The effect of religion remains, but it is small compared with the effects of other factors: the cultural shift of attitudes between 1960 and 1970, social class differences (at an earlier period), or the difference in the USA between whites and blacks, the latter being both more religious and more permissive. Females are less permissive than males, though this too is changing (Reiss, 1967).

Masturbation was less frequent for the devout in Kinsey's surveys, for both sexes, and for both married and single people.

Homosexuality was slightly less frequent for the devout; the rate was particularly low for Jews and high for Catholics, particularly non-practising Catholics.

Nocturnal emissions for Kinsey's devout males were insignificantly more frequent, for his devout females sex dreams to the point of orgasm were less frequent.

Sex play of different degrees of intimacy, short of intercourse, is less frequent for religious people. Schofield (1965) found a clear negative correlation between degrees of sex play and frequency of church attendance.

Summary

Clearly there is less sexual activity on the part of religious people. This is particularly true of premarital intercourse, and other forms of sexual activity disapproved of by churches. However, this effect is smaller than that of other social factors.

Many religions impose restrictions on sexual activity, and this is particularly true of Christianity. While there are historical reasons for this, there may also be psychological reasons. Wallin (1957) found that among couples with low sexual gratification, the religious couples were much happier with their marriages, as if religion was a kind of substitute for sex. It may also be the case that sexual deprivation is one of the roots of religion, a theory we shall discuss later (p. 198f).

Birth control

A number of studies show that Catholics are more likely to use the rhythm method (safe period) or withdrawal (*coitus interruptus*), and less likely to use contraception, compared with non-Catholics. However, the gap is closing fast, as American surveys of married women carried out in 1960 and 1965 show (Table 9.2). In the same study it was found that the greatest change had taken place in educated Catholic women and in those who went to church less frequently.

TABLE 9.2   *Attitudes to contraception in the USA in 1960 and 1965*

| | Protestants | | Catholics | |
	1960	1965	1960	1965
	%	%	%	%
In favour of birth control	91	92	52	70
In favour of rhythm method only	5	4	33	23
Against birth control	3	4	9	6

Source: Westoff and Ryder (1971).

Similar findings were obtained in British studies of different samples of women. Catholics were much less likely to use the sheath (42 per cent v. 61 per cent for non-Catholics), and slightly less likely to use the pill (16 per cent v. 19 per cent), or diaphragm (9 per cent v. 16 per cent), in a survey of middle-aged women, asked to report on their use of different methods throughout their married lives (Langford, 1969). Comparable results were obtained by Gorer (1971) and Cartwright (1970). Social Surveys (1964) found that 46 per cent of British Catholics disapproved of birth control compared with 8 per cent for the whole population.

Sexual attitudes

Religious people of different denominations are found to have characteristic attitudes on all aspects of sexual behaviour.

Premarital and extramarital intercourse   As would be expected from the reported behaviour, religious people disapprove more of these kinds of behaviour, as shown in Table 9.3. In this British survey there was a clear effect both of nominal affiliation and regular attendance, while nonconformists were most likely to disapprove.

TABLE 9.3   *Disapproval of premarital and extramarital intercourse by nominal and regular members of churches*

| | All | C. of E. | | Noncon. | | R.C. | | No rel. |
		nom.	reg.	nom.	reg.	nom.	reg.	
	%	%	%	%	%	%	%	%
Disapprove of PMI	64	64	79	70	90	71	84	36
Disapprove of EMI	82	82	91	85	97	87	92	69

Source: Social Surveys (1964).

155

Reiss (1967) found more permissive attitudes in the USA in liberal Protestant groups like Presbyterians and Episcopalians. Wright and Cox (1971), in a study of British 17- to 19-year-old students, found that attitudes to the morality of premarital sexual intercourse were strongly related to religious beliefs. The more religious respondents held more negative attitudes towards premarital intercourse. Nevertheless, Wright and Cox report a significant change in attitudes between 1963 and 1970, even for the group with conventional religious beliefs.

Guilt about sex This is more common among religious people. Peterson (1965), in a study of 420 married people, found the rates of guilt set out in Table 9.4

TABLE 9.4   *Sex guilt in married people*

	%
Sect-Conservative	29
Institutional-Authoritarian	21
Liberal	11
Jewish	10
No church—Agnostic	6

Source: Peterson (1965).

Divorce Chesser (1956) found that only 5 per cent of Catholics would seek divorce if their marriage proved unsatisfactory, compared with 32 per cent of members of the Church of England. Similarly, only 14 per cent of those from a religious background said they would seek divorce, compared with 37 per cent of those from a non-religious background. In his factor analysis of the opinions of 700 people, Eysenck (1944) found that there was a high negative correlation between being in favour of easier divorce laws and agreeing with various religious propositions.

Homosexuality and prostitution Homosexuality is disapproved of by Catholics, especially by regular attenders. Membership of other churches makes no difference. Prostitutes are disapproved of by Catholics, especially by regular attenders, 53 per cent of whom would like prostitutes punished by law (compared with 39 per cent for the whole population). Membership of other churches has no effect on attitudes to prostitutes, but regular attendance does, creating more disapproval, especially for nonconformists (Social Surveys, 1964).

156

Abortion In the USA there is a positive correlation between religious activity and opposition to abortion, but this does not seem to vary with denomination (Finner and Gamache, 1969). In Britain Cartwright (1970) found that about 50 per cent of Catholics were opposed to abortion, compared with 25 per cent of non-Catholics. These attitudes were shared by Catholic doctors and health visitors.

Summary

Religious people are against pre- and extramarital intercourse, and feel guilty about sex, especially if they belong to strict sects as opposed to liberal churches. Catholics are more opposed to birth control, divorce, homosexuality and prostitution, and other regular church members share disapproval of the last three in lesser degree.

Marital adjustment

Several investigators have examined the factors associated with marital happiness or 'adjustment', this being measured by means of self-ratings. In all of the studies in which religious variables have been included, the more religious people have claimed to be more happily married. The differences are not large, but they are highly consistent. Chesser (1956) found that 91 per cent of his English married women who were regular church attenders were 'exceptionally or very happy' as compared with 62 per cent of non-attenders. Landis and Landis (1953) in a study of 409 American couples found that 54 per cent of regular attenders were 'very happy' as opposed to 43 per cent of those who went occasionally or never. Burgess and Cottrell (1939) found a 'good' marital adjustment in 50 per cent of couples married in church compared with about 37 per cent of those married elsewhere. When couples from a religious background are compared with others, the result is not so definite: Chesser found such marriages were happy slightly more frequently —79 per cent compared with 67 per cent; and Terman (1938) found a curvilinear relationship, so that those with a strict religious training or with no religious training were less happily married than those with an intermediate amount. Masters and Johnson (1970) find that a strict religious upbringing is one of the main causes of sexual problems in marriage.

There are also denominational differences in marital happiness. Peterson (1965) found that members of liberal churches and Jews were most satisfied, followed by those with no church, sect members and Catholics; the differences were greater for women. In England Chesser (1956) found that nonconformists were most happily married, followed by members of the Church of England, and Catholics; the non-religious were least satisfied.

157

The divorce rate is lower for church members. Catholics have a lower rate of divorce, and those with no religious affiliation a rate about three times that of those belonging to churches, in the USA. The following table presents data on the percentage of marriages ending in divorce by religious affiliation and non-affiliation.

TABLE 9.5 *Success of marriage by religious composition of partners in the USA*

Religious composition of family	Landis-Landis Study*		Weeks Study†		Bell Study‡	
	Divorced	Intact	Divorced	Intact	Divorced	Intact
	%	%	%	%	%	%
Both Catholic	4·4	95·6	3·8	96·2	6·4	93·6
Both Protestant	6·0	94·0	10·0	90·0	6·8	93·2
Both Jewish	5·2	94·8	—	—	4·6	95·4
Both independent	17·9	82·1	23·9	76·1	16·7	83·3

* Study of 4,108 marriages of parents of college students in Michigan, 1958.
† Study of 6,548 public and parochial school children in Spokane, Wash., 1943.
‡ Study of 13,528 families in Maryland in 1938.
Source: Vernon (1968).

It is not very clear why religious people should be more happily married than others. Perhaps they only say they are. Perhaps religion draws them together, in a context where the ideals of love and family life are prominent. Other studies show that Catholics compensate for their low divorce rate by a higher rate of desertion and separation. Catholics often belong to the working class, in which these ways of ending marriage are more common.

Agreement over religion is an important factor in marital happiness. Locke (1951) found that 'very happy' marriages were much more common when there was agreement about religion: 65 per cent compared with 9 per cent of his 544 couples in the early years of marriages. Fisher (1948) in a study of the parents of college students found evidence that similarity of religious values was more important for the success of marriage than similarity of other values on the Vernon-Allport scale. Burchinal (1957) has pointed out, on the other hand, that agreement on such matters as finance and how to spend time together emerge as more important predictors of marital adjustment than agreement on religion. In other studies (e.g. Landis, 1949) in which American children were asked about their parents, the divorce rate was highest for mixed Protestant-Catholic marriages, and conflict over the religious training of the children seemed to be the main source of trouble in these families. Monahan and Kephart

(1954) in a careful study of desertion and non-support cases in Philadelphia did not find any more desertions in mixed marriages; Mowrer (1927) analysed 2,661 marriages in Chicago and found that mixed religion was only a minor factor in desertion for partners of the same race, differences of nationality outweighing differences of religion.

Religious people are more happily married than non-religious, and less likely to divorce. But a strict religious upbringing can create sexual problems later. Agreement over religion is an even more important factor.

Fertility

It is found in many parts of the world that Catholics have more children than Protestants, and Protestants more than Jews. This is partly because rural families have larger families, and Catholics came later to the towns. Goldberg (1959) found that first-generation urban Catholic families in Detroit had 3·40 children, compared with 2·49 for Protestants. In second-generation families, the Catholics had 2·37 children, the Protestants 2·00. The Catholic-Protestant differential remained in the city, but was much reduced. Another problem is that people of less education and lower social class have larger families. However, large-scale fertility surveys of national samples of American women show that actual and expected family size are greater for Catholics within every occupational, educational and income group (see Table 9.6).

TABLE 9.6   *Expected number of children for Catholics and Protestants*

Occupation (of husband)	Prot.	Cath.	Education (of wife)	Prot.	Cath.
Upper white collar	2·8	3·9	College	2·8	4·1
Lower white collar	2·8	3·6	High school 4	2·7	3·5
Upper blue collar	3·1	3·5	High school 1–3	3·1	3·5
Lower blue collar	3·1	3·7	Grade school	3·3	4·2
Farm	3·3	4·5			
Other	2·8	3·9			

Source: Whelpton *et al.* (1966).

There are variations between Protestant groups, the Hutterites, Mormons and Baptists having the largest families. And there are variations between Catholic groups of different national origins, the Irish Americans having more children than the Italian Americans, though the Irish in Ireland have fewer.

The main reason for these differences is that members of different

159

religious groups have different preferences for family size: there is a high correlation between preferred size and actual size (Whelpton *et al.*, 1966). Stokes (1972) carried out a study of 304 couples in Kentucky, in which social class and education were held constant. He found that the Catholic couples wanted to have an average of 4·5 children, compared with a figure of 2·9 for the Protestants. At the time of the survey the Catholics had 2·6, the Protestants 2·0 children. These preferences can in turn be related to the teaching of different churches, though this teaching can change. American Catholics who go to church once a week or more expect to have 4·4 children; while those who do not go to church expect to have 3·2. There are no similar differences for Protestants (Whelpton *et al.*, 1966), though in the Appalachians there is a similar link between degree of fundamentalism and preferred number of children (De Jong, 1965). Among older Orthodox Jews there is a connection between orthodoxy and fertility, but not for younger ones (Lazerwitz, 1970).

A second factor consists of the different attitudes towards birth control. Whelpton *et al.* (1966) conclude that this is not an important factor in explaining Protestant-Catholic differences in the USA since parents have the number of children they want; this factor does, however, explain class differences in family size. As we have seen, Catholics have been changing their attitudes towards birth control quite rapidly.

A further factor is the age of marriage: Protestants on average marry later, since they are more concerned about their education. The Irish Catholic church recommended late marriage in order to limit family size under poor economic conditions.

10   Social and economic factors

Social class and religiosity

The relationship between religiosity and social class has not always been found to be uniform or clear. Demerath (1965) after summarizing a large number of studies, which sometimes produced contradictory results, suggested that social class affects the way in which religiosity is expressed. Thus, we can expect different results in studies of social class and religiosity, according to the measure used.

Social status and formal participation

Formal participation, i.e. church attendance and church membership, is the first aspect of religious activity to be considered. A clear, positive relationship between social status and church attendance in the USA has been reported by Lazerwitz (1961a), Lenski (1963), and others.

TABLE 10.1   *Church attendance and social class* (*subjective identification*) *in Great Britain, 1957*

Class	Percentage attending at least 'now and again'
Upper	73 (26)
Upper-middle	71 (138)
Middle	56 (474)
Lower-middle	52 (283)
Working	39 (748)

Source: Stark (1964).

Members of the middle class are more likely to attend church or become church members, and the finding in most American studies has been that members of the lower class are least likely to be church members or to attend church services (Burchinal, 1959; Hollingshead, 1949; Lenski, 1953). Studies of church attendance in Great Britain show a similar positive correlation between social class and church attendance (see Table 10.1).

Religious beliefs

In the USA, members of the lower class are less likely to be church members, but those of this class who are, are more likely to have fundamentalist religious beliefs (Demerath, 1965). Class differences in religiosity as measured by religious beliefs were commented on by Lynd and Lynd (1929):

> Members of the working class show a disposition to believe
> their religion more ardently and to accumulate more
> emotionally charged values around their beliefs. Religion
> appears to be operate more prominently as an active agency
> of support and encouragement among this section of the city
> [p. 329].

Demerath (1965) also found that middle- and upper-class Protestants hold more liberal beliefs, and approve of church involvement in social issues, while working-class Protestants hold more traditional beliefs and disapprove of any church involvement in secular affairs.

Johnson (1962) showed that members of the working class were more likely to hold fundamentalist religious beliefs, which in turn were related to conservative political attitudes. Dynes (1955) found that lower socio-economic status was significantly related to a greater acceptance of a sect type of religious organization on an attitude scale. Using a measure of religious attitudes, Almquist (1966) found that social class was the best predictor of religiosity. When respondents were divided into upper-middle-class, lower-middle-class, and lower-class, lower-class members scored higher than the other two groups.

Differences in fundamentalism of religious beliefs among Americans in the Southern Appalachian region are presented in Table 10.2. It should be noted that this region is dominated by fundamentalist Protestantism (De Jong and Ford, 1965), but even within its population there is a strong negative relationship between socio-economic status and fundamentalism of beliefs. The status categories used in the table were based on income, occupation, education, household equipment and self-identification.

TABLE 10.2   *Religious fundamentalism and socio-economic status, southern Appalachian region, 1958*

Socio-economic status	Respondents No.	%	Total	Low	Moderate	High	Very High
				Percentage distribution			
All respondents	1445	100·0	100·0	16·3	23·5	42·4	17·8
Lower	408	28·2	100·0	3·4	12·7	51·5	32·4
Lower-middle	493	34·1	100·0	8·9	20·1	52·1	18·9
Upper-middle	355	24·6	100·0	25·6	34·4	31·5	8·5
Upper	189	13·1	100·0	46·0	34·9	18·0	1·1

Degree of religious fundamentalism

Source: De Jong and Ford (1965).

One way of looking at the difference in style of religious activity between middle- and upper-class church members and lower-class church members is that of seeing church members with higher status as involved with a religion of 'doing', while those with lower status are involved in a religion of 'feeling'. Thus, we should predict a greater frequency of religious experiences among the lower classes, and indeed, in three Gallup Polls asking respondents whether they had had any religious or mystical experiences, those with lower income more frequently reported such experiences. Thus, in a 1967 poll in the USA, 51·0 per cent of respondents with incomes below $3,000 and only 39·7 per cent of those with incomes above $3,000 reported mystical experiences (Back and Bourque, 1970).

TABLE 10.3   *Religious beliefs and social class in Great Britain, 1957*

Class	Life after death	The Devil	Christ's divinity
	Percentage who believe in:		
	%	%	%
Upper	85 (26)	50 (26)	88 (26)
Upper-middle	60 (138)	40 (134)	79 (138)
Middle	56 (474)	33 (474)	72 (474)
Lower-middle	54 (284)	34 (279)	67 (285)
Working	49 (767)	32 (758)	70 (768)

Source: Stark (1964).

In Great Britain the relationship between social class and traditional beliefs is rather different. Here adherence to religious beliefs is positively correlated with class position, and members of the working class are likely to be less conservative in their beliefs (see Table 10.3).

Sectarianism

Sectarianism as a form of religious organization and expression is typical of the lower classes. Goldschmidt (1944) saw Protestant denominationalism in the USA as a reflection of the class structure and social segregation based on class. He suggested that while traditional churches meet the needs of the upper classes, evangelical sects meet working-class needs by offering them a fantasy world. Dynes (1955, 1956) reported that sectarianism as a social attitude, i.e. preference for sect-type religious activities, was correlated with lower socio-economic status. A study of a snake-handling cult in the USA (La Barre, 1962) showed that members of this group came from among the poorest whites, described as the rural proletariat of southern USA. The lower-class and minority-group origins of sects and cults in the USA have been well documented (Yinger, 1957; Boisen, 1939, 1955). In Great Britain small sects are mostly drawn from among the very poor and members of minority groups, with the exception of Christian Science (Gorer, 1955; Wilson, 1961).

Summary and explanation

We can summarize the American findings by stating that they reveal a difference in the nature of religious involvement in different classes in the USA. Members of the middle class score higher on measures of institutional participation: church attendance and church membership. Members of the lower class score higher on measures of traditional beliefs and reported religious experiences. They are also more likely to become sect members, with a subsequent intense psychological and social involvement.

One explanation for social class differences in religious participation is that lower-class people tended to participate less often in all types of voluntary organizations (Lenski, 1963). Membership in churches, like membership in any kind of voluntary organization, is directly related to social class (Demerath, 1965). We may hypothesize that middle-class people in the USA are 'joiners'; and so they join many organizations, including churches. Herberg (1955) stated that involvement in church activity is part of the middle-class life-style. Goode (1966) found that middle-class people tend to join voluntary organizations, and middle-class life-style explains activity and involvement in church organizations. The findings on the relationship between class and religious activity can be explained in this way. If we control for general associational activity of church members, the original correlation disappears.

Another explanation is that different social classes have different styles of religious expression (Demerath, 1965). Thus, middle- and upper-class Protestant church members stress formal, organized participation in church activities, while working-class Protestant church members stress the spontaneous, emotional aspects of religious behaviour. Membership in the main denominations in the USA expresses little more than social conventionality, while sect membership usually means extreme personal commitment and involvement, and is more likely to affect other areas of life. Membership in sects, as opposed to churches, entails a much greater psychological involvement on the part of the individual (Wilson, 1970; Schwartz, 1970), and is often marked by a rejection of past experience and 'bridge-burning' acts (Hine, 1969).

Goode (1966) suggested that the findings on the correlation of social class and church activity have implications in terms of the meaning of church participation to different social classes in the USA. The interpretation offered by Goode was that church activity has become secularized for the middle class. The lower class, on the other hand, manifests a lower level of formal activities, but a higher level of religiosity and psychological involvement in religion.

An explanation of various types of religious participation in terms of social privilege and social deprivation was offered by Campbell and Fukuyama (1970). Using several measures of privilege and deprivation the major finding was that more privileged people prefer organizational religion, while the deprived prefer traditional beliefs and a devotional orientation. The findings on socio-economic status and its effects on religious behaviour can be accounted for by the privilege-deprivation framework. Goode (1968) has also suggested a deprivation explanation of social-class differences in religious participation, since religious styles seem to be related to the felt needs and tensions in the life of various classes. Lower-class people, who are more frustrated, will opt for a more involved religious style.

Another motive for socially underprivileged people to join sects is that they achieve an increase of status; not only are they accepted as social equals but they become part of a spiritual élite (Stark, 1967). Some sects indeed condemn all those outside the sect as sinners. It is important to remember that both the lower and the upper classes have other means of satisfying their respective needs and relieving their respective frustrations. This may explain why

more members of the lower classes do not join religious sects.
The relationship of religious involvement and social class in
Great Britain shows a completely different pattern. In Great Britain
both church attendance and religiosity as measured by beliefs are
positively correlated with social class. The explanation for this
difference between USA and Great Britain is part of the general
explanation for the differences in the pattern of secularization in
the two countries. As we suggested in Chapter 2 above, the secularization of the working class in Great Britain is related to historical
and political factors which did not exist in the USA. Among them are
the greater political consciousness and activity of the British working
class (as compared with the American lower class), and the historical
tradition of religious dissent in Britain (Wilson, 1966). Churches
have been a middle-class institution in Great Britain at least since
the nineteenth century, supporting other middle-class values and
institutions (Inglis, 1963; Wickham, 1957).

Denomination and social class

The fact that members of religious denominations often have in
common not only faith, but also similar socio-economic status, has

TABLE 10.4   *Social class profiles of American religious groups*

Denomination	Upper	Class Middle	Lower	N
	%	%	%	
Christian Scientist	24·8	36·5	38·7	137
Episcopal	24·1	33·7	42·2	590
Congregational	23·9	42·6	33·5	376
Presbyterian	21·9	40·0	38·1	961
Jewish	21·8	32·0	46·2	537
Reformed	19·1	31·3	49·6	131
Methodist	12·7	35·6	51·7	2100
Lutheran	10·9	36·1	53·0	723
Christian	10·0	35·4	54·6	370
Protestant (small bodies)	10·0	27·3	62·7	888
Roman Catholic	8·7	24·7	66·6	2390
Baptist	8·0	24·0	68·0	1381
Mormon	5·1	28·6	66·3	175
No preference	13·3	26·0	60·7	466
Protestant (undesignated)	12·4	24·1	63·5	460
Atheist, agnostic	33·3	46·7	20·0	15
No answer or Don't know	11·0	29·5	59·5	319

Source: Schneider (1952).

166

been observed, especially in the case of American multi-denominational Protestantism (e.g. Niebuhr, 1929; Pope, 1948; Lazerwitz, 1961b). The close relationship between social and church affiliation in the USA was expressed by Winter (1962) as follows: 'The Church is now a reflection of the economic ladder. Ascent on this ladder is validated by escalation to congregations of higher social and economic rank. For every rung on the ladder there is an appropriate congregation, with ushers of slightly more refined dress, and somewhat more cultivated ladies' affairs' (p. 77).

Tables 10.4 and 10.5 present socio-economic status data for American denominations, in the form of social class membership, and in the form of socio-economic indices. Using religious grouping as the independent variable, we may examine its influence on socio-economic positions of individuals. Warren (1970) reported that

TABLE 10.5 *Socio-economic characteristics of fifteen religious groups in Detroit, 1966*

Religious group	Total N	Median family income	Median occupational status*	Median school years completed
Protestant	499	$10,117	45·3	12·0
Congregational	10	17,500	82·7	16·5
Episcopal	34	13,000	59·9	13·0
Presbyterian	75	11,667	60·3	13·5
Nondenom. Protestant	10	11,250	39·9	11·8
Methodist	93	10,703	45·0	12·1
Lutheran	110	10,375	42·9	12·0
Protestant, no denomination specified	32	9,727	48·8	11·5
Baptist	104	9,311	28·6	11·4
Church of Christ	16	8,636	23·3	11·5
Other fundamentalist	15	7,938	26·4	11·0
Roman Catholic	427	9,999	43·2	12·0
Eastern Orthodox	13	9,999	55·0	12·6
Jew	29	14,688	65·0	15·7
No preference, other	38	10,357	55·0	12·1
Not ascertained	7			
Grand total	1,013	$10,177	45·2	12·0

*The current occupation of the respondent was first coded into the 6-digit detailed occupation-industry code of the US Bureau of the Census and then recoded by computer to the 2-digit code of Duncan's Index of Socio-economic Status (cf. Duncan, 1961).

Source: Laumann (1969).

167

Jews, Presbyterians, and Episcopalians are above the average socio-economic status, Methodists and Catholics are close to average, and Baptists are below the average. On the basis of socio-economic survey data, Lazerwitz (1964) presented the following hierarchy of American denominations:

Top:	Episcopalians
	Presbyterians
	Jews
Middle:	Methodists
	Lutherans
	Roman Catholics
Bottom:	White Baptists
	Negro Baptists

Whether religion is a determinant of status, i.e. whether religious factors are responsible for the observed difference in social-class standing among religious groups, has been called into question. Gockel (1969) and others have argued that socio-economic status differences among members of religious groups can be explained by differences which are educational, occupational or regional, but not religious in themselves. Our discussion of the Protestant ethic thesis, in Chapter 6 above, showed that this is likely to be the case. Thus, social standing can lead to a certain style of religious behaviour, but the opposite is less likely to occur. Still, it is possible that religious influences, interacting with social conditions, will influence the extent to which socio-economic status of denominations will remain stable over time. This is one way of interpreting some of the findings which show persistence in the socio-economic status of religious groups over time (e.g. Lenski, 1963).

In Britain, earlier studies showed that the Church of England had a higher proportion of upper- and middle-class members, the nonconformists had more working-class members, while the

TABLE 10.6 *Percentages of social-class ratings in religious denomination, Great Britain, 1964*

Denomination Class rating	Total	Church of England	Nonconformist	Roman Catholic
	%	%	%	%
Average+	4	3	4	4
Average	25	26	24	19
Average−	64	65	66	69
Very poor	7	6	6	8

Source: Social Surveys (1964). Ratings done by interviewer.

Catholic faith appealed to all sections of the population (BIPO, 1950). However, recent surveys show that there are now no class differences between denominations. The relationship between denomination and social class in Great Britain is shown in Table 10.6.

Minority-group membership

Differences of race or caste are similar to social class differences, except that in these cases the barriers are almost impossible to cross. Most findings on the connection between race and religious behaviour are from the USA, comparing whites and Negroes. All aspects of religious activity are much higher for American Negroes, compared with American whites. Roucek (1968) reported that in 1963 there were 55,000 Negro churches in the USA, which makes for a ratio of one church for every 200 Negro churchgoers, compared with one church for every 400 white churchgoers. Formal church membership among Negroes would be expected to be lower because of their lower status, but there is evidence that it is higher than among whites. Negroes usually belong to all-Negro denominations, and their church services tend to be less formal (Glenn, 1964). Even within the Negro caste itself, as Billings (1934) observed, there are social class differences, and the functions the religious group serves at every class level are different. While the lower-class sects serve as an outlet for deprivation and conflict, middle- and upper-class churches serve as social centres and sources of respectability. Church attendance rates for US blacks are higher than those for whites as Table 10.7 illustrates.

TABLE 10.7   *Comparison of responses to the question: 'How often have you attended religious services in the last year?' for blacks and whites in Los Angeles, 1965–6*

Response	Negroes	Whites
	%	%
More than once a week	13	11
Once a week	25	18
Two or three times a month	18	8
Once a month	8	6
A few times per year	26	31
Never	8	25
No answer	2	1
Total	100	100
N	586	586

Note: χ^2 for Once a month or more versus less than that $= 52 \cdot 8$. d.f. $= 1$, p. $< 0 \cdot 001$. Source: McConahay (1970).

In terms of their beliefs, American Negroes are consistently found to be more traditional (Glenn, 1964), and in this respect they parallel lower-class whites. Using the Allport-Vernon Study of values, Pugh (1951) found that the religious scale was highest for three groups of Negroes, which included ministers, church members and non-church members. Cameron (1969) found that Negroes rated all

TABLE 10.8   *Comparison of responses to the question: 'How important was religion to you when you were growing up?' for blacks and whites in Los Angeles, 1965–6*

Response	Negroes	Whites
	%	%
Very important	81	53
Somewhat important	15	33
Not important	3	14
No answer	1	0
Total	100	100
N	586	586

Note: χ^2 for Very important versus Somewhat $+$ Not $= 101\cdot6$. d.f. $= 1$, p. $<0\cdot001$. Source: McConahay (1970).

dimensions of religion as more important in their lives, compared with a matched group of whites, and in Gallup Polls dealing with religious experiences, Negroes reported such experiences more often than whites (Back and Borque, 1970). Tables 10.8 and 10.9 contain comparative data on the significance of religion among blacks and whites in the USA.

Another major characteristic of black religion is the existence

TABLE 10.9   *Negro-white differences in responses to the question 'How strongly do you feel about your religious beliefs?' in a sample of American adults, 1965*

Response	Very strongly	Strongly	Moderately	Less than moderately	N
Race	%	%	%	%	
White	44	22	27	7	1,198
Black	62	20	14	4	204

Source: Alston (1973).

of small sects and splinter groups, often organized around a charismatic leader (Glenn, 1964; Dollard, 1949). Services of worship in these sects often provide outlets for frustrated personal and group needs, through emotionality and cohesiveness. The prevalence and functions of religious sects, and intense religious experiences among American Negroes, have most often been explained on the basis of their lower social status and many frustrations. Alland (1962) describes a revivalistic Negro church which was created in the midst of a deprived community, and where services emphasize joy and ecstasy, with resulting trance states. Cameron (1971), adopting the Marxist position (cf. Chapter 11) simply asserts that 'their social situation in the USA requires more "opiate"' (p. 73). Findings on the political consequences of black religion were presented in Chapter 7 above.

The increasing number of black immigrants in Great Britain, especially those from the West Indies, has created a visible racial minority, similar to the one in the USA, and has given rise to new religious groups. West Indian immigrants, generally rejected by the established churches, have formed new sectarian groups (Hill, 1970). It is interesting to note that they did not join existing British sects, but formed their own. Hill (1971) reported that many of the West Indian immigrants used to be church members in their home country, but changed their religious patterns when they came to Great Britain and joined Pentecostal sects. The explanation offered by Hill is in terms of the status loss which occurred with immigration, rather than in terms of economic deprivation.

Urban–rural differences

Differences in religious behaviour between town and country have been found in a number of surveys, in which this particular breakdown was included. Gorer (1955) found more religious activity among those living in communities with a population of fewer than 10,000 persons in Great Britain (see Table 10.10). Ogburn and Tibbits (1933) and Lenski (1953) found clear evidence of more church attendance in smaller communities in the USA. Glock and Stark (1966) found in a nationwide US survey that residence in a small community was positively correlated with holding traditional beliefs. Similarly, an analysis of Gallup Polls showed that rural residents showed more conservatism in religious beliefs (Nelsen et al., 1971). Light (1970) reported that religion was likely to have more effect on the lives of rural, as compared with urban, adolescent girls. More residents of cities with populations below 50,000 reported having had mystical experiences than residents of larger cities (Back and Bourque, 1970).

171

TABLE 10.10 *Community size and indicators of religiosity in Great Britain, 1955, in percentages*

	Size of community			
	Under 10,000	*10,000– 100,000*	*100,000– 1,000,000*	*over 1,000,000*
No religion	14	21	23	29
Weekly attendance	17	15	15	12
Daily prayers	48	43	42	40

Source: Gorer (1955).

Table 10.11, below, shows differences in religious activity and religious beliefs between farmers and non-farmers in the USA. The comparison has been made on the basis of occupational groups. On the whole, the data in Table 10.11 'indicate that the popular stereotypes and the impressions of social scientists are surprisingly accurate' (Glenn and Alston, 1967, p. 384). Farmers appear to be more traditional and fundamentalist in their beliefs than any other

TABLE 10.11 *Differences in indices of religiosity among occupational groups in the USA, in percentages*

Religious beliefs, practices, and affiliations	*Upper non-manual**	*Lower non-manual†*	*Upper manual‡*	*Lower manual§*	*Farmers*
Attended church in last seven days (Gallup, 1965)	51·6	40·8	42·8	39·7	45·2
Regularly watch or listen to religious services on television or radio (Gallup, 1957)	24·0	30·8	32·3	38·5	43·9
Are members of a church or synagogue (Gallup, 1954)	80·5	80·1	77·9	72·5	68·7
Are members of the Roman Catholic Church (Gallup, 1954)	17·4	17·7	26·6	19·1	4·5
Are members of the Baptist Church (Gallup, 1954)	10·8	9·2	13·3	18·7	17·9
Are members of the Presbyterian or Episcopal Church (Gallup, 1954)	10·2	9·9	4·5	3·6	5·4
Believe that Jesus Christ was the Son of God (Christians only, Gallup, 1957):	79·1	89·2	91·6	93·6	94·9
Believe that there is a Devil (Gallup, 1957):	47·3	55·2	61·0	68·3	76·8
Believe that there is life after death (Gallup, 1957):	69·4	73·5	71·6	78·3	82·6
Believe that Jesus Christ will return to earth (Christians only, Gallup, 1959):	43·6	52·3	57·9	60·1	72·9

* Professional and semi-professional workers, businessmen, and executives.
† Clerical and sales workers.
‡ Craftsmen and foremen.
§ Operatives, service workers, and non-agricultural labourers.
‖ Farm owners, tenants, and managers. According to the 1960 census, only about 1 per cent of 'farmers and farm managers' are managers.
Source: Glenn and Alston (1967).

occupational group, despite the fact that they are less likely to be church members. In many respects they appear to be most similar to the group of lower manual workers. If we look at the other end of the rural-urban continuum we can see that less traditional religious behaviour is more typical of large cities. Nationwide public opinion polls in the USA indicate that respondents from large cities report less orthodox religious activity and beliefs compared with those from smaller cities and rural areas (Marty *et al.*, 1968). Educational and social class-differences probably account for much of these findings.

Such differences may be due to various historical processes. The greater religious activity in British country areas and small towns could be due to cultural lag, large towns taking the lead in a decline of religion, as in other matters. The American results can be similarly explained: Glenn and Alston (1967) explained the persistence of urban-rural differences as due to the 'time lag' factor in the diffusion of innovation and change to the rural areas. These include changes in religious beliefs and traditions, and in general social attitudes. Support for this explanation is given by findings which show farmers to be more ethno-centric and isolationist.

Social disorganization

People are said to be socially disorganized if there are no strong links of friendship, or persistent patterns of social interaction, between them. The term can be applied to individuals who live alone and do not belong to, or are not accepted by, social groups or organizations; it can be applied to social groups where the members do not like one another—the reverse of 'cohesiveness'; it can be applied to areas or organizations where there is little formation of social groups or friendships. The level of mental disorder increases with social disorganization, including people who are unmarried, immigrants, people in areas of low population density, and dwellers in the disorganized central sectors of large cities (Hare, 1952). In this section we shall see if social disorganization affects religion.

Most of the data we have on the effects of social disorganization and rapid social change are based on studies of small religious sects and millennial religious movements. The rise of religious sects in large US cities in this century, together with the existence of small rural sects, whose beliefs and traditions are extreme compared with those of most of the population, have both been explained in terms of social disorganization and dislocation. Cantril and Sherif (1938) regarded the Father Divine sect in the urban USA as providing security and meaning in a complex, confusing environment. Holt (1940) concluded that Holiness sects grew up among Southern whites migrating to large cities in an attempt to establish cohesion and structure in the life of uprooted people. Fauset (1944) described similar developments among urban blacks, who were both minority-group members and immigrants to the large cities, and thus lived under multiple stress. Boisen (1955) regarded social crisis as one of the main causes in the development of new religious movements.

A conceptualization of Jehovah's Witnesses as a reaction to the complexity and pace of social change in modern society was offered by Bram (1956). Cohn (1957) in a study of millenial movements in medieval Europe found that they generally started under conditions of social disorganization, resulting from social change. Poblete and O'Dea (1960) suggested that the formation of religious sects is a response to the anxieties of social and cultural change in deprived groups. In a study of sects among Puerto Rican immigrants in New York, they described the formation of sects as the reaction to anomie and an attempt to redevelop a sense of community. Photiadis and Schweiker (1970) suggested that in a period of fast social change membership in authoritarian churches and sects will rise, and presented data to support this suggestion.

Prophetic religious leaders, who often organize new sects, are likely to appear in periods of social disorganization or of rapid social change. Hoult (1958) suggests that prophets arise among minorities subjected to value conflicts and external pressures. He quotes as examples Old Testament prophets, American Indian prophets, and American black sect leaders.

The studies reviewed in this section all suggest that conditions of extreme social disorganization for minority groups and individuals caught in social changes, for which they are unprepared, lead to the growth of religious sects. It is clear that, since the conditions that give rise to such groups are extreme, the religious reactions to the felt crisis may also seem extreme. Such religious groups are themselves subject to the conditions of social pressure and disorganization, and are thus not likely to survive in their original form.

Economic conditions

It has sometimes been thought that religion prospers in times of economic depression. An attempt has been made to test this hypothesis by plotting curves of *per capita* personal incomes (at constant prices) against the membership statistics for various churches. These curves are not reproduced here because they show virtually no relationship between the two variables. In Great Britain there has been a general increase in prosperity since 1925, accompanied by a fall in religious activity, while in America prosperity was for a time accompanied by a rise in the level of religion. In neither country is there any detailed correspondence between the fluctuations in the curves, as would be expected if there were any causal connection, as is found, for example, between indices of economic prosperity and suicide rates (Henry and Short, 1954).

The greatest change in the level of economic prosperity since 1900 took place during the depression years of 1929–33 in Great Britain and 1930–5 in USA. The depression was welcomed by some religious leaders who thought that people would turn to the churches. In Great Britain there was a slight rise in the membership figures of the Church of England and the Roman Catholic Church, but none for the nonconformist bodies (see p. 9).

The American changes have been analysed in detail by Kincheloe (1937), and his main results will be reported here. During the depression there was no change in membership in the major bodies. However, there was a 10 per cent rise in voluntary contributions from 1929 to 1932, followed by a drop to 25 per cent below the initial figure in 1935; but the rise was probably due to an active drive for funds by the churches at that time. A survey of 678 Congregational churches showed a small temporary rise of attendance (Kincheloe, 1937), but a survey of rural churches showed a decline of attendance during this period (Brunner and Lorge, 1937). Attendance of Jews at the synagogue however dropped about 30 per cent. It seems that the influence of the depression on the main religious bodies was to produce a small initial increase of activity in some but not others; the overall effect was slight.

Several writers have reported that the small Protestant sects in America expanded during the depression (e.g. Boisen, 1955). The best available figures for testing this hypothesis are to be found in the *Census of Religious Bodies*: Table 10.12 shows the

TABLE 10.12   *American sects and the depression*

	1906	1916	1926	1936	1953
Assemblies of God (thousands)		6·7	47·9	148	370
Church of God (thousands)		7·8	23·2	44·8	66·3
Church of the Nazarene (thousands)	6·7	32·3	64	136	250
Evangelical Pillar of Fire	230	1,129	2,442	4,044	5,100
Seventh Day Adventists (thousands)	62·2	79·3	111	133	261
The Pentecostal Holiness Church (thousands)		5·6	8·1	12·9	43·9
Pilgrim Holiness Church (thousands)	2·7	5·3	15·0	20·1	30·9

Based on *Census of Religious Bodies* (1906–36) and *Yearbook of American Churches* (1955).

175

membership returns to the *Census* between 1906 and 1936 for a number of sects which did increase during the depression. It can be seen that they were increasing at much the same rate both before and after the depression. This is consistent with Kincheloe's estimate that sect members increased from 150,000 in 1920 to 400,000 in 1930, and 550,000 in 1935.

There is some evidence about the British sects. Wilson (1961) reports that the evangelist campaigns of the Elim Foursquare Gospel movement were most successful during the depression years.

The other large change in economic conditions has been the post-war boom, particularly in the USA. This has been accompanied by an increase in religious activity for all groups, including the sects (see Table 10.12). In Great Britain there has been an increase in religion from 1950 to 1960.

Sales (1972) suggested that only certain churches become more attractive in times of insecurity, such as the great depression of the 1930s. Other churches seem to have more appeal during times of prosperity. In an empirical test of this hypothesis he tested religious conversion rates during the period 1920–39 in four authoritarian churches and four non-authoritarian churches. These rates were correlated with changes in personal disposable income, and the results are presented in Table 10.13.

TABLE 10.13 *Correlations between estimated per capita disposable income and estimated conversion ratios in four authoritarian and four nonauthoritarian denominations*

Denomination	r between estimated per capita disposable income and estimated conversion ratio
Authoritarian	
Church of Jesus Christ of Latterday Saints	$-0\cdot460\ddagger$
Roman Catholic Church	$-0\cdot456\ddagger$
Seventh-day Adventist Church	$-0\cdot867\,\S$
Southern Baptist Convention	$-0\cdot193$
Non-authoritarian	
Congregational Christian Church	$0\cdot503\ddagger$
Northern Baptist Convention	$0\cdot403\dagger$
Presbyterian Church in the United States of America	$0\cdot533\,\S$
Protestant Episcopal Church	$0\cdot312*$

$* p < 0\cdot10.$ $\dagger p < 0\cdot05.$ $\ddagger p < 0\cdot015.$ $\S p < 0\cdot01.$

Source: Sales (1972).

The results clearly support the hypothesis, and were interpreted in terms of the theory that people are drawn to authoritarian churches in times of stress and insecurity. A smaller replication of the first American depression study, covering an economically depressed area in the USA, showed similar results.

In summary we can say that, while conditions of economic depression as observed in the USA in the 1930s do not bring about major changes in religious activity, it seems that they bring about increases in certain religious bodies, namely authoritarian ones. While it is true that the American sects flourished during the depression, their rate of increase was much the same before and after.

It is argued elsewhere (p. 191f) that economic and social-status deprivation is an important factor in small sect religion; it would be expected from this that the sects would have expanded during the depression. Similarly Henry and Short (1954) account for the lack of increase in the working-class suicide rate by suggesting that 'relative status' is in fact raised for this group by the decline of middle-class prosperity. This suggests that it may be deprivation of status rather than money that is the more important in producing sects. The idea of relative, rather than absolute, deprivation has been used increasingly to explain the growth of sects, and seems relevant to this case. Schwartz (1970) postulates relative deprivation to explain why people join religious sects: 'People join sects because they seek to redress the lack of deference and esteem they feel is rightfully theirs' (pp. 40–1).

11   Theories of religious behaviour

In this final chapter we propose to test some empirical hypotheses derived from theories of religious behaviour against the evidence which has been presented in previous chapters. Before we proceed, however, we should point out some of the limitations and constraints under which the tests will be conducted. One problem encountering all workers in this area is that some of the most provocative and insightful statements about religious behaviour are not actually taken from systematic theoretical presentations. There are very few systematic theories of religious behaviour, and many of those that exist are merely descriptive. As a result some interesting theoretical insights are hard to test empirically.

The derivation of empirical propositions from theoretical statements, especially those that are not comprehensive or systematic, involves the risk of losing most of the insights offered, unless the nature of the empirical test is well specified. Often an hypothesis is taken out of context, and other aspects of the theory are not considered. Sometimes what is tested is the letter, rather than the spirit, of a great idea. In order not to be guilty of these shortcomings which we have found in others we will try to specify the explanatory aims and limits of the theoretical propositions with which we are dealing. Naturally, the selection of propositions reflects our own view of the field, and our judgment as to what can be tested and what evidence can be brought forth to support a given proposition.

The method of testing these theories is much the same in each case, though the details differ. The theory is stated as precisely as possible, and deductions are made about what would be expected in terms of individual differences in religious behaviour and of the type of beliefs that would be present. For example if religion is due to frustration then people who are deprived of the gratification of needs should be more religious, while their beliefs should form some kind of compensation for their frustrations. This theory could be put forward as the sole explanation of religion, in which case there should be an exact correspondence between the degree of frustration and the amount of religious behaviour; or it could be put forward as one process amongst others, in which case a significant correlation of undetermined size would be expected between frustration and religion. In the case of most theories considered in this chapter it is the second interpretation that will be given, whatever may have been the intention of earlier writers.

There are several difficulties that arise in the course of these verifications. (1) The same empirical result sometimes follows from more than one theory. There are two main possibilities here: either two separate processes are operating together, or one theory includes the other by providing a wider range of successful predictions. If one theory can account for all the phenomena that the other explains, together with further results, then the narrower theory can be discarded. However, if the result that is jointly explained is one of the few points of overlap, it is more likely that two separate processes are at work, and both theories should be retained. The result in question is in this case 'overdetermined'. (2) Some of the verifications may be successful and others not. We shall deal with this by showing the areas over which the theory applies. For example, the theory may fit perfectly for certain religious groups, or for people of a certain age-range, but not for others. Furthermore, the theory may have to be made more specific in terms of the particular drives that are being frustrated, coming into conflict, and so forth. (3) The direction of causation may be specified in the prediction, but be unknown for the empirical data. In such a case we shall simply accept the verification as successful but weak.

We selected several general theories of the origins and functions of religion, and also several more specific propositions about the motivation for, and sources of, religious activities and practices. A psychological outlook on religious behaviour often leads to a natural emphasis on motivation: why are some people more religious and why do they engage in certain practices? From the findings we have presented so far it seems plausible to assume that every kind of religious activity is motivationally overdetermined. Personal history, situational factors and personality dynamics all combine in determining why certain people will engage in religious activities. That is why we decided to present several 'mini-theories', which may contribute to an overall understanding of a person or a group.

Theories of religious behaviour (those that are not theologically based) can be divided on the basis of several possible categories: there are *theories of origin*, which attempt to explain how religion first arose; there are *theories of maintenance*, which attempt to explain why certain individuals, or certain societies, hold certain belief systems; and there are *theories of consequence*, which deal with the effects of religious behaviour for either individuals or social groups.

The best-known theories of origin are psychological, and among them we shall examine those that propose projection, cognitive need, and reaction to frustration as explaining the sources of religion. Sociological theories often deal with the maintenance and function of religion, and among them we shall examine those that emphasize deprivation and integration.

Psychological theories of maintenance emphasize social learning and partial motivations such as guilt or sexual needs. The material on individual differences in religiosity and their correlates naturally relates to maintenance theories. As we shall see later, several theories of religious behaviour have aroused considerable interest and generated much writing and research. Such are Freud's (1913) theory of its origin as due to paternal projection, and Marx's (Marx and Engels, 1957) maintenance theory of deprivation and compensation. Since both Freud and Marx offered some additional hypotheses about religious behaviour, we shall examine those as well.

How much can the findings contribute to a definite validation of the theories? In some cases such a validation is difficult, as in the case of theories of the origins of religion as a belief system. Explaining the behaviour of humans at the hypothetical point in time at which religion first appeared is by necessity speculative. Any verification of such theories must be done by historical, archaeological and anthropological methods. Findings on the social and individual psychology of religion in modern society may only be suggestive in this respect, and may say more about the interaction between cultural traditions and present-day individuals. Such findings, however, are much more pertinent to theories that try to explain the maintenance of religious belief systems.

THEORIES OF ORIGIN

Cognitive need theories

Research on attitudes and beliefs by social psychologists has shown that beliefs often satisfy cognitive needs; that is, they provide a coherent, partly rational, account of some range of phenomena (e.g. Smith, Bruner and White, 1956; Katz and Stotland, 1959). Many studies have shown the importance of pressures towards cognitive consistency, including pressures to adopt beliefs which are compatible with one another as well as with experience (Abelson *et al.*, 1968). Here is the basis for some of the main psychological theories of religious beliefs: they are developed and accepted because they provide a coherent explanation of some aspects of experience. However, belief systems are not acceptable to most people unless they are shared with members of a social group; many social psychology studies have shown the influence of group norms on the acceptance of beliefs. The beliefs that are accepted may be true, they may be false (as in the spread of rumours and delusions), or they may be arbitrary ways of categorizing and interpreting reality.

Developmental psychologists, especially followers of Piaget, have observed how adolescents are not only capable of abstract thought, but also have a desire for a rational explanation of everything; theology offers such an explanation (Elkind, 1971). This line of thought suggests that the cognitive-need theory applies particularly to adolescents. Another version of it is that religion helps to provide a solution for this age-group to individual problems of identity and purpose in life.

The main sociological theories of religion make similar points, but emphasize that religion offers a socially shared set of meanings. Weber (1922) maintained that religion is concerned with the meaning of those irrational aspects of life — evil, suffering and death — that are insoluble by science. Durkheim (1915) maintained that religious symbols, representing society, serve to control egocentric impulses and provide a disciplined guide to life. Bellah (1967) adds that religion provides a sense of identity for individuals and groups, i.e. a definition of self as well as environment. These sociological theories can be put together to say that religion provides a socially shared set of cognitions which provide an interpretation of reality, a definition of self, and a guide to life (Berger and Luckmann, 1967).

The cognitive problems that can be met by religion are of several kinds. (1) Intellectual problems such as 'How did the world begin?', 'What is the purpose of life?' etc. to which no answer is provided by science or common sense. (2) Unacceptable aspects of life, such as suffering and death. (3) Particular forms of frustration and unfairness, such as the lot of underprivileged individuals and groups. (4) Natural phenomena not yet explained by the local scientists, e.g. eclipses of the sun and lightning, for primitive tribes. (5) Natural phenomena perhaps inexplicable by science, as we know it: consciousness, creativity, aesthetic and mystical experiences. (6) Problems of identity and goals in life, phrased as cognitive issues.

Some support may be provided for the cognitive theory by Thouless's interesting finding (1935) that people are more certain of the truth of religious propositions than of factual ones of the type 'Tigers are to be found in some parts of China'. Subjects recorded their agreement or disagreements with the items on a seven point scale: judgments of the religious items showed a stronger tendency towards the two extremes of judgment, disbelief being as dogmatic as belief. This finding was replicated much later by Brown (1962). Sanai (1952) in a similar study of adult students found a W-shaped distribution for religious items, a normal distribution for factual items (e.g. tigers in India), and a U-shaped distribution for political items. The U-shaped political distribution probably reflects the existence of two political parties, as Sanai points out. The distributions for religious items are also probably affected by the existence of two or three shared views about religion, so that it is difficult to say how far the results are due to a 'tendency to certainty in religious belief'.

Adolescents and students are commonly observed to move from one coherent set of beliefs, or disbeliefs, to another. During adolescence they are converted and deconverted (p. 65). Students develop modified beliefs which take some account of the other point of view (p. 34f). During this second stage a tendency to certainty seems to be replaced by a gradual accommodation of beliefs, for example towards believing in a vital force or spirit rather than in a personal God.

There is no clear evidence that religion helps with problems of individual identity and purpose. Nevertheless it is significant that there is a peak of interest in religion, especially in its intellectual aspects, at or shortly before the age at which identity problems reach their height. Erikson (1958) has applied his ideas about identity formation in adolescence to individuals in the past, including Martin Luther. Erikson shows how Luther resolved his conflicts and identity problems through the development of religious ideas.

The beliefs of scientists and other academics are of interest here. The least religious are psychologists, followed by social scientists (p. 88f); they already have a fairly coherent account of life, which is different from the religious account. Much more religious are those in the physical sciences and humanities, whose subject-matter offers no such competing system of explanation (see p. 92f).

Sociological and historical studies have shown clearly how particular sets of religious ideas act to provide socially shared meanings and goals. We have discussed the Protestant ethic (p. 82f), which legitimated business activities and provided a guide to conduct in this area. Small sects provide a definition of their members as a special spiritual élite, and lay down strict rules of conduct. However, it is not clear that the majority churches at the present time do very much to affect behaviour, except in certain limited spheres (Chapter 9). What they still do is to provide some kind of solution to problems of death and suffering. While the cognitive-need theory deals with the intellectual side of these problems, they can also be examined from the point of view of fear and frustration, as we shall do later in this chapter.

Schweiker (1969) tested the hypothesis that religion 'acts as a superordinate meaning system capable of endowing secular activity with greater and more integrative meaning'. He found that there was a stronger correlation between membership of secular groups and various measures of lack of anomie, for church members. Festinger et al. (1956) found that when physical support for religious beliefs failed, a sect went out to increase its membership (p. 40), showing the importance of social support for religious beliefs.

The cognitive-need theories appear to be broadly correct, though there is not a great deal of detailed evidence. They appear to apply more strongly to young people. In addition there is an overlap with theories based on fear or frustration, since there is a cognitive component to the religious response. These theories do not provide much explanation for other aspects of religious activity: ritual, prayer or church membership. It has been suggested that words are unsuitable for expressing religious ideas, and that non-verbal expression such as ritual and music has greater power here (Langer, 1942). It is suggested that subjective experiences and the direction of behaviour, which form the subject-matter of religion, are not readily codable into words. However, since non-verbal communication is vague, rituals nearly always have to be supplemented by words. It is in this verbal, cognitive sphere, that there is need for a socially shared interpretation of experience that provides a guide to life, which for some people is provided by religion. Recent research on the relative dominance of the two hemispheres of the brain may be relevant here. There is evidence that the left hemisphere is dominant for verbal and allied cognitive activities, while the right is dominant for spatial, aesthetic, and other intuitive, analogical, non-verbal operations (for right-handed males at least) (Ornstein, 1973). There is also evidence that religious people tend to be right hemisphere dominant (Bakan, 1971). This suggests that religious attitudes and ideas are primarily produced by the non-verbal right hemispheres, but are supplemented by the verbal activities of the left.

The father-projection theory

Among the various Freudian hypotheses regarding the sources and the functions of religion, the one suggesting the connection between one's earthly father and the idea of a divine father has been most testable and the most tested. In *Totem and Taboo* (1913), where it was first stated, Freud suggested rather emphatically that 'God is in every case modelled after the father, and that our personal

183

relation to God is dependent upon our relation to our physical father, fluctuating and changing with him, and that God at bottom is nothing but an exalted father' (p. 244). The same idea was expressed in Freud's other major writings on religion (1927, 1939). A more general version of this suggestion was presented by Jones (1951) as follows: 'The religious life represents a dramatization on a cosmic plane of the emotions, fears and longings which arose in the child's relation to his parents' (p. 195).

The most general version of the parental-projection hypothesis states that there is in every society a connection between early socialization experiences and beliefs regarding supernatural beings (Spiro and D'Andrade, 1958). This hypothesis stems from viewing religion as a cultural projective system (Kardiner and Linton, 1939). For religious individuals in contemporary Western societies, similarity between the images of the deity and parental or father images in general are to be expected on cultural grounds, since these similarities are openly expressed as part of many religious traditions. References to 'Our Father in heaven', 'Holy Mother' and 'the Holy Family' are frequent in prayers and sermons (Warner, 1961). It might be argued that these references in themselves lend support to the family-projection hypothesis, even without any further psychological findings. Since parental descriptions of deity are part of religious traditions, we can assume that in many individuals they are simply learnt. We may suppose that the similarity between parental images and deity images is the result of interaction between cultural tradition and the individual's own experiences, which are a result of universal family situations. An added factor is the observation that religious traditions themselves are learned from the parents.

What we are dealing with, then, is an interaction between a cultural belief system and individual personality system. Borrowing from Spiro and D'Andrade (1958), we can state two assumptions: that (1) belief systems are not created anew by each individual as he grows up, but are transmitted from generation to generation; and that (2) belief systems endure because the private fantasies and images of individuals correspond to these cultural traditions.

Several empirical studies have tested the hypothesis of similarity between parental images and deity images. The findings can be summarized as follows:

(1) Attitudes towards God are closer to attitudes towards the opposite sex parent (Godin and Hallez, 1964; Strunk, 1959). Attitudes towards God and father were most similar for nuns ($r = 0.65$), followed by unmarried girls, followed by older women (Godin and Hallez, 1964).

(2) God is described as, and attitudes towards God are similar

to, those towards the preferred parent (Nelson, 1971; Godin and Hallez, 1964). Two studies (Godin and Hallez, 1964; Nelson, 1971) report that with respondents reporting no preference for one parent, the correlations between the deity image and the images of both parents are very similar (see Table 11.1).

TABLE 11.1 *Correlations between perception of God and parents*

Father—God	Mother—God	
0·54*	0·26	prefer father
0·26	0·58*	prefer mother
0·64*	0·64*	no preference

In a sample of 30 Belgian males, 40 females. * = statistically significant at p <0·01. Source: Godin and Hallez (1964).

(3) God is seen as similar to both mother and father. If a descriptive, cognitive measure is used, rather than attitudes, God is seen as primarily paternal (Vergote *et al.*, 1969): father-God correlations for 180 American students, of both sexes, were 0·70, mother-God correlations were 0·37.

(4) There is some evidence that Catholics see God as more similar to mother, than Protestants (Rees, 1967).

These findings, which seem to indicate a general parental projection, rather than a specific paternal projection, bring us back to the original psychoanalytic formulations. How do these stand now in the light of the findings? While only one study gives clear support to the paternal-projection hypothesis in its original form, other studies indicate a considerable degree of maternal projection as well. The relative importance of mother and father as sources of the God image evidently varies between different groups. At the same time the tendency to indicate similarity between the deity and opposite-sex parent or preferred parent can be related to Jones's (1951) formulation quoted above, and to Freud's more general view of religion as a consequence of the Oedipal situation. In the study by Vergote *et al.* (1969), in which descriptive rather than objective terms were used, a stronger link between the images of God and of father was found. However, a number of subjects had images of God which contained conventional paternal elements, but which were unlike their conceptions of their own fathers. Comparing this study with the others, it seems possible that the paternal image of God is carried by the culture while the affective attitude towards God is derived from relations with parents.

Related studies which provide additional support for psychoanalytic formulations are those by Spiro and D'Andrade (1958), using cross-cultural data, and by Larsen and Knapp (1964) using semantic differential ratings of symbolic stimuli. Larsen and Knapp found that the deity image as rated by females was more benevolent, while males rated it as more punitive; they interpreted the difference as supporting the Oedipal theory of the image origin of the deity. We can conclude that the evidence presented so far does lend support to the hypothesis that parental projections play a part in the religious ideas of adolescents and adults in Western societies. This tells us something about the content of religious images, but does not deal directly with their sources and development in the individual. The most obvious derivations of the parental projection hypothesis would lead us to examine supernatural beliefs in children and their developmental sequence.

The findings on the concept of the deity in children are as follows. Harms (1944) reported on the observed tendency of young children to view God as their own father, without any statistical analysis. Deconchy (1967), in a study of 4,660 French Catholic children aged 8 to 16, obtained descriptions of God. Among boys, the percentage describing God as like their fathers varied with age, showing a general upward trend. The lowest percentage (7 per cent) was at age 9, and the highest (25 per cent) at age 13. Among girls, the same upward trend was observed, reaching a higher level than for the boys during adolescence. The lowest point for girls (9 per cent) was at age 9, and the highest point (39 per cent) at age 15. In a further analysis of the data from this project, Deconchy (1968) reported that the image of God in boys was more often connected with the maternal image of the Virgin Mary and less often with the image of Christ, while for girls the opposite connection was found. These findings, limited as they are, seem to offer additional corroboration of the earlier ones for adults, and are quite consistent with the parental-projection hypothesis.

The empirical findings can be summarized by saying that they give definite support to psychoanalytic notions about the impact of family relationships on religious ideas. Vergote *et al.* concluded: 'we may acknowledge an extraordinary analogy between the Oedipus structure and the structuring of the religious attitude' (1969, p. 87). Freud's hypothesis regarding the special impact of the father image received only limited support, but wider notions such as those of Jones (1951) and Spiro and D'Andrade (1958) were closely supported.

The findings of a relationship between the image of God and the image of the opposite-sex or preferred parent lend support to the notion that the deity is a projected love-object, and that positive qualities are projected more than negative ones. Freud emphasized the ambivalence toward both father and God, while the subjects in most studies project a totally positive picture.

186

Projection of maternal attributes seems to be another bit of evidence which goes against the original formulations. Freud himself admitted that 'I am at a loss to indicate the place of the great maternal deities who perhaps everywhere preceded the paternal deities' (1913, p. 247). The connection between mother image and deity image found in several studies may be interpreted as supporting a Jungian interpretation of religion. The maternal projection evident in the data, together with the undifferentiated parental projection, can be attributed to cultural and historical factors. One may even hypothesize about the resurfacing of the Great Mother, long suppressed in Judaic and Protestant traditions.

Before reaching a conclusion about the implications of the findings for the original Freudian hypothesis, we should examine the nature of the theory and the evidence required to support it. What Freud presented in his major writings on religion was an attempt to reconstruct the events that led to the formation of monotheistic religion. The validity of Freud's theory of the origin of religion will not be established by psychological studies of contemporary individuals. Findings of such studies are only suggestive in this respect, and say more about the interaction between cultural traditions and individuals. Such findings may be more relevant to theories which try to explain contemporary religious beliefs in individuals. They support and corroborate Freud's clinical insights, which were partly based on observations of contemporary individuals. The findings suggest that psychological mechanisms similar to those involved in a historical creation of religion can be shown to exist. The findings support the Kardiner and Linton theory (1939) of religion as a 'projective system'.

In conclusion, it is important to emphasize that the research done so far has been extremely limited, sometimes showing an unsophisticated interpretation of Freudian concepts.

The super-ego projection theory

This theory has been proposed by Flugel (1945), among others, and postulates that the psychological construct of the super-ego is 'projected' on to God. The basic theory of the super-ego can be summarized briefly as follows: the child is punished by its parents, either physically or by the withdrawal of love, for indulging in certain behaviour, and it experiences anxiety when it does so because of the anticipated punishment. The child identifies itself with the parents and wishes to be like them and conform to their demands. Thus the parental requirements become 'internalized', and the child now feels guilty even if the parents are absent. The psychological mechanism which represents the parental demands is called the super-ego. The super-ego is harsh and irrational, because aggression towards the parents is redirected on to the self; this is particularly likely to happen when the parents are kind, but frustrating in subtle ways. When physical punishment is used, children feel more able to express their frustration in outward aggression.

A later formulation of the super-ego projection hypothesis states that 'There is a being, God, and an institution, religion, that serve the adult as magnified parents who enter the conscience and punish and reward, helping to maintain the adult's typical balance between desire, morality, and action' (Ostow and Sharfstein, 1954, p. 76).

The super-ego is likely to come into conflict with instinctive desires, particularly sexual and aggressive desires. Flugel's theory (1945) is that this conflict is relieved by projection of the super-ego which now appears as God. Projection, or externalization, is a defence mechanism: an internal process or property is reacted to as if it were outside the individual. For example, the super-ego can be projected on to a doctor, teacher, leader or priest; the repressive demands of the super-ego are then thought to be prohibitions imposed by the person in question, who is felt to be coercing and looking down on the subject. Alternatively, the instinctive desires can be projected on to groups of people such as Jews or Negroes, who are then thought to be highly sexed and aggressive. The gains for the individual are that the conflict is reduced through being no longer an inner one, while he feels that he can deal with the situation by overt action, instead of by changing himself (cf. Horney, 1946). In Flugel's formulation a more radical type of projection is postulated, in which the super-ego is projected on to the Universe as a God, and the instinctive desires similarly as the Devil (Flugel, 1945; Fenichel, 1945).

If the instincts are opposed by the super-ego in religious people, this should result in a diminution of the forbidden instinctive activity. Sexual activity is lower for devout religious people, whether Catholics, Protestants or Jews (p. 152f), and these religions are preoccupied with sexual prohibitions.

Confirmation of another kind is provided by Unwin's study (1934) of 80 primitive societies: he rated each society for the degree of restriction on sexual behaviour and for the development of religion; the two variables were found to be highly correlated with each other. Aggressive behaviour too would be expected to be lower in religious people: research shows that regular churchgoers are less delinquent, though this is not true of church members or those who merely hold orthodox beliefs (p. 148f).

It would also be expected that religion will be associated with guilt feelings. As we have seen, there is a correlation between guilt and church attendance for Protestant females, and the same group score high in intro-punitiveness (p. 99). Other studies found that people 'converted' at evangelical campaigns had often been suffering from guilt feelings beforehand (p. 45). Protestant doctrines and evangelical addresses emphasize sin, guilt and salvation. These data suggest that the theory under discussion may apply particularly to Protestants. The reason that these results apply particularly to women may simply be that females have stronger guilt feelings.

If religious behaviour is derived from the super-ego in some way, religion should have an irrational super-ego quality about it. There are several ways in which this proves to be true. Funk (1956) discovered that a majority of students thought that they were not as strict in their religion as they ought to be, and wished that they were perfectly sure that religion was true. Secondly, religion always has an ethical flavour, in which powerful moral demands are made, and sin is condemned. Thirdly, God is often perceived as a forbidding, punishing figure. Religious people are more authoritarian than non-religious people, and authoritarians perceive God very much in this awesome way.

On the basis of the super-ego projection theory, we should also predict that women would show greater religiosity, since, according to psychoanalytic theory, internalization processes which form the super-ego are incomplete in women. It is possible to interpret the greater religiosity of women as a result of stronger internalization, followed by projection.

From the above findings we have established some evidence for the super-ego projection theory, and especially for the view that much religious ideology reflects a struggle between the instincts and the super-ego.

THEORIES OF MAINTENANCE

Social learning

This theory states that religious behaviour, beliefs and experiences are simply part of the culture, and are regularly transmitted from generation to generation, in the same way as any other customs. This view has of course been widely held, and there is much obvious evidence for it, for example the fact that children reared in different parts of the world tend to acquire the local religious beliefs. To some extent we assume this theory when we talk of the different religions of different countries, for it is assumed that these are relatively unchanging and will persist in time. This is clearly a 'same-level'

189

explanation, postulating that religion is learnt by the same processes of socialization as any other attitudes and beliefs.

The whole of Chapter 3 on environmental factors provides direct evidence for the social learning theory, and shows in detail how the learning takes place. It is found, for example, that children acquire much the same beliefs as their parents, particularly if they like them and continue to live at home. The same is true, to much the same extent, of attitudes on political and other matters. Religious attitudes and beliefs are modified by membership of educational and other social groups, in the same way that other attitudes are affected. There is some evidence that the content of mystical experiences depends on the beliefs which are held beforehand, and that the stigmata have occurred as a result of suggestion in hysterical personalities. No one experienced this before St Francis, though several hundred have done so since that time (Thurston, 1951).

While there is a good deal of evidence in support of the social learning theory, its limitations are obvious. In the first place, it cannot account for any of the very considerable individual differences in religious activity within the culture, variations due to age, personality and social class in particular. This is because the theory shows how religion is passed on but does not show the motivational forces maintaining it: behaviour is not learned unless a need is satisfied, though several different ways of satisfying the same need may be learned. The theory obviously provides one important postulate of a more complete account. Sex differences can be partly explained: females become better socialized during childhood than males. Personality differences in religion are not very great, as we have seen.

The other important limitation of the theory is that it predicts, if anything, that all religious movements will remain unchanged by time; it cannot account for the initiation of new movements or for the decline of old ones. The state of the churches in a country at a particular point in time is the result of a long and complex history of the rise and fall of movements, influenced by different religious leaders, partly reacting to historical circumstances, partly affecting history themselves. The small sects are of great interest today, because here we can see new religious movements being born—the Pentecostal revival began in 1901—and we can see them growing and changing into churches.

Despite the cross-cultural and historical evidence for the diversity of religious beliefs, there are also some universal features: gods are envisaged as invisible spiritual forces with some of the properties of persons, who are good and powerful; they are usually thought of as male. The main alternative view in the modern world is that there are no such beings, though many who hold this view subscribe to the idea that there is some vital purpose in the universe (p. 13). These universal features could be explained by social learning, in terms of cultural diffusion. Alternatively these universal factors may be due to innate features of the human mind (approximately the Jungian view), or widely-shared aspects of human experience (the Freudian view). If the universal features reflect innate aspects of human nature, there may have been natural selection, due to some survival value found in religion (Hardy, 1966).

Deprivation and compensation

Theories linking religious activity to deprivation have been quite common in the literature, ever since Marx formulated the best known among them: 'Religious suffering is at the same time an expression of real suffering and a protest against real suffering. Religion is the sigh of the oppressed creature, the heart of a heartless world, and the soul of soulless conditions. It is the opium of the people' (1964, pp. 43–4). Freud (1927) developed a similar view of religious beliefs as reactions to both individual and social deprivations, and as a way of keeping the masses under control.

The sociological deprivation-compensation theory of religious involvement was most clearly expressed by Davis (1948), as follows: 'The greater his [man's] disappointment in this life, the greater his faith in the next. Thus the existence of goals beyond this world serves to compensate people for frustrations they inevitably experience in striving to reach socially acquired and socially valuable ends' (p. 532).

TABLE 11.2 *Proposed relationships between deprivation and the development of religious groups*

Type of deprivation	Form of religious group	Success expectations
Economic	Sect	Extinction or transformation
Social	Church	Retain original form
Organismic	Healing movement	Becomes cult-like or is destroyed by medical discoveries
Ethical	Reform movements	Early extinction due to success, opposition or becoming irrelevant
Psychic	Cult	Total success resulting in extinction through transformation, or failure due to extreme opposition

Source: Glock (1964).

In this way Glock (1964) distinguishes between five kinds of deprivations which may give rise to religious reactions: economic, social, organismic, ethical and psychic. Their relationships to religious groups are shown in Table 11.2. Religious reactions to deprivations are likely to appear, according to Glock, when the causes of deprivation are either inaccurately perceived or are beyond the control of those subject to it. Therefore, states Glock, religious activities 'are likely to compensate for feelings of deprivation rather than to eliminate its causes' (p. 29).

The validity of the deprivation-compensation hypothesis can be tested as follows. We can try to locate those who are more deprived, those 'oppressed creatures', and see if they are more religious, compared with less deprived people. Deprivation can be defined, and has been defined, and in many different ways, as the table by Glock (1964) indicates. A combination of several deprivation factors has been proposed by Campbell and Fukuyama (1970). They defined social deprivation on the basis of age, sex, education, socio-economic status, and place of residence (rural or urban). Using this combined index, they found that participation in organized church activities was positively correlated with privilege, and not deprivation. When religiosity was measured by traditional beliefs and devotionalism, the opposite pattern emerged. Traditional beliefs and devotional orientation were stronger among older people, females, less educated people, and the poor and the rural. The conclusion was that social deprivation was related to a particular style of religious activity, which emphasizes devotion and traditional beliefs.

In a study of American Roman Catholics, Christopher *et al.* (1971) used a similar combined index of social deprivation, including indices of sex, age and education, which was found to be positively correlated with several measures of religiosity. Evidence on the effects of the deprivation factors proposed by Campbell and Fukuyama (1970) can be found in previous chapters. The findings presented earlier demonstrate that there is a relationship between measures of deprivation and traditional beliefs in most populations studied. Support for the deprivation-compensation view of religious activity has been offered in both the psychological context (religiosity and religious activity as reactions to individual frustration) and the sociological context (religious groups as organized attempts to deal with felt deprivation).

The view that religious organizations of the sect kind represent attempts to deal with various kinds of deprivation has been suggested by Glock (1964) and Wilson (1961). Marx described the projective element in religion not as a direct reflection of reality in any way, but as an 'inverse world', in which fantasy compensates for real suffering (Marx and Engels, 1957). From this claim we would predict that such fantasy gratification will be part of religious beliefs among deprived social groups.

Clark (1965) summarized the common characteristics of 200 American sects and concludes that their beliefs are compensatory. (1) Their belief in the speedy ending of this world and the coming of the next where the rich shall be cast down and the humble and meek raised up. (2) Their puritan morality in which a virtue is made of frugality, humility and industry, while luxuries and worldly amusements are vices. (3) The stress on simplicity of worship and opposition to expensive equipment: the Churches of Christ opposed missionary activity because of the cost involved. (4) The Church of the Nazarene openly states that its mission is to the poor, others to Negroes. As Clark says, it is curious that none of these bodies is interested in social reform. It seems that there are two opposed types of response to economic and social status deprivation: an other-worldly fantasy response, and a left-wing political action response. We may conclude that there is good evidence for the truth of this theory in the case of the small sect.

It is possible that many people get adjusted to their economic and social status, and only experience frustration or satisfaction when it changes. Lenski (1953) found that people who had moved downwards in social status compared with their parents were more interested in religion than those who had kept the same position, and that the latter were more interested than those who had moved upwards. Since changes of prosperity in the business cycle produce no general change in the level of religious activity, it is likely that Lenski's results reflect changes of status rather than changes of prosperity. Unfortunately no differential analysis of beliefs is available here. According to the present hypothesis underprivileged minority groups should be more religious than other people. It is the case that American Negroes, for example, are considerably more religious than the main population (p. 169f), and it should be noted that their religion tends to be of the small sect and ecstatic type. It is common for political groups to develop in response to frustration; our problem is whether this is also true of religious movements, which try to bring about their ends by means of prayer, belief and ceremony.

Nottingham (1954) suggests that the beliefs associated with the Hindu caste system developed to ease its stresses. It is believed that a person's position in the system is merited by his performance in previous incarnations; social discontent is averted by these beliefs. This theory, that beliefs are generated to relieve the frustrations of the social and political order, has some support. Nottingham gives other examples, and Kardiner et al. (1945) trace the development of

193

Jewish-Christian beliefs in these terms. Similar considerations apply to Pfister's interesting demonstrations (1948) that the Jewish-Christian community has always become more ritualistic in times of stress.

The greater level of church membership and church attendance among those with higher socio-economic status in both the USA and Great Britain has been used as an argument against the validity of deprivation theories of religiosity. This argument can be countered on two grounds: first, the nature of middle-class religious activity; and second, the possibility that it may still be a response to some kind of deprivation. As was shown in Chapter 10, middle-class religiosity in the USA is a rather formal and secularized affair. Goode (1966), after studying class differences in religiosity, suggested that church attendance should not be used as a measure of religious behaviour, since it has become a totally secular activity, reflecting only the greater tendency of the middle class to be active in voluntary associations. If middle-class church attendance is indeed a voluntary social activity, as many observers suggest, then it fits quite well with Glock's (1964) view of the church as responding to social deprivation (see Table 11.2). Carlos (1970), in studying religious activities in the suburbs of large cities, suggested the satisfaction of social needs as explaining the higher rates of church attendance in the suburbs.

The effects of social deprivation in the case of individuals are quite clear. Those without established families tend to be more active religiously. Chapter 3 provides evidence to confirm this trend from studies which show that widows, single people and married women without children are more active than others in church affairs. Social deprivation explanations of religious activity are supported by findings on affiliative behaviour (Schachter, 1959). These findings show that stress leads to affiliative behaviour, which reduces anxiety. Since most religious activities are group activities, we can expect people in stress situations to turn to them.

An illustration of the role of organismic deprivation in religious activities is supplied by the case of Christian Science. This is the major middle-class sect in the USA, and was described by Wilson (1970) as manipulationist, offering its members relief for a specified problem. Since the problem which Christian Science deals with is illness, we can expect sect members to be suffering from health problems and other deprivations. England (1954), in a study of Christian Science testimonial letters, found that most of the letters came from elderly females, who suffered from a variety of physical and mental problems, some of which would be regarded as psychosomatic or hysterical. Table 11.3 shows two aspects of Christian Science membership: being female and concerned with health.

194

TABLE 11.3 *Factors sustaining interest in Christian Science, by sex and problem*

Problem	Sex	
	Male	Female
Health	75 (79·8%)	392 (96·5%)
Other	19 (20·2%)	14 (3·5%)
Total	94	406

$\chi^2 = 33·85$ significant at the 0·05 level. Source: England (1954).

The greater religious activity of women may be due to frustration. Women as a group are less educated, and wield much less economic and political power, thus being less able to satisfy personal needs and ambitions. Bourque and Back (1968) suggest that religious experiences are 'structured group attempts to overcome feelings of frustration and alienation' (p. 38). In a survey of reported religious experiences in the USA (Back and Bourque, 1970) it was found that members of less privileged groups, including women and blacks, reported having more religious experiences than all other groups.

Relief of guilt

Several psychoanalytic writers mention the function of religion in relieving guilt feelings (e.g. Pfister, 1948). Guilt feelings have often been interpreted as the direction of aggression towards the self, and there is evidence that it is connected with internal conflicts between the self and the ego-ideal or the conscience (Flugel, 1945; Rosenzweig, 1945). Guilt feelings are strongest in those whose parents used strict discipline and are stronger in females than in males (Wright, 1971). Ostow and Sharfstein (1954) suggest that guilt is used by churches as a means of controlling people, in the interests of both religion and social control.

One prediction from this theory is that people with guilt feelings should be attracted towards Christianity with its doctrine of forgiveness. Starbuck (1899) obtained some evidence that young people converted at a revival often had strong guilt feelings before this happened. Clark (1929) found that 55 per cent of his sudden converts suffered from a sense of sin, compared with 8·5 per cent for the total sample of converts. Fifty-seven per cent of the sudden converts experienced subsequent joy, compared with 14 per cent for the total.

195

If religion succeeded in relieving guilt feelings, there would be no difference between religious people and others. In fact, as we have seen, religious people do have stronger guilt feelings, as a number of studies of young people have found (p. 99). They also have stronger self-ideal self conflicts (p. 126f).

A second prediction which can be made is that those who are drawn to Protestantism will have stronger guilt feelings than those drawn to Catholicism. There are differences in guilt feelings between the two groups, which may be due to the influences of the respective churches. As we have seen, young Protestants do have somewhat stronger guilt feelings; there is some evidence that they are more intro-punitive, at least for females (p. 99). While the suicide rate used to be higher for Protestants, this is no longer so (p. 142f). There is another interpretation of these findings; Protestant rituals tend to dwell on sin and guilt, so might increase guilt feelings; Catholic practices include confession, so might reduce it. There are no data to test these possibilities as yet.

We have seen that if this theory is correct, it applies more to Protestants than to Catholics. We should expect it to apply particularly to more extreme Protestant groups, like sects, since they place more emphasis on sin and salvation. There are no data to test this directly, but one of the implications of this hypothesis will be examined in connection with sex differences.

There is fairly extensive evidence that women have stronger guilt feelings, and are more intro-punitive than men (Wright, 1971; Bernard, 1949). This may provide an explanation of the greater religious activity of women. Taken together with the previous point, it leads to the prediction that there should be an increasing proportion of female members along the Catholic-Protestant dimension. We have seen that this is the case (p. 75f). We have also seen that women are particularly active in private rather than public worship (p. 73). This suggests that relief of guilt, if that is what is going on, takes place in private rather than in public.

It also seems likely that this mechanism operates for the young rather than the old. This would be expected, since sex is one of the main sources of guilt feelings. Another source is conflict between career and altruism values, which affects those of student age. At evangelical meetings, where conversions are largely brought about by arousal of guilt feelings, it is almost entirely young people who are converted (p. 61).

There does appear to be a certain body of evidence to suggest that the relief of guilt theory applies to young, female, members of Protestant groups, in particular those which emphasize sin and salvation.

Fear of death

Anthropologists such as Malinowski (1925) have stressed the functions of religion in helping those facing death to adjust to the situation, as well as in helping those who are bereaved. This can be regarded as an anticipated frustration, in so far as all the satisfactions of life are about to be ended. There is often anxiety about what is to come next. Or it may be experienced as a cognitive problem: the sudden ending of life is felt not to make sense. The predictions and findings may be summarized as follows:

(1) It would be expected that people would become progressively more religious as they get older. As has been shown (p. 68f), there is an increasing amount of religious concern from the age of sixty onwards; there is also increasing belief in an after-life: 100 per cent of people over ninety were certain of an after-life in one survey; there is an increase in private prayer. Churchgoing declines but is partly replaced by radio and television services. The number of people who said they went to church 'for reassurance of immortality' increased progressively with age.

(2) It would be predicted that people exposed to great danger would become more religious. Surveys of soldiers in World War II showed that about three-quarters of those who had been under fire said that they were greatly helped by prayer; it was also found that ex-servicemen were more religious than before, especially if they had been in action. These men were more religious in the sense of believing more in God and being more concerned with religious questions, but their church attendance was not affected (p. 52f).

(3) We have seen that old people who are religious are also better adjusted and happier. They are less apprehensive about death, and even look forward to it (p. 55).

(4) It would be expected that the after-life to which people look forward would be a pleasant one. At the present time most of those who do believe in an after-life think that it will either be like this one, or will be a pleasanter version of life (p. 13).

On the other hand 20 per cent in Britain and 65 per cent in the USA say that they believe in hell, which would not be expected at all on the present theory, unless hell is reserved for other people. Belief in hell requires some further explanation. One is that there is a widespread desire for fair play, and an equitable division of rewards, as studies of children's games and industrial workers show. Life is manifestly unfair, so that punishments as well as rewards are needed in the after-life. A second explanation of hell would be that some people have such strong guilt feelings that they feel in need of further punishment. Fewer Catholics believe in hell than Protestants (15 per cent v. 19 per cent; Gorer,

1955), but the difference is small, and can be explained by differences in education. If this mechanism operates at all it probably applies to a very small number of people.

Apart from the complications introduced by belief in hell, this group of studies provides very strong support for the theory that fear of death is a basis for religious beliefs.

Sexual motivation

The sex-repression theory of the origin of religion proposes that religious activities are sublimations of sexual impulses. Leuba (1925), who supported this view, pointed to the prominence of sexual symbolism in religion, which seems to be almost universal, and the erotic nature of religious frenzy. Mol (1970) and Taylor (1959) suggested that sex and religion were two alternative, mutually exclusive ways of self-expression and satisfaction. On the basis of a study correlating sexual attitudes and religiosity Mol (1970) suggested that religion and sex are alternative forms of commitment, and that sexual indulgence is a form of self-integration which is competitive with religious activities. Wallin (1957) found evidence that religious activity provided a substitute for sexual satisfaction in marriage, and more so for women than for men (p. 154f).

There is plentiful evidence, mainly from case studies and observation, regarding the role of sexual impulses in various forms of religious ritual and religious experience. The analysis in most of these cases is based on clinical inferences (Schroeder, 1932; Wedemeyer, 1949), but it is also supported by the religious traditions themselves. Scenes of sexual excitement during religious rituals are rarer today, but by no means non-existent. La Barre (1962) reports on sexual responses displayed by women members of a snake-handling cult during services. More sublimated forms of sexual expression can be observed in more reserved groups of believers. Religious literature throughout history has been filled with descriptions of love, devotion and yearning, which must be regarded as related to human experiences of intimacy and attachment. Not only the famous mystics but also common believers in every age have expressed erotic urges through their religious devotion.

Some of the evidence presented in Chapter 5 (on sex differences) and Chapter 9 (on sex and marriage) above is relevant to the question of sexual motivation in religious behaviour. Chapter 5 showed that women score higher than men on all measures of religiosity. Women are also less free to express their sexual impulses. Throughout history there is evidence that women have invested much of their energy in religious devotion, and this has sometimes reached hysterical frenzy. It seems possible that this devotion was motivated in part by diverted sexual energy, which otherwise could not be expressed. Chapter 9 showed that a higher degree of religiosity is correlated with a lower level of sexual activity. This supports the hypothesis that religious activities and sexual activities may be alternative ways of satisfying similar needs.

If sexual deprivation is a factor in religious activity, unmarried people should be more religious than married, since it may be assumed that in general their opportunities for sexual outlet are less. Social surveys show that single people are slightly more religious than married (p. 51f); again this is consistent with the hypothesis, but could be explained in other ways. It should also be remembered that old age is the most religious time of life, when the sexual instinct is greatly weakened. It is likely that sudden conversions during adolescence may be due to sexual guilt feelings which come to a height during this time.

The clearest instance of a sexual content to religious activities is provided by some of the classical saints and mystics. As has been demonstrated by Leuba (1925) and Thouless (1923), many of the writings are full of scarcely disguised sexual symbolism. When we consider that these people had no overt sexual satisfaction at all, it seems very likely that frustration or internal inhibition of this instinct is partly responsible for their religious activities. Thouless (1924) regards the great emphasis placed on chastity as evidence of the sexual basis of religion.

To conclude this section on the sexual motivation hypothesis, there is evidence in the case of the mystics that frustration or internal inhibition is operative; the greater religious activity of unmarried people and those with little sexual activity also supports one or other of these theories. The most important evidence, which can be observed most easily, is the use of terms of endearment, tenderness and devotion in religious literature, and the emotional attachments of people everywhere to their religious symbols and practices. Speaking of just sexual motivation in this case may lead to misinterpretations, since we are dealing here with erotic expressions and attachments in more sublimated forms.

Obsessional behaviour

Freud (1907) pointed to a number of descriptive similarities between obsessional neuroses and religious ritual, and Reik (1951) has elaborated upon this. But Philp (1956) opposed the theory by pointing to differences between the two phenomena. However, there seems to be some measure of agreement between these writers about the similarities and differences between rituals and obsessions, so we shall summarize these briefly in order to clarify the theory.

199

(1) The psychoanalytic theory of obsessional neurosis is that obsessions are distorted symbolic versions either of instinctive desires forbidden by the super-ego, or of the super-ego's prohibitions themselves. The obsessions and compulsions simultaneously allow some substitute gratification both of the desire and of its prohibition: Fenichel suggests pleasureless compulsive masturbation as an example of such a compromise (1945). Reik (1951) similarly traces the development of ideas about the Trinity as a compromise between ideas of filial rebellion and veneration for the father. (2) The neurotic's rituals have a compulsive character, in that he must carry them out conscientiously and experiences guilt if he fails to do so: this is to some extent true of religious rituals too. (3) In religion there are taboos: of Sunday work, food before communion, and so forth; obsessional neurotics also have things that they must avoid touching or thinking about. Flugel (1945) suggests that the taboo of the king in primitive religion, together with the rituals he must perform, serve the functions of honouring and protecting him, but at the same time of limiting his power making his life a burden, another compromise mechanism. Reik (1951) points out that the taboos surrounding religious dogma develop as a defence against scepticism; at the same time the dogma is developed in absurd detail, reflecting an underlying contempt for it. (4) The real conflict in neurotics becomes displaced on to trivial details and verbal matters; this is also the case with religion, where the dogmas and rituals become elaborated in enormous detail, minute parts of which may become the basis for schisms and persecutions.

So much for the similarities which have been claimed; now we turn to the differences. (1) The most important difference is that neurotic obsessions are individual, while religious rituals are collective actions of a social group, carried out in public. (2) Freud maintained (1907) that whereas obsessional neurosis is due to inhibition of the sexual instinct, religious ritual is due to the suppression of egoistic and anti-social needs. Fenichel (1945) maintains that obsessionals often have conflicts about submission and rebellion, cruelty and gentleness, as a result of regression to the anal-sadistic stage of development.

Freud's observations on the similarities between religious acts and obsessional behaviour are a good example of a mini-theory of religious behaviour. It does have value in explaining the psychological motives of some religious acts, and it does shed light on the cultural nature of religion as opposed to neurosis. Much of what Freud says has parallels in religious literature. The concept and the emotion of obsessions are certainly not alien to those who hold their faith with fervour. The theoretical formulations, however, are very difficult to verify by the use of the social psychological data presented in the previous chapters. They may be more useful to historians of culture and religion, since they deal mostly with origins of religious practices. The studies by Reik (1951) are psycho-historical in nature, and should be regarded as such. It is possible that at some stage studies of this kind will reach the quantification stage, thus allowing us to make more definite statements.

THEORIES OF CONSEQUENCE

Individual integration

The notion that the function of religion for the individual is better personal integration and personal adjustment is a reflection of older religious traditions, but has also been stated in modern psychological terms (e.g. Allport, 1950). Hartmann (1958) saw the main function of religion in the individual as the integrative function, through which the inner mental processes are synthesized with social adaptation. Another view of the integrative function was offered by Draper (1969), who emphasized the sublimation of aggressive and libidinal drives through religion. While many writers have emphasized the positive role of religion in the integration of the individual, others, viewing religion itself as something to be overcome, suggested that religious beliefs will be accompanied by a lesser degree of individual integration. If religious belief is seen as a refusal to face reality, as Freud (1927) saw it, then we should predict that religious people will be more dependent and less adequate or assertive. They should also suffer more from guilt and anxiety. Marx (in Marx and Engels, 1957) similarly saw religious devotion as taking away from man's esteem for himself, and leading to less independence and integration.

We shall first review the evidence related to individual integration, which was presented in previous chapters. On the positive side (i.e. religion as contributing to personality integration) there are several consistent findings. Church members and church attenders in the USA are better adjusted on measures of psychiatric impairment, and religious activity is positively related to adjustment in old age. Regular church attenders also enjoy better physical health and are less likely to commit suicide (Chapter 8). Religious individuals may be able to face better some life crises and especially death (Chapters 3 and 8). They are less likely than the non-religious to abuse alcohol (Chapter 8), and are better adjusted in marriage (Chapter 9). In addition, sect members are probably helped by being given an identity as members of a spiritual élite, by an acceptable

201

cognitive interpretation of their underprivileged social position, and by the cathartic group experiences (Chapter 10). Church members in the USA are possibly also supported in terms of individual identity and community feeling (Chapter 2).

On the negative side (i.e. religion as related to deficient personality integration) there are the following findings. Religiosity has been found to be tied to narrowness of perspective, which is reflected in measures of authoritarianism and dogmatism (Chapter 6). Religious people have been found to be more suggestible and dependent (Chapter 6). A high degree of religious orthodoxy is likely to interfere with scientific achievement (Chapter 6), and may lead to some sex problems (Chapters 8 and 9). Religious students have been found to report a greater degree of personal inadequacy and anxiety, in studies using psychological inventories (Chapter 8).

Both positive and negative effects of religion are partly due to its positive effects for social integration. A properly functioning society needs a certain kind of personality; people must succeed in developing a personality structure, which is directed towards long-term goals, and takes sufficient concern for the needs of others. As children grow up, they are expected to persist in the pursuit and attainment of long-term goals, instead of being dominated by immediate desires. This is often supported by religion; for example, Protestant ideas of a 'calling', and of being judged on one's life-work, emphasize the importance of such long-term plans.

The ego-centric and antisocial impulses of children are disciplined by parents and other representatives of society; the restraining forces are to differing degrees internalized by children; religious ideas are partly based on the parents (according to Freud) or on society at large (according to Durkheim), and religion sides with these restraints.

The integration of personality can be seen as the control of lower and more basic needs by higher-level and longer-term plans. These long-term plans may be provided by developing an identity which is committed to a certain way of life, and certain goals and values. Society provides a number of ready-made identities, and religion makes a contribution here, by offering models with a coherent identity and way of life, varying somewhat between different churches. The impact is greatest perhaps for the sects, since they make the greatest demands, and also have the most to offer by way of a positive religious self-image; however, members of all churches can if they wish make this a central part of their identity.

Integration and control of the personality are partly done by the development of cognitive structures: ideas and beliefs about the self and its place in the world, for example. In this sphere religion can provide meaning, purpose and identity (p. 180f). It can also contribute to conflict and confusion, as in the conflict between science and religion.

Social integration

Sociologists of religion, ever since Durkheim (1915), have explained the function of religion in terms of its ability to provide legitimation for social arrangements or 'social constructions of reality' (Berger and Luckmann, 1967). By providing a unified and unifying value system, religion is supposed to contribute to the integration of the whole society and the functioning of other social institutions. Religion has been described as 'the most general mechanism for integrating meaning and motivation in action systems' (Bellah, 1970, p. 12). As such, it will contribute to social stability and to better adaptation of the whole social system.

Parsons (1960) described the 'core' function of religion in the social system as 'the regulation of the balance of the motivational commitment of the individual to the values of his society—and through these values to his role in it' (p. 302). Yinger (1957) offered a more limited theory of integration, emphasizing the role of religion in creating political stability. Similarly, Ostow and Sharfstein (1954) offered a psychological version of the integration-through-control theory. They suggest that since most members of a stable society must be obedient and accepting, religion is used to make them this way.

Herberg (1955) and Bellah (1967) described secularized American religion, which integrates society through its emphasis on shared beliefs. In this respect we can talk about religious uniformity in the USA. There is evidence that most of the population supports this 'civil religion', and it is clear that non-support implies rejection of other central American values. Glock and Stark (1966) defined the limits of American 'pluralism', which seems to correspond to 'civil religion'. Those who are beyond the pale of American pluralism, i.e. atheists and agnostics, are subject to hostility and criticism (Glock and Stark, 1965, 1966). While these findings support the notion of religion as an integrative force in American society, what is unclear is the extent to which allegiance to the civil religion has any social significance or practical consequences (Wilson, 1966).

A civil religion similar to the one described in the USA can probably be outlined in Great Britain, or in most other modern societies. The question still remains: how religious is such an integrative ideology, and what are its practical consequences? Eister (1957) showed that general theories about the integrative and supportive functions of religion for the whole society do not lend themselves to easy confirmation in a complex secularized society, and that most of the evidence goes against them.

The extent of secularization in the USA and Great Britain, as described in Chapter 2, tends to cast doubt on the idea that modern societies are indeed integrated through a central religious value system. Fenn (1972) made a convincing case for the argument that modern society is not held together by a common set of values; and that if there is such a set of values, it is not a religious one. While social control in secularized societies seems to be quite effective, other mechanisms, such as mass media, have taken the place of religion as controller and integrator (Marcuse, 1964). While the discussion in Chapter 2 would indicate that the role of religion in the total integration of society is declining, evidence about the consequences of religion as an integrative social force is to be found elsewhere in this book, especially Chapters 7 and 10. If we regard individual and social conformity and conservatism as contributing to social integration and stability, as indeed we may, the evidence is both plentiful and convincing to show that religiosity is related to both. Chapter 7 shows that religious people tend to be more conservative politically, and to support existing social arrangements rather than new ones. The evidence linking religiosity and conservative social attitudes extends across the areas of ethno-centrism, social issues and political attitudes.

Chapters 7 and 10 also show that among members of the lower class and of minority groups, those who are more religious tend to accept their social and economic circumstances more easily. The kind of religious activities that disadvantaged people engage in seems to be more committed and more psychologically involving. There is a great deal of emotionality, and Wilson (1966) suggested that 'the opportunity for emotional expression in the religious context might be seen as a deflection of concern from social inequalities' (p. 105). Other-worldly religious orientation is more likely to be found among the lower classes.

Pope (1942) showed how different types of religious organizations prevent radical social change and contribute to the maintenance of the *status quo*. It was shown that churches openly and directly co-operated with the industrial owners, while sects directed the concerns of the industrial workers from this world to the next. Awareness of the powerful controlling functions of religion is indicated by the financial and public support given to churches by the American 'robber barons' of the nineteenth and twentieth centuries (Josephson, 1962).

While most of the findings indicate that religious involvement would tend to steer a person away from actions to improve his conditions in this world, religious involvement may lead to improvement via conformity and better adjustment. Schwartz (1970), for example, showed that in some instances religious reactions to deprivation may be instrumental in improving the realistic situation of their followers. Moreover, several investigators have suggested that some religious sects socialize or resocialize their members in the direction of the central norms of society, and in this way contribute to an improved adjustment of their members (Robbins, 1968).

Johnson (1961) showed that some sects help to resocialize their members according to middle-class values with their emphasis on 'clean living' (cf. Alland, 1962) and asceticism. This in turn helps sect members in their daily lives and improves their economic situation. Holt (1940) similarly described sects as helping in adjustment to the social environment. At the same time, this kind of adherence to central values is likely to prevent any basic social changes and contributes to the maintenance of the existing power relations in society (Yinger, 1957).

But what about those members of society who are not involved in sectarian activities, and who are not among the deprived and powerless? How does religion influence their integration in society? As shown above, those who are more religious tend to be more conforming and less deviant, *vis-à-vis* society in general. We may also expect them to feel more integrated and less alienated, compared with people who are less religious.

If we assume that religion helps social integration, then we should expect those who are better integrated in the society to exhibit a greater degree of religiosity. This position was taken by Swanson (1971), who found that to some extent those who were more socially involved (i.e. members of the racial majority and native-born Americans) were more likely to accept some religious beliefs.

The effects of religion as an integrative force could be observed in cases of religious uniformity or plurality in small groups or small societies. Such minor societies are created when a Utopian community separates from the larger society around it. In a survey of Utopian societies in the USA between 1776 and 1900, it was shown that those with a single religious faith survived longer than those with several religious faiths or no religious orientation at all (Stephan and Stephan, 1973). While this finding could apply quite well to other small groups, and could have been predicted on the basis of what we know about group dynamics, it has only a limited application to wider and larger societies. One might say that religious uniformity in any society is a cohesive factor, which is certainly true, but societies where such a uniformity is possible are becoming rare. History provides many examples where religious differences have been the cause of divisions and conflicts. The potential of

205

religion as a divisive factor was observed above in the section on ethno-centrism (Chapter 7).

In summary, we are able to say that despite the decline of religion as a common belief system and a meaningful mechanism for integration in modern societies, some of its social effects as an integrative force can still be seen. One example is the general conservatism and conformity related to religiosity, which in turn lead to greater stability of the whole social system. Another case is that of reducing the potential for political action on the part of deprived groups, either by turning them away from social conditions, or by helping them to adjust to the social system. Nevertheless, these effects, even when they are observed, must be regarded as residual.

BEYOND PSYCHOLOGY

In this chapter so far we have considered only 'reductive' theories, that attempt to explain religious phenomena in terms of familiar psychological or social processes. Some of these accounts recognize the importance of historical religious traditions, and do not always try to explain these too. And it is usually recognized that because there is a psychological explanation for a belief, the belief is not necessarily false.

Some of the main psychological writers on this topic have not supposed that religion could be explained in psychological terms. William James (1902), for example, thought that religion was something outside man, and that religious experiences could not be explained by psychology. Jung's views (e.g. 1933) on religion are difficult to interpret, but he evidently thought that his archetypes were more than psychological projections (cf. Bertocci, 1971). Nuttin (1962) saw religion as integration with an absolute order of existence, and contact with a spiritual environment. The reason that we have not considered such theories so far in this book is that they take us beyond psychology, and therefore cannot be verified by empirical methods. We have seen that there is a considerable degree of empirical support for some of the reductive theories which we have considered, but that does not mean to say that this is the whole story.

Research and thinking in other areas of psychology has led many psychologists to recognize that there are limits to psychology. Psychology does not include mathematics, for example, though it can say something about the thought processes involved, can measure mathematical ability, and so on. Mathematics is an autonomous sphere of knowledge, with principles and methods of its own. The same is true of physics and other branches of science. But it is in the humanities that the limits of psychology are even more evident: psychology can make only minor and peripheral contributions to music, art and literature. Artistic creations produce aesthetic experiences and commentaries on life in ways that psychology comprehends only dimly, and cannot itself create. Religious experience has something in common with aesthetic experience: in both cases there is a quality of subjective experience which cannot be grasped or explained in psychological categories.

Whether or not religion finally turns out to be, as Freud thought, an illusion, it creates a special quality of experience which is not immediately reducible to psychological terms; in some people it is able to generate a certain quality or style of life, though, as we have seen, the effects on behaviour are slowly diminishing.

Many psychologists today have come to realize that psychology, as it has been developed so far, cannot do justice to all aspects of human nature. Psychology has come a very long way since the days of early behaviourism, and rats in mazes. Research is now being carried out into, for example, conscious experiences, creativity, and religious beliefs. However, humanistic, existentialist and other psychologists feel that psychology needs to extend its philosophical base further, to take more seriously the possibility that man is free, creative, and not wholly predictable, that conscious experiences are perhaps not wholly reducible to neurological events, and may indeed be causes of behaviour (Maslow, 1962). While these ideas offer a more satisfactory model of man than that of traditional psychology, they have not led so far to experimental research. If and when psychologists develop an extended view of human nature, and research methods to go with it, the relation between psychology and religion may be very different.

Bibliographical Index

Figures in square brackets indicate the page in this book where the reference is cited.

AARONSON, B. and OSMOND, H. (1971), *Psychedelics*. London: Hogarth Press. [47, 50]

ABELSON, R. P. *et al.* (eds) (1968), *Theories of Cognitive Consistency: a Sourcebook*. Chicago: Rand McNally. [180]

ABRAMSON, H. A. (ed.) (1967), *LSD in Psychotherapy and Alcoholism*. Indianapolis: Bobbs-Merrill. [50]

ACUFF, G. and GORMAN, B. (1967), 'Emeritus professors: The effect of professional activity and religion on "meaning" ', *Sociological Quarterly*, 9, pp. 112–15. [130]

ADORNO, T. W. *et al.* (1950), *The Authoritarian Personality*. New York: Harper. [82, 96, 113, 116]

ALEXANDER, I. E. and ADLERSTEIN, A. M. (1959), *The Meaning of Death*. New York: McGraw-Hill. [56]

ALFORD, R. R. (1963), *Party and Society*. Chicago: Rand McNally. [102, 104]

ALLAND, A., JR. (1962), 'Possession in a revivalistic Negro church', *Journal for the Scientific Study of Religion*, 1, pp. 204–13. [74, 108, 138, 171, 205]

ALLEN, D. E. and SANDHU, H. S. (1967), 'A comparative study of delinquents: family affect, religion and personal income', *Social Forces*, 46, pp. 263–9. [150]

ALLEN, R. O. and SPILKA, B. (1967), 'Committed and consensual religion: A specification of religion-prejudice relationships', *Journal for the Scientific Study of Religion*, 6, pp. 191–206. [114, 116]

ALLINSMITH, W. and ALLINSMITH, B. (1948), 'Religious affiliation and politico-economic attitude: A study of eight major US religious groups', *Public Opinion Quarterly*, 12, pp. 377–89. [103, 106]

ALLISON, J. (1967), 'Adaptive regression and intense religious experiences,' *Journal of Nervous and Mental Disease*, 145, pp. 452–63. [140]

208

ALLISON, J. (1969), 'Religious conversion: regression and progression in an adolescent experience', *Journal for the Scientific Study of Religion*, 8, pp. 23–38. [60]

ALLPORT, G. W. (1950), *The Individual and His Religion*. New York: Macmillan.

ALLPORT, G. W. (1966), 'The religious context of prejudice', *Journal for the Scientific Study of Religion*, 5, pp. 447–57. [113, 114, 115]

ALLPORT, G. W., GILLESPIE, J. M. and YOUNG, J. (1948), 'The religion of the post-war college student', *Journal of Psychology*, 25, pp. 3–33. [31, 35, 53, 54, 64, 73]

ALLPORT, G. W. and KRAMER, B. M. (1946), 'Some roots of prejudice', *Journal of Psychology*, 22, pp. 9–39. [113]

ALLPORT, G. W. and ROSS, J. M. (1967), 'Personal religious orientation and prejudice', *Journal of Personality and Social Psychology*, 5, pp. 432–43. [114]

ALLPORT, G. W., VERNON, P. E. and LINDZEY, G. (1960), *Manual for the Study of Values: A Scale for Measuring the Dominant Interests in Personality*, 3rd edn. Boston: Houghton Mifflin. [4]

ALMQUIST, E. M. (1966), 'Social class and religiosity', *Kansas Journal of Sociology*, 2, pp. 90–9. [162]

ALSTON, J. P. (1973), 'Review of the polls', *Journal for the Scientific Study of Religion*, 12, pp. 109–11. [22, 170]

ALSTON, J. P., PEEK, C. W. and WINGROVE, C. R. (1972), 'Religiosity and Black militancy: A reappraisal', *Journal for the Scientific Study of Religion*, 11, pp. 252–61. [110]

ANDERSON, C. H. (1968), 'Religious community among white Protestants, Catholics, and Mormons', *Social Forces*, 46, pp. 501–8. [104]

ANDERSON, D. C. (1966), 'Ascetic Protestantism and political preference', *Review of Religious Research*, 7, pp. 167–70. [105]

ARGYLE, M. and DELIN, P. (1965), 'Non-universal laws of socialization', *Human Relations*, 18, pp. 77–86. [80, 99]

ARSENIAN, S. (1943), 'Change in evaluative attitudes during four years of college', *Journal of Applied Psychology*, 27, pp. 338–49. [36]

ASTIN, A. W. (1968), 'Personal and environmental determinants of student activism', *Measurement and Evaluation in Guidance*, 1, pp. 149–62. [108]

BABCHUK, N., CROCKETT, H. J. JR. and BALLWEG, J. A. (1967), 'Change in religious affiliation and family stability', *Social Forces*, 45, pp. 551–5. [141]

BACK, C. W. and BOURQUE, L. B. (1970), 'Can feelings be enumerated?', *Behavioral Science*, 15, pp. 487–96. [74, 163, 170, 171, 195]

BAER, D. J. and MOSELE, V. F. (1971), 'Political and religious beliefs of Catholics and attitudes toward involvement in the Vietnam war', *Journal of Psychology*, 78, pp. 161–4. [105]

BAGLEY, C. (1970), 'Relation of religion and racial prejudice in Europe', *Journal for the Scientific Study of Religion*, 9, pp. 219–25. [122, 113]

BAHR, H. M. (1970), 'Aging and religious disaffiliation', *Social Forces*, 49, pp. 59–71. [66]

209

BAKAN, P. (1971), 'The eyes have it', *Psychology Today*, *4*, pp. 64–7.

BALFOUR, A. and HAMILTON, C. M. (1963), 'Attempted suicide in Glasgow', *British Journal of Psychiatry*, *109*, pp. 609–15. [144]

BARBER, B. (1941), 'Acculturation and messianic movements', *American Sociological Review*, *6*, pp. 663–9. [136]

BARRON, M. L. (1961), *The Aging American*. New York: Crowell. [69]

BARRY, H. III, BACON, M. K. and CHILD, I. L. (1957), 'A cross-cultural study of sex differences in socialization', *Journal of Abnormal and Social Psychology*, *55*, pp. 327–32. [77]

BASS, B. (1956), 'Development and evaluation of a scale for measuring social acquiescence', *Journal of Abnormal and Social Psychology*, *53*, pp. 296–9. [98]

BATEMAN, M. M. and JENSEN, J. S. (1958), 'The effect of religious background on modes of handling anger', *Journal of Social Psychology*, *47*, pp. 133–41. [99]

BEALER, R. C. and WILLETS, F. K. (1967), 'The religious interests of American high school youth: a survey of recent research', *Religious Education*, *62*, pp. 435–44. [64, 65]

BECKER, R. J. (1971), 'Religion and psychological health', in Strommen (1971). [126]

BELL, H. M. (1938), *Youth Tell Their Story*. New York: American Council on Education. [31, 32]

BELLAH, R. N. (1967), 'Civil religion in America', *Daedalus*, *96*, pp. 1–21. [27, 181, 203]

BELLAH, R. N. (1968), 'Religion: The sociology of religion', *International Encyclopaedia of the Social Sciences*, *13*, pp. 406–14.

BELLAH, R. N. (1970), *Beyond Belief*. New York: Harper & Row. [203]

BELLO, F. (1954), 'The young scientists', *Fortune*, *49*, pp. 142–3. [88]

BENDER, I. E. (1958), 'Changes in religious interest: A retest after 15 years', *Journal of Abnormal and Social Psychology*, *57*, pp. 41–6. [66]

BENDER, I. E. (1968), 'A longitudinal study of church attenders and non-attenders', *Journal for the Scientific Study of Religion*, *7*, pp. 230–7. [67, 94, 105]

BENDER, I. E. and KAGIWADA, G. (1968), 'Hansen's law of "Third-Generation Return" and the study of American religio-ethnic groups', *Phylon*, *29*, pp. 360–70. [28]

BEREITER, C. and FREEDMAN, M. B. (1962), 'Fields of study and the people in them', in N. Sanford (ed.), *The American College*. New York: Wiley [92]

BERGER, P. L. (1961), *The Noise of Solemn Assemblies*. New York: Doubleday. [27, 29]

BERGER, P. L. and LUCKMANN, T. (1963), 'Sociology of religion and sociology of knowledge', *Sociology and Social Research*, *47*, pp. 417–27. [26]

BERGER, P. L. and LUCKMANN, T. (1967), *The Social Construction of Reality*. New York: Doubleday. [181, 203]

BERNARD, J. (1949), 'The Rosenzweig picture frustration-study: I. Norms, reliability, and statistical evaluation', *Journal of Psychology*, *28*, pp. 325–32. [196]

BERTOCCI, P. A. (1971), 'Psychological interpretations of religious experience', in Strommen (1971). [206]

BIERSDORF, J. E. and JOHNSON, J. R. (1966), 'Religion and physical disability', *Rehabilitation Record*, 7, pp. 1–4. [141]

BILLINGS, R. A. (1934), 'The Negro and his church', *Psychoanalytic Review*, 21, pp. 425–41. [169]

BIPO (1948, 1950, 1957), British Institute of Public Opinion. Unpublished reports of surveys. [72, 169]

BLAU, P. M. (1953), 'Orientation of college students toward international relations', *American Journal of Sociology*, 59, pp. 205–19. [107]

BOCHEL, J. M. and DENVER, D. T. (1970), 'Religion and voting: a critical review and a new analysis', *Political Studies*, 18, pp. 205–19. [103, 104]

BOCK, D. C. and WARREN, N. C. (1972), 'Religious belief as a factor in obedience to destructive commands', *Review of Religious Research*, 13, pp. 185-91. [122]

BOEHM, L. (1962), 'The development of conscience: A comparison of students in Catholic parochial schools and in public schools', *Child Development*, 23, pp. 591–602. [122]

BOEHM, L. (1963), 'The development of conscience: a comparison of upper middle class academically gifted children attending Catholic and Jewish parochial schools', *Journal of Social Psychology*, 59, pp. 101–10. [122]

BOISEN, A. T. (1939), 'Economic distress and religious experience: a study of the Holy Rollers', *Psychiatry*, 2, pp. 185–94. [139, 164]

BOISEN, A. T. (1955), *Religion in Crisis and Custom*, New York: Harper. [134, 136, 164, 174, 175]

BONGER, W. A. (1943), *Race and Crime*. New York: Columbia University Press. [148, 149]

BOSE, R. G. (1929), 'Religious concepts of children', *Religious Education*, 24, pp. 831–7. [59, 62, 63]

BOUMA, G. D. (1970), 'Assessing the impact of religion: a critical review', *Sociological Analysis*, 31, pp. 172–9. [1]

BOURQUE, L. B. (1969), 'Social correlates of transcendental experience', *Sociological Analysis*, 30, pp. 151–63. [5]

BOURQUE, L. B. and BACK, K. W. (1968), 'Values and transcendental experiences', *Social Forces*, 47, pp. 34–8. [74, 78, 111, 195]

BRAM, J. (1956), 'Jehovah's Witnesses and the values of American culture', *Transactions of the New York Academy of Sciences*, 19, pp. 47–54. [174]

BREWER, D. L. (1970), 'Religious resistance to changing beliefs about race', *Pacific Sociological Review*, 13, pp. 163–70. [116]

BRIGHTWELL, L. E. (1962), 'A study of religious delusions', *Bulletin of the Tulane Medical Faculty*, 21, pp. 159–72. [135]

BRONFENBRENNER, U. (1958), 'Socialization and social class through time and space', in E. E. Maccoby, T. M. Newcomb and E. L. Hartley (eds), *Readings in Social Psychology*, 3rd edn. New York: Holt. [82]

BROOM, L. and GLENN, N. (1966), 'Religious differences in reported attitudes and behavior', *Sociological Analysis*, 27, pp. 187–209. [84]

BROWN, D. and FREEDMAN, M. B. (1962), in N. Sanford, (ed.) *The American College*, New York: Wiley. [39]

BROWN, D. G. and LOWE, W. L. (1951), 'Religious beliefs and personality characteristics of college students', *Journal of Social Psychology*, *33*, pp. 103–29. [81, 93, 97]

BROWN, L. B. (1962), 'A study of religious belief', *British Journal of Psychology*, *53*, pp. 259–72. [80, 94, 95, 182]

BROWN, L. B. (1965), 'Aggression and denominational membership', *British Journal of Social and Clinical Psychology*, *4*, pp. 175–8. [95, 96, 99]

BROWN, L. B. and PALLANT, D. J. (1962), 'Religious belief and social pressure', *Psychological Reports*, *10*, pp. 269–70. [38]

BROWN, R. (1965), *Social Psychology*. New York: Free Press.

BRUNNER, E. DE S. and LORGE, I. (1937), *Rural Trends in Depression Years*. Columbia University Press. [175]

BUCKE, R. M. (1901), *Cosmic Consciousness*. New York: Dutton. [67]

BURCHINAL, L. G. (1957), 'Marital satisfaction and religious behavior', *American Sociological Review*, *22*, pp. 306–10. [158]

BURCHINAL, L. G. (1959), 'Some social status criteria and church membership and church attendance', *Journal of Social Psychology*, *49*, pp. 53–64. [162]

BURGESS, E. W. and COTTRELL, L. S. (1939), *Predicting Success or Failure in Marriage*. New York: Prentice-Hall. [157]

BURGESS, J. H. and WAGNER, R. L. (1971), 'Religion as a factor in extrusion to public mental hospitals', *Journal for the Scientific Study of Religion*, *10*, pp. 237–40. [132]

BURNHAM, K. E., CONNORS, J. F. III, and LEONARD, R. C. (1969), 'Religious affiliation, church attendance, religious education and student attitudes toward race', *Sociological Analysis*, *30*, pp. 235–44. [113]

BURTT, H. E. and FALKENBURG, D. R. JR. (1941), 'The influence of majority and expert opinion on religious attitudes', *Journal of Social Psychology*, *14*, pp. 269–78. [38]

BUTLER, D. E. and STOKES, D. (1969), *Political change in Britain*. London: Macmillan. [14, 102, 103]

CAHALAN, D., CISIN, I. H. and CROSSLEY, H. M. (1969), *American Drinking Practices*. New Brunswick, N.J.: Rutgers Center for Alcohol Studies. [147]

CAMERON, P. (1969), 'Valued aspects of religion to Negroes and whites', *Proceedings of the 77th Annual Convention of the American Psychological Association*, *4*, pp. 741–2. [67, 170]

CAMERON, P. (1971), 'Personality differences between typical urban Negroes and whites', *Journal of Negro Education*, *40*, pp. 66–75. [171]

CAMPBELL, A. (1971), *White Attitudes Toward Black People*. Ann Arbor, Michigan: Institute for Social Research, University of Michigan. [119]

CAMPBELL, A. *et al.* (1960), *The American Voter*. New York: Wiley. [100]

CAMPBELL, T. C. and FUKUYAMA, Y. (1970), *The Fragmented Layman*, Philadelphia: Pilgrim Press. [78, 165, 192]

CANTRIL, H. (1941), *The Psychology of Social Movements*. London: Chapman & Hall. [46]

CANTRIL, H. (1943), 'Educational and economic composition of religious groups', *American Journal of Sociology*, 48, pp. 574–9. [34]

CANTRIL, H. (ed.) (1951), *Public Opinion 1935–1946*. Princeton University Press. [20]

CANTRIL, H. and SHERIF, M. (1938), 'The kingdom of Father Divine', *Journal of Abnormal and Social Psychology*, 33, pp. 147–67. [173]

CARLOS, S. (1970), 'Religious participation and the urban-suburban continuum', *American Journal of Sociology*, 75, pp. 742–59. [194]

CARMAN, R. S. (1971), 'Expectations and socialization experiences related to drinking among US service men', *Quarterly Journal of Studies on Alcohol*, 32, pp. 1040–7. [147]

CARNEY, R. E. and MCKEACHIE, W. J. (1962), 'Religion, sex, social class, probability of success, and student personality', *Journal for the Scientific Study of Religion*, 2, pp. 32–42. [84]

CARTWRIGHT, A. (1970), *Parents and Family Planning Services*. London: Routledge & Kegan Paul. [155, 157].

CAUTER, T. and DOWNHAM, J. S. (1954), *The Communication of Ideas*. London: Chatto & Windus. [33, 65]

CAVAN, R. S. (1928), *Suicide*. University of Chicago Press. [142]

CAVAN, R. S. *et al.* (1949), *Personal Adjustment in Old Age*. Chicago: Science Research Associates. [68, 69]

CAVANAUGH, J. J. (1939), 'Survey of fifteen surveys', *Bulletin of the University of Notre Dame*, 34, pp. 1–128. [30, 32, 39]

CENSUS (1906, 1916, 1926, 1936, 1940), *Census of Religious Bodies*. US Department of Commerce, Bureau of the Census. [15, 71, 72, 75, 175, 176]

CENTERS, R. (1949), *The Psychology of Social Classes*. Princeton University Press. [101]

CHADWICK, W. O. (1966), *The Victorian Church*, vol. 1. London: Black. [11]

CHESSER, E. (1956), *The Sexual, Marital and Family Relationships of the English Woman*. London: Hutchinson. [32, 33, 38, 51, 152, 156, 157]

CHRISTENSEN, C. W. (1965), 'Religious conversion in adolescence', *Pastoral Psychology*, 16, pp. 17–28. [140]

CHRISTIE, R. and JAHODA, M. (1954), *Studies in the Scope and Method of the 'Authoritarian Personality'*. Chicago: Free Press. [96]

CHRISTOPHER, S., FEARON, J., MCCOY, J. and NOBBE, C. (1971), 'Social deprivation and religiosity', *Journal for the Scientific Study of Religion*, 10, pp. 385–92. [192]

CLARK, E. T. (1929), *The Psychology of Religious Awakening*. New York: Macmillan. [61, 195]

CLARK, E. T. (1965), *The Small Sects in America*. New York: Abingdon Press. [193]

CLARK, W. H. (1950), 'The psychology of religious values', in *Personality Symposium No 1*. New York: Grune & Stratton. [74]

CLARK, W. H. (1955), 'A study of some of the factors leading to achieve-

213

ment and creativity, with special reference to religious scepticism and belief', *Journal of Social Psychology*, *51*, pp. 57–70. [88]

CLARK, W. H. (1958), *The Psychology of Religion*. New York: Macmillan. [136]

CLARK, W. H. (1971), 'Intense religious experience', in Strommen (1971). [50]

CLARK, W. H. and RASKIN, M. (1971), 'LSD as a means of exploring the non-rational consciousness', reported by Clark in Strommen (1971). [48]

CLARK, W. H. and WARNER, C. M. (1955), 'The relation of church attendance to honesty and kindness in a small community', *Religious Education*, *50*, pp. 340–2. [121]

CLINE, V. B. and RICHARDS, J. M. (1965), 'A factor analytic study of religious beliefs and behavior', *Journal of Personality and Social Psychology*, *1*, pp. 569–78. [120, 121]

COE, G. A. (1916), *The Psychology of Religion*. University of Chicago Press. [97]

COHN, H. (1957), *The Pursuit of the Millennium*. London: Secker & Warburg. [112, 174]

COLQUHOUN, F. (1955), *Harringay Story*. London: Hodder & Stoughton. [42, 61, 77]

COMSTOCK, G. W. and PARTRIDGE, K. B. (1972), 'Church attendance and health', *Journal of Chronic Diseases*, *25*, pp. 665–72. [124, 125, 143]

CONGER, J. J. and MILLER, W. (1966), *Personality, Social Class and Delinquency*. New York: Wiley. [150]

CONNORS, J. F. III, LEONARD, R. C. and BURNHAM, K. E. (1968), 'Religion and opposition to war among college students', *Sociological Analysis*, *29*, pp. 211–19. [107]

COWEN, E. L. (1954), 'The negative concept as a personality measure', *Journal of Consulting Psychology*, *18*, pp. 138–42. [126]

COX, E. (1967), *Sixth Form Religion*. London: SCM Press. [74]

CRANDALL, V. C. and GOZALI, J. (1969), 'The social desirability responses of children of four religious-cultural groups', *Child Development*, *40*, pp. 751–62. [59, 121]

CRAWFORD, B. F. (1938), *Religious Trends in a Century of Hymns*. New York: Carnegie Press. [24]

CRESPI, L. (1963), 'Occupational status and religion', *American Sociological Review*, *28*, p. 131. [85]

CROOG, S. H. and LEVINE, S. (1972), 'Religious identity and response to serious illness: A report on heart patients', *Social Science and Medicine*, *6*, pp. 17–32. [54]

CURRIE, R. and GILBERT, A. (1972), 'Religion', in A. H. Halsey (ed.), *Trends in British Society since 1900*. London: Macmillan. [9, 10]

DALY, R. J. and COCHRANE, C. M. (1968), 'Affective disorder taxonomies in middle-aged females', *British Journal of Psychiatry*, *14*, pp. 1295–7. [135]

D'ANDRADE, R. G. (1967), 'Sex differences and cultural institutions', in E. E. Maccoby (ed.), *The Development of Sex Differences*. London: Tavistock. [77]

DARLEY, J. M. and BATSON, C. D. (1973), ' "From Jerusalem to Jericho":
a study of situational and dispositional variables in helping behavior',
Journal of Personal and Social Psychology, 27, pp. 100–8. [121]

DATTA, L. E. (1967), 'Family religious background and early scientific
creativity', *American Sociological Review, 32*, pp. 626–35. [92]

DAVENPORT, F. M. (1906), *Primitive Traits in Religious Revivals*. New
York: Macmillan. [41]

DAVIS, K. (1948), *Human Society*. New York: Macmillan. [191]

DAYTON, N. A. (1940), *New Facts on Mental Disorders*. Springfield, Ill.:
Charles C. Thomas. [131]

DEBORD, L. W. (1969), 'Adolescent religious participation: An examination of sib-structure and church attendance', *Adolescence, 16*,
pp. 557–70. [60]

DECONCHY, J. P. (1967), *Structure génétique de l'idée de Dieu*. Brussels:
Lumen Vitae. [186]

DECONCHY, J. P. (1968), 'God and parental images: the masculine and
feminine in religious free associations', in A. Godin (ed.), *From Cry
to Word*. Brussels: Lumen Vitae. [186]

DEIKMAN, A. J. (1963), 'Experimental meditation', *Journal of Nervous
and Mental Disease, 136*, pp. 329–73. [50]

DE JONG, G. F. (1965), 'Religious fundamentalism, socio-economic
status, and fertility attitudes in the southern Appalachians',
Demography, 2, pp. 540–8. [160]

DE JONG, G. F. and FAULKNER, J. E. (1967), 'The church, individual
religiosity, and social justice', *Sociological Analysis, 28*, pp. 34–43.
[119]

DE JONG, G. F. and FORD, T. R. (1965), 'Religious fundamentalism and
denominational preference in the southern Appalachian region',
Journal for the Scientific Study of Religion, 5, pp. 24–33. [162, 163]

DEMERATH, N. J. III (1965), *Social Class in American Protestantism*.
Chicago: Rand McNally. [161, 162, 164, 165]

DEMERATH, N. J. III (1968), 'Trends and anti-trends in religious change',
in E. B. Sheldon and W. E. Moore (eds), *Indicators of Social Change*.
New York: Russell Sage Foundation. [17]

DEMERATH, N. J. III (1969), 'Irreligion, a-religion, and the case of the
religionless church: Two case studies in organizational convergence',
Sociological Analysis, 30, pp. 191–203. [107]

DEMERATH, N. J. III and HAMMOND, P. E. (1969), *Religion in Social
Context*. New York: Random House. [20]

DEMERATH, N. J. III and LEVINSON, R. M. (1971), 'Baiting the dissident
hook: Some effects of bias on measuring religious beliefs', *Sociometry, 34*, pp. 346–59. [20]

DITTES, J. E. (1969), 'Psychology of religion', in G. Lindzey and E.
Aronson (eds), *The Handbook of Social Psychology*, 2nd edn, vol. 5.
Reading, Mass.: Addison-Wesley. [126]

DITTES, J. E. (1971a), 'Psychological characteristics of religious professionals', in Strommen (1971). [137]

DITTES, J. E. (1971b), 'Religion, prejudice and personality', in Strommen
(1971). [116]

DOLLARD, J. (1949), *Caste and Class in a Southern Town*. New York: Doubleday. [108, 171]

DOMHOFF, G. W. (1967), *Who Rules America?* Englewood Cliffs, N.J.: Prentice-Hall. [104]

DOUVAN, E. and ADELSON, J. (1966), *The Adolescent Experience*. New York: Wiley. [78]

DRAPER, E. (1969), 'Religion as an intrapsychic experience', *Clinical Journal of Medicine*, *19*, pp. 111–19. [201]

DREGER, R. M. (1952), 'Some personality correlates of religious attitudes as determined by projective techniques', *Psychological Monographs*, *66*, No. 3. [126]

DROBA, D. D. (1932), 'Churches and war attitudes', *Sociology and Social Research*, *16*, pp. 547–52. [107]

DUBLIN, L. I. (1933), *To be or not to be*. New York: Smith & Haas. [142]

DUKE, J. D. (1964), 'Placebo reactivity and tests of suggestibility', *Journal of Personality*, *32*, pp. 227–35. [98]

DUNCAN, O. D. (1961), 'A socio-economic index for all occupations', in A. J. Reiss (ed.) *Occupations and Social Status*. Chicago: Free Press. [167]

DUNN, R. F. (1965), 'Personality patterns among religious personnel', *Catholic Psychological Record*, *3*, pp. 125–37. [137]

DURKHEIM, E. (1897), *Suicide*. London: Routledge & Kegan Paul. [142, 144]

DURKHEIM, E. (1915), *The Elementary Forms of the Religious Life*. London: Allen & Unwin. [181, 203]

DYNES, R. R. (1955), 'Church-sect typology and socio-economic status', *American Sociological Review*, *20*, pp. 555–60. [162, 164]

DYNES, R. R. (1956), 'Rurality, migration and sectarianism', *Rural Sociology*, *21*, pp. 24–8. [164]

ECKHARDT, K. W. (1970), 'Religiosity and civil rights militancy', *Review of Religious Research*, *11*, pp. 197–203. [118, 119]

EHRLICH, H. J. (1973), *The Social Psychology of Prejudice*. New York: Wiley. [116]

EISTER, A. W. (1957), 'Religious institutions in complex societies: difficulties in the theoretic specification of functions', *American Sociological Review*, *22*, pp. 387–91. [203]

ELDER, G. H. JR. (1965), 'Family structure and educational achievement: a cross-national analysis', *American Sociological Review*, *30*, pp. 81–95. [81, 86]

ELINSON, H. (1965), 'Implications of Pentecostal religion for intellectualism, politics, and race relations', *American Journal of Sociology*, *70*, pp. 403–15. [111]

ELKIND, D. (1964), 'Age changes in the meaning of religious identity', *Review of Religious Research*, *6*, pp. 36–40. [59]

ELKIND, D. (1971), 'The origins of religion in the child', *Review of Religious Research*, *12*, pp. 35–42. [181]

ENGLAND, R. W. (1954), 'Some aspects of Christian Science as reflected in letters of testimony', *American Journal of Sociology*, 59, pp. 448–53. [194, 195]

EPPS, P. (1957), 'Women in prison on "attempted suicide" charges', *Lancet*, 273, ii, pp. 182–4. [144]

ERICKSON, D. (1962), 'Differential effects of public and sectarian schooling on the religiousness of the child', cited by A. M. Greeley and G. L. Gockel in Strommen (1971). [31, 32]

ERIKSON, E. H. (1958), *Young Man Luther: A Study in Psychoanalysis and History*. New York: Norton. [182]

ERSKINE, H. G. (1960), 'The polls: Presidential election', *Public Opinion Quarterly*, 25, pp. 128–39. [101]

EYSENCK, H. J. (1944), 'General social attitudes', *Journal of Social Psychology*, 19, pp. 207–27. [156]

EYSENCK, H. J. (1947), *Dimensions of Personality*, London: Kegan Paul. [97, 98]

EZER, M. (1962), 'The effect of religion upon children's responses to questions involving physical causality', in J. F. Rosenblith and W. Allinsmith (eds), *The Causes of Behavior*. Boston: Allyn & Bacon. [59]

FAGAN, J. and BREED, G. (1970), 'A good, short measure of religious dogmatism', *Psychological Reports*, 26, pp. 533–4. [73]

FARR, C. B. and HOWE, R. L. (1932), 'The influence of religious ideas on the etiology, symptomatology, and prognosis of the psychoses, with special reference to social factors', *American Journal of Psychiatry*, 11, pp. 845–65. [134]

FAULKNER, J. E. and DE JONG, G. F. (1968), 'A note on religiosity and moral behavior of a sample of college students', *Social Compass*, 15, pp. 37–44. [121]

FAUSET, A. H. (1944), *Black Gods of the Metropolis: Negro Religious Cults of the Urban North*. Philadelphia: University of Pennsylvania Press. [174]

FEAGIN, J. R. (1964), 'Prejudice and religious types: A focused study of southern fundamentalists', *Journal for the Scientific Study of Religion*, 4, pp. 3–13. [114]

FEATHER, N. T. (1964), 'Acceptance and rejection of arguments in relation to attitude strength, critical ability and intolerance of inconsistency', *Journal of Abnormal and Social Psychology*, 69, pp. 127–36. [97]

FEATHERMAN, D. L. (1971), 'The socio-economic achievement of white religio-ethnic subgroups: Social and psychological explanations', *American Sociological Review*, 36, pp. 207–22. [87]

FEIFEL, H. et al. (1967), 'Physicians consider death', *Proceedings of the 75th Convention of the APA*, 2, pp. 201–2. [56]

FEIFEL, H. and JONES, R. B. (1968), 'Perception of death as related to nearness of death', *Proceedings of American Psychological Association*, pp. 545–6. [56]

FELDMAN, K. A. (1969a), 'Change and stability of religious orientations during college: Part 1. Freshman-senior comparisons', *Review of Religious Research*, 11, pp. 40–60. [34]

217

FELDMAN, K. A. (1969b), 'Change and stability of religious orientations during college: Part II. Social-structural correlates', *Review of Religious Research, 11*, pp. 103–28. [36]

FELDMAN, K. A. and NEWCOMB, T. M. (1969), *The Impact of College on Students*. San Francisco: Jossey-Bass. [35, 37]

FENICHEL, O. (1945), *The Psychoanalytic Theory of Neurosis*. New York: Norton. [188, 200]

FENN, R. K. (1972), 'Toward a new sociology of religion', *Journal for the Scientific Study of Religion, 11*, pp. 16–32. [204]

FERGUSON, T. (1952), *The Young Delinquent in his Social Setting*. London: Oxford University Press. [150]

FERMAN, L. A. (1960), 'Religious change on a college campus', *Journal of College Student Personnel, 1*, pp. 2–12. [34, 35]

FESTINGER, L., RIECKEN, H. W. and SCHACHTER, S. (1956), *When Prophecy Fails*. Minneapolis: University of Minnesota Press. [40, 183]

FICHTER, J. H. (1952), 'The profile of Catholic religious life', *American Journal of Sociology, 58*, pp. 145–9. [51, 76]

FICHTER, J. H. (1954), *Social Relations in the Urban Parish*. University of Chicago Press. [65, 66, 67]

FINNER, S. L. and GAMACHE, J. D. (1969), 'The relation between religious commitment and attitudes toward induced abortions', *Sociological Analysis, 30*, pp. 1–12. [157]

FISCHER, E. H. and COHEN, S. L. (1972), 'Demographic correlates of attitudes toward seeking professional psychological help', *Journal of Consulting and Clinical Psychology, 39*, pp. 70–4. [133]

FISHER, S. (1964), 'Acquiescence and religiosity', *Psychological Reports, 15*, p. 784. [98]

FISHER, S. C. (1948), 'Relationships in attitudes, opinions and values among family members', *University of California Publications in Culture and Society, 2*, pp. 29–100. [158]

FLUGEL, J. C. (1945), *Man, Morals and Society*. London: Duckworth. [187, 188, 195, 200]

FORBES, G. B., TEVAULT, R. K. and GROMOLL, H. F. (1971), 'Willingness to help strangers as a function of liberal, conservative or Catholic church membership: a field study with the lost-letter technique', *Psychological Reports, 28*, pp. 947–9. [121]

FORD, T. R. (1960), 'Status, residence and fundamentalist religious beliefs in the Southern Appalachians', *Social Forces, 39*, pp. 41–9. [34]

FOX, W. S. and JACKSON, E. F. (1973), 'Protestant-Catholic differences in educational achievement and persistence in school', *Journal for the Scientific Study of Religion, 12*, pp. 65–84. [87]

FRANK, J. D. (1961), *Persuasion and Healing*. Baltimore: Johns Hopkins Press. [44, 126]

FRANZBLAU, A. N. (1934), *Religious Beliefs and Character Among Jewish Adolescents*. New York: Columbia University Teachers College. [121]

FREUD, S. (1907), 'Obsessive acts and religious practices', *Collected Papers, 2*, pp. 25–35. [199, 200]

FREUD, S. (1913), *Totem and Taboo*. London: Hogarth Press. [180, 183, 187]

FREUD, S. (1922), *Group Psychology and the Analysis of the Ego.* London: Hogarth Press. [115]

FREUD, S. (1927), *The Future of An Illusion.* London: Hogarth Press. [184, 191, 201]

FREUD, S. (1939), *Civilization and Its Discontents.* London: Hogarth Press. [184]

FRIEDRICHS, R. W. (1959), 'Christians and residential exclusion: an empirical study of a northern dilemma', *Journal of Social Issues*, 15, pp. 14–23. [121]

FRIEDRICHS, R. W. (1971), 'Decline in prejudice among churchgoers following clergy-led open housing campaign', *Journal for the Scientific Study of Religion*, 10, pp. 152–6. [117, 118]

FRITSCH, D. and HETZER, H. (1928), 'Die religiose Entwicklung des Jugendlichen', *Archiven f.d. ges. Psychol.*, 62, pp. 409–42. [62, 63]

FRY, C. L. (1933), 'The religious affiliations of American leaders', *Scientific Monthly*, 36, pp. 241–9. [87, 93]

FUCHS, L. H. (1956), *The Political Behavior of American Jews.* Chicago: Free Press. [112]

FUKUYAMA, Y. (1961), 'The major dimensions of church membership', *Review of Religious Research*, 2, pp. 154–61. [6]

FUNK, R. A. (1956), 'Religious attitudes and manifest anxiety in a college population', *American Psychologist*, 11, p. 375. [126, 189]

FUSE, T. (1968), 'Religion, war and the institutional dilemma: a sociological interpretation', *Journal of Peace Research*, 2, pp. 196–210. [107]

GABENNESCH, H. (1972), 'Authoritarianism as world view', *American Journal of Sociology*, 77, pp. 857–75. [96]

GALLENMORE, J. L. JR., WILSON, W. P. and RHOADS, J. M. (1969), 'The religious life of patients with affective disorders', *Diseases of the Nervous System*, 30, pp. 483–7. [135]

GALLUP, G. H. (1972), *The Gallup Poll: Public Opinion 1935–1971.* New York: Random House. [15, 17, 19, 20, 34, 72, 73, 102, 113, 146, 163, 172]

GANNON, T. M. (1967), 'Religious attitude and behavior changes of institutional delinquents', *Sociological Analysis*, 28, pp. 215–25. [150]

GARAI, J. E. (1970), 'Sex differences in mental health', *Genetic Psychology Monographs*, 81(2), pp. 123–42. [77]

GARAI, J. E. and SCHEINFELD, A. (1968), 'Sex differences in mental and behavioral traits', *Genetic Psychology Monographs*, 77, pp. 169–299. [77, 78]

GARFIELD, S. J., COHEN, H. A. and ROTH, R. M. (1967), 'A correlative study of cheating in college students', *Journal of Educational Research*, 61, pp. 172–3. [121]

GARGAN, E. T. (1961), 'Radical Catholics of the right', *Social Order*, 11, pp. 409–19. [106]

GARRISON, K. C. (1951), *Psychology of Adolescence.* New York: Prentice-Hall. [62]

GELFAND, D. M., GELFAND, S. and RARDIN, M. W. (1965), 'Some personality factors associated with placebo responsivity', *Psychological Reports*, *17*, pp. 555–62. [98]

GIBBONS, D. and DE JARNETTE, J. (1972), 'Hypnotic suggestibility and religious experience', *Journal for the Scientific Study of Religion*, *11*, pp. 152–6. [98]

GILLIN, J. L. (1945), *Criminology and Penology*. New York: Appleton-Century-Crofts. [148]

GLENN, N. D. (1964), 'Negro religion and Negro status in the United States', in L. Schneider (ed.), *Religion, Culture and Society*. New York: Wiley. [169, 170, 171]

GLENN, N. D. and ALSTON, J. P. (1967), 'Rural-urban differences in reported attitude and behavior', *The Southwestern Social Science Quarterly*, *47*, pp. 381–400. [172, 173]

GLENN, N. D. and HYLAND, R. (1967), 'Religious preference and worldly success: Some evidence from national surveys', *American Sociological Review*, *32*, pp. 73–85. [85]

GLENN, N. D. and WEINER, D. (1969), 'Some trends in the social origins of American sociologists', *American Sociologist*, *4*, pp. 291–302. [89]

GLOCK, C. Y. (1959), 'The sociology of religion', in R. K. Merton *et al.* (eds), *Sociology Today*, New York: Basic Books. [52]

GLOCK, C. Y. (1962), 'On the study of religious commitment', *Religious Education*, *57*, Research Suppl. pp. 98–110. [5, 6, 42]

GLOCK, C. Y. (1964), 'The role of deprivation in the origin and evolution of religious groups', in R. Lee and M. E. Marty (eds), *Religion and Social Conflict*. New York: Oxford University Press. [191, 192, 194]

GLOCK, C. Y., RINGER, B. B. and BABBIE, E. R. (1967), *To Comfort and to Challenge*. Berkeley: University of California Press. [52, 110, 116]

GLOCK, C. Y. and STARK, R. (1965), *Religion and Society in Tension*. Chicago: Rand McNally. [27, 105, 111, 203]

GLOCK, C. Y. and STARK, R. (1966), *Christian Beliefs and Anti-Semitism*. New York: Harper & Row. [5, 21, 116, 171, 203]

GLUECK, S. and GLUECK, E. (1950), *Unravelling Juvenile Delinquency*. London: Oxford University Press. [149, 150]

GOCKEL, G. L. (1969), 'Income and religious affiliation: A regression analysis', *American Journal of Sociology*, *74*, pp. 632–47. [168]

GODIN, A. and HALLEZ, M. (1964), 'Parental images and divine paternity', in A. Godin (ed.), *From Religious Experience to a Religious Attitude*. Brussels: Lumen Vitae. [184, 185]

GOLDBERG, D. (1959), 'The fertility of two-generation urbanites', *Population Studies*, *12*, pp. 214–22. [159]

GOLDBERG, P. H. and STARK, M. (1965), 'Johnson or Goldwater? Some personality and attitude correlates of political choice', *Psychological Reports*, *17*, pp. 627–31. [106]

GOLDMAN, R. J. (1964), *Religious Thinking from Childhood to Adolescence*. London: Routledge & Kegan Paul. [58]

GOLDMAN, R. J. (1965), 'Do we want our children taught about God?', *New Society*, 27 May 1965. [11, 12]

GOLDSCHEIDER, C. and SIMPSON, J. E. (1967), 'Religious affiliation and juvenile delinquency', *Sociological Inquiry*, *37*, pp. 297–310. [149]

GOLDSCHMIDT, W. R. (1944), 'Class denominations in rural California churches', *American Journal of Sociology*, *49*, pp. 348–55. [164]

GOLDSEN, R. K., ROSENBERG, M., WILLIAMS, R. M. JR. and SUCHMEN, E. A. (1960), *What College Students Think*. Princeton: Van Nostrand. [121]

GOLDSTEIN, S. (1969), 'Socioeconomic differentials among religious groups in the United States', *American Journal of Sociology*, *74*, pp. 612–31. [85]

GOODE, E. (1966), 'Social class and church participation', *American Journal of Sociology*, *72*, pp. 102–11. [164, 165, 194]

GOODE, E. (1968), 'Class styles of religious sociation', *British Journal of Sociology*, *19*, pp. 1–16. [165]

GOODMAN, F. (1972), *Speaking in Tongues: a Cross-cultural Study in Glossolalia*. Chicago University Press. [139]

GORER, G. (1955), *Exploring English Character*. London: Cresset. [4, 9, 12, 13, 33, 40, 51, 52, 55, 56, 65, 66, 67, 68, 69, 72, 73, 122, 164, 171, 172, 198]

GORER, G. (1965), *Death, Grief, and Mourning*. New York: Doubleday. [57]

GORER, G. (1971), *Sex and Marriage in England Today*. London: Nelson. [153, 155]

GRAFF, R. W. and LADD, C. E. (1971), 'POI [Personality Orientation Inventory] correlates of a religious commitment inventory', *Journal of Clinical Psychology*, *27*, pp. 502–4. [98, 127]

GRAY, J. A. (1971), 'Sex differences in emotional behaviour in mammals including man: endocrine basis', *Acta Psychologica*, *35*, pp. 29–46. [77]

GREELEY, A. M. (1963), 'The influence of the "religious factor" on career plans and occupational values of college graduates', *American Journal of Sociology*, *68*, pp. 658–71. [84, 86]

GREELEY, A. M. (1967), 'Religion and academic plans: A note on progress', *American Journal of Sociology*, *72*, pp. 668–72. [91]

GREELEY, A. M. and ROSSI, P. H. (1966), *The Education of Catholic Americans*. New York: Doubleday. [33]

GREGORY, W. E. (1957), 'The orthodoxy of the authoritarian personality', *Journal of Social Psychology*, *45*, pp. 217–32. [95]

GRIER, W. H. and COBBS, P. M. (1971), *The Jesus Bag*. New York: McGraw-Hill. [108]

GROUP FOR THE ADVANCEMENT OF PSYCHIATRY (1968), 'The use of religion in mental illness', *Group for the Advancement of Psychiatry: Reports and Symposium*, *6*, pp. 664–88. [135]

GURIN, G., VEROFF, J. and FIELD, S. (1960), *Americans View Their Mental Health*. New York: Basic Books. [127]

HADDEN, J. K. (1963), 'An analysis of some factors associated with religion and political affiliation in a college population', *Journal for the Scientific Study of Religion*, *2*, pp. 209–14. [105, 118]

HADDEN, J. K. (1969), 'Theological beliefs and political ideology among Protestant clergy', in J. Price (ed.), *Social Facts*. London: Collier-Macmillan. [106, 110]

HALBWACHS, M. (1930), *Les Causes du suicide*. Paris: Librairie Félix Alcan. [142]

HAMBURG, D. A. (1967), *Report of the Ad Hoc Committee on Central Fact-Gathering Data*. New York: American Psychoanalytic Association. [133]

HAMILTON, R. F. (1968), 'A research note on the mass support for "tough" military initiatives', *American Sociological Review*, *33*, pp. 439–45. [107]

HAMILTON, T. (1942), 'Social optimism and pessimism in American Protestantism', *Public Opinion Quarterly*, *6*, pp. 280–3. [110]

HANSEN, M. L. (1952), 'The problem of the third generation immigrant', *Commentary*, *14*, pp. 492–500. [28]

HARDY, A. (1966), *The Divine Flame*. London: Collins. [191]

HARE, E. H. (1952), 'The ecology of mental illness', *Journal of Mental Science*, *98*, pp. 579–94. [173]

HARMS, E. (1944), 'The development of religious experience in children', *American Journal of Sociology*, *50*, pp. 112–22. [58, 186]

HART, H. (1933), 'Changing social attitudes and interests', Chapter 8 in *Recent Social Trends in the United States*. New York: McGraw-Hill. [5, 23, 24]

HART, H. (1942), 'Religion', *American Journal of Sociology*, *47*, pp. 888–97. [24]

HARTMANN, G. W. (1936), 'A field experiment on the comparative effectiveness of "emotional" and "rational" political leaflets in determining election results', *Journal of Abnormal and Social Psychology*, *13*, pp. 54–7. [44]

HARTMANN, H. (1958), *Ego Psychology and the Problem of Adaptation*. New York: International Universities Press, pp. 74–9. [201]

HARTNETT, R. T. and PETERSON, R. E. (1968), 'Religious preference as a factor in attitudinal and background differences among college freshmen', *Sociology of Education*, *41*, pp. 227–37. [120]

HARTSHORNE, H. and MAY, M. A. (1928), *Studies in Deceit*. New York: Macmillan. [120, 121]

HASSENGER, R. (ed.) (1967), *The Shape of Catholic Higher Education*. University of Chicago Press. [90]

HAVENS, J. (1963), 'The changing climate of research on the college student and his religion', *Journal for the Scientific Study of Religion*, *3*, pp. 52–69. [37, 39]

HAVINGHURST, R. J. and ALBRECHT, R. (1953), *Older People*. London: Longman. [68]

HAVINGHURST, R. J. and KEATING, B. (1971), 'The religion of youth', in Strommen (1971). [5]

HEALY, W. and BRONNER, A. F. (1923), *New Light on Delinquency and its Treatment*. New Haven: Yale University Press. [150]

HEATH, D. H. (1969), 'Secularization and maturity of religious beliefs', *Journal of Religion and Health*, *8*, pp. 335–58. [22]

HEIST, P. *et al.* (1961), 'Personality and scholarship', *Science*, *133*, pp. 362–7. [88]

HENDERSON, D. and GILLESPIE, R. D. (1956), *A Textbook of Psychiatry*. London: Oxford University Press. [134]

HENNESSEY, B. C. (1965), *Public Opinion*. Belmont, California: Wadsworth. [110, 112]

HENRY, A. F. and SHORT, J. F. (1954), *Homicide and Suicide*, Chicago: Free Press. [175, 177]

HENRY, W. E., SIMS, J. H. and SPRAY, S. L. (1971), *The Fifth Profession*. San Francisco: Jossey-Bass. [90, 133]

HERBERG, W. (1955), *Protestant, Catholic, Jew*. New York: Doubleday. [19, 27, 28, 29, 164, 203]

HERRON, S. (1955), 'What's left of Harringay?', *British Weekly*, 10 February. [41, 43]

HESS, R. D. and TORNEY, J. V. (1962), 'Religion, age and sex in children's perceptions of family authority', *Child Development, 33*, pp. 781–9. [81]

HIGHET, J. (1957), 'The churches in Glasgow', *British Weekly*, 22, 29 August. [42]

HILL, C. (1970), 'Some aspects of race and religion in Britain', in D. Martin (ed.), *Sociological Yearbook of Religion in Britain 3*. London: SCM Press. [171]

HILL, C. (1971), 'From church to sect: West Indian religious sect development in Britain', *Journal for the Scientific Study of Religion, 10*, pp. 114–23. [171]

HINE, V. H. (1969), 'Pentecostal glossolalia: toward a functional interpretation', *Journal for the Scientific Study of Religion, 8*, pp. 211–26. [139, 140, 165]

HINKLE, L. E. and WOLFF, H. G. (1957), 'Health and the social environment: experimental investigations', in A. H. Leighton *et al.* (eds), *Explorations in Social Psychiatry*. London: Tavistock. [124]

HIRSCHBERG, G. and GILLILAND, A. R. (1942), 'Parent-child relations in attitudes', *Journal of Abnormal and Social Psychology, 37*, pp. 125–30. [32]

HIRSCHI, T. and STARK, R. (1969), 'Hellfire and delinquency', *Social Problems, 17*, pp. 202–13. [151]

HOGE, D. R. (1971a), 'College students' value patterns in the 1950's and the 1960's', *Sociology of Education, 44*, pp. 170–97. [22, 106, 111]

HOGE, D. R. (1971b), 'Religious commitments of college students over five decades', *International Yearbook for the Sociology of Religion, 7*, pp. 184–211. [22, 106, 111]

HOLE, G. (1971), 'Some comparisons among guilt feelings, religion and suicidal tendencies in depressed patients', *Life-Threatening Behavior, 1*, pp. 138–42. [145]

HOLLINGSHEAD, A. B. (1949), *Elmtown's Youth*. New York: Wiley. [162]

HOLLINGSHEAD, A. B. and REDLICH, F. (1958), *Social Class and Mental Illness*. New York: Wiley. [133]

HOLLINGWORTH, L. S. (1933), 'The adolescent child', pp. 882–908 in C. A. Murchison (ed.), *A Handbook of Child Psychology*. Worcester, Massachusetts: Clark University Press. [62, 63]

HOLT, J. B. (1940), 'Holiness religion: cultural shock and social reorganization', *American Sociological Review, 5*, pp. 740–7. [173, 205]

HORNEY, K. (1946), *Our Inner Conflicts*. London: Lund Humphries. [188]

HORTON, P. B. (1940), 'Student interest in the churches', *Religious Education*, *35*, pp. 215–19. [65]

HOULT, T. F. (1958), *The Sociology of Religion*. New York: Holt. [174]

HOVLAND, C. I. (1954), 'Effects of the mass media of communication', Chapter 28 in G. Lindzey (ed.), *Handbook of Social Psychology*. Cambridge, Mass.: Addison-Wesley. [46]

HOWELLS, T. H. (1928), 'A comparative study of those who accept as against those who reject religious authority', *University of Iowa Studies in Character*, *2*, No 2. [93, 97]

HUNT, R. A. (1968), 'The interpretation of the religious scale of the Allport-Vernon-Lindzey Study of Values', *Journal for the Scientific Study of Religion*, *7*, pp. 65–77. [4]

HUNT, R. A. and KING, M. (1971), 'The intrinsic-extrinsic concept: a review and evaluation', *Journal for the Scientific Study of Religion*, *10*, pp. 339–56. [115]

HUNTER, W. W. and MAURICE, H. (1953), *Older People tell their Story*. University of Michigan Press. [68]

HUTT, C. (1972), 'Sex differences in human development', *Human Development*, *15*, pp. 153–70. [78]

HUXLEY, A. (1954), *Doors of Perception*, London: Chatto & Windus. [47]

HYDE, K. E. *et al.* (1956), *Sunday Schools Today*. London: Free Church Federal Council. [33]

INFORMATION SERVICE (1954), *Trends in giving to 14 religious bodies*. National Council of the Churches of Christ in the USA. [23]

INGLIS, K. S. (1963), *Churches and the Working Class in Victorian England*. London: Routledge & Kegan Paul. [166]

ITA (1970), *Religion in Britain and Northern Ireland*. London: Independent Television Authority. [12, 13, 15, 57, 122, 141]

JACKSON, E. F. and CROCKETT, H. J. (1964), 'Occupational mobility in the USA: a point estimate and trend comparison', *American Sociological Review*, *29*, pp. 5–15. [84]

JACKSON, E. F., FOX, W. S. and CROCKETT, H. J. (1970), 'Religion and occupational achievement', *American Sociological Review*, *35*, pp. 48–63. [84, 85]

JACO, E. G. (1960), *The Social Epidemiology of Mental Disorders*. New York: Russell Sage. [133]

JAMES, W. (1902), *The Varieties of Religious Experience*. New York: Longman. [60, 136, 137, 206]

JANET, P. M. F. (1907), *Major Symptoms of Hysteria*. New York: Macmillan. [97]

JANOWITZ, M. and SEGAL, D. R. (1967), 'Social cleavage and party affiliation: Germany, Great Britain, and the United States', *American Journal of Sociology*, *72*, pp. 601–18. [104]

JEFFERS, F. C., NICHOLS, C. R. and EISDORFER, C. (1961), 'Attitudes of older persons toward death: a preliminary study', *Journal of Gerontology*, *16*, pp. 53–6. [55]

JOHNSON, B. (1961), 'Do holiness sects socialize in dominant values?', *Social Forces*, *39*, pp. 309–17. [205]

JOHNSON, B. (1962), 'Ascetic Protestantism and political preference', *Public Opinion Quarterly*, *26*, pp. 35–46. [6, 105, 162]

JOHNSON, B. (1966), 'Theology and party preference among Protestant clergymen', *American Sociological Review*, *31*, pp. 200–8. [105, 106, 110]

JOHNSON, W. T. (1971), 'The religious crusade: revival or ritual?', *American Journal of Sociology*, *76*, pp. 873–90. [45]

JOHNSTONE, R. (1966), *The Effectiveness of Lutheran Elementary and Secondary Schools as Agencies of Christian Education*. St Louis: Concordia Seminary. [33]

JONES, D. C. (1934), *Social Survey of Merseyside*, vol. 3. London: Hodder & Stoughton. [11, 76]

JONES, E. (1951), 'The psychology of religion', in E. Jones (ed.), *Essays in Psychoanalysis*. London: Hogarth Press. [130, 184, 185, 186]

JONES, V. (1970), 'Attitudes of college students and their changes: a 37-year study', *Genetic Psychology Monographs*, *81*, pp. 3–80. [35, 75, 93]

JONES, W. L. (1937), *A Psychological Study of Religious Conversion*. London: Epworth Press. [61]

JOSEPHSON, M. (1962), *The Robber Barons*. New York: Harcourt, Brace & World. [204]

JUNG, C. G. (1933), *Modern Man in Search of a Soul*. London: Kegan Paul. [206]

KANTNER, J. F. and ZELNIK, M. (1972), 'Sexual experience of young unmarried women in the United States', *Family Planning Perspectives*, *4*, pp. 9–18. [153]

KARDINER, A. and LINTON, R. (1939), *The Individual and His Society*. New York: Columbia University Press. [184, 187]

KARDINER, A. *et al.* (1945), *The Psychological Frontiers of Society*. New York: Columbia University Press. [193]

KARLSSON, G. (1957), *Adaptability and Communication in Marriage*. Uppsala: Almquist & Wiksells Boktrycheriab. [52]

KATZ, D. and ALLPORT, F. H. (1931), *Students' Attitudes*. Syracuse, New York: Craftsman Press. [75, 76]

KATZ, D. and STOTLAND, E. (1959), 'A preliminary statement to a theory of attitude structure and change', in S. Koch (ed.), *Psychology: A Study of a Science*, vol. 3. New York: McGraw-Hill. [180]

KAUFMAN, M. R. (1939), 'Religious delusions in schizophrenia', *International Journal of Psycho-Analysis*, *20*, pp. 363–76. [134]

KELLEY, M. W. (1958), 'Depression in the psychoses of members of religious communities of women', *American Journal of Psychiatry*, *115*, pp. 72–5. [138]

KELLY, E. L. (1955), 'Consistency of the adult personality', *American Psychologist*, *10*, pp. 659–81. [66, 67]

KELMAN, H. C. (1961), 'Processes of attitude change', *Public Opinion Quarterly*, *25*, pp. 57–78. [40]

225

BIBLIOGRAPHICAL INDEX

KENYON, F. E. (1971), 'The life and health of Joan of Arc', *Practitioner*, *207*, pp. 835–42. [136]

KIEV, A. (1964), 'Psychotherapeutic aspects of Pentecostal sects among West Indian immigrants to England', *British Journal of Sociology*, *15*, pp. 129–38. [139]

KILPATRICK, D. G., SUTKER, L. W. and SUTKER, P. B. (1970), 'Dogmatism, religion, and religiosity: a review and re-evaluation', *Psychological Reports*, *26*, pp. 15–22. [96, 97]

KINCHELOE, S. C. (1937), *Research Memorandum on Religion in the Depression*. SSRC Bulletin, No 33. [175, 176]

KING, S. H. and FUNKENSTEIN, D. H. (1957), 'Religious practice and cardiovascular reactions during stress', *Journal of Abnormal and Social Psychology*, *55*, pp. 135–7. [99]

KINGSBURY, F. A. (1937), 'Why do people go to church?', *Religious Education*, *32*, pp. 50–4. [68]

KINSEY, A. C., POMEROY, W. B. and MARTIN, C. E. (1948), *Sexual Behavior in the Human Male*. London: Saunders. [152, 153, 154]

KINSEY, A. C. et al. (1953), *Sexual Behavior in the Human Female*. London: Saunders. [152, 154]

KIRKPATRICK, C. (1949), 'Religion and humanitarianism: a study of institutional implications', *Psychological Monographs*, *63*, No 309. [4, 120]

KLAF, F. C. and HAMILTON, J. G. (1961), 'Schizophrenia—a hundred years ago and today', *Journal of Mental Science*, *107*, pp. 819–27. [135]

KLEINER, R. J., TUCKMAN, J. and LAVELL, M. (1959), 'Mental disorder and status based on religious affiliation', *Human Relations*, *12*, pp. 273–6. [131, 132]

KNAPP, R. H. and GOODRICH, H. B. (1951), 'The origins of American scientists', *Science*, *113*, pp. 543–5. [87]

KNUPFER, G. and ROOM, R. (1967), 'Drinking patterns and attitudes of Irish, Jewish and White Protestant American men', *Quarterly Journal of Studies on Alcohol*, *28*, pp. 676–99. [145, 146]

KOSA, J. (1969), 'The medical student: his career and religion', *Hospital Progress*, *50*, pp. 51–3. [89, 91, 92]

KOSA, J. and NUNN, C. Z. (1964), 'Race deprivation and attitude toward Communism', *Phylon*, *25*, pp. 337–46. [106]

KOSA, J. and SCHOMMER, C. O. (1961), 'Religious participation, religious knowledge and scholastic aptitude: an empirical study', *Journal for the Scientific Study of Religion*, *1*, pp. 88–97. [93]

KRAMER, M., POLLACK, E. S., REDICK, R. W. and LOCKE, B. Z. (1972), *Mental Disorders/Suicide*. Cambridge, Mass.: Harvard University Press. [142, 143]

KRANITZ, L., ABRAHAMS, J., SPIEGEL, D. and KEITH-SPIEGEL, P. (1968), 'Religious beliefs of suicidal patients', *Psychological Reports*, *22*, p. 936. [144]

KUHLEN, R. G. and ARNOLD, M. (1944), 'Age differences in religious beliefs and problems during adolescence', *Journal of Genetic Psychology*, *65*, pp. 291–300. [63, 64]

226

KUPKY, O. (1928), *The Religious Development of Adolescents*. New York: Macmillan. [59]

KUSHNER, A. W. (1967), 'Two cases of auto-castration due to religious delusions', *British Journal of Medical Psychology*, 40, pp. 293–8. [134]

LA BARRE, W. (1938), *The Peyote Cult*. New Haven: Yale University Press. [48]

LA BARRE, W. (1962), *They shall take up Serpents*. Minneapolis: University of Minnesota Press. [164, 198]

LAMBERT, W. W., TRIANDIS, L. M. and WOLF, M. (1959), 'Some correlates of beliefs in the malevolence and benevolence of supernatural beings', *Journal of Abnormal and Social Psychology*, 58, pp. 162–9. [33]

LANDIS, J. T. (1949), 'Marriages of mixed and non-mixed religious faith', *American Sociological Review*, 14, pp. 401–7. [38, 158]

LANDIS, J. T. and LANDIS, M. G. (1953), *Building a Successful Marriage*. Englewood Cliffs, N. J.: Prentice-Hall. [157]

LANG, K. and LANG, G. E. (1960), 'Decisions for Christ: Billy Graham in New York City', in M. Stein, A. J. Vidich and O. M. White (eds), *Identity and Anxiety*. Chicago: Free Press. [42, 45]

LANGER, S. K. (1942), *Philosophy in a New Key*. Cambridge, Mass.: Harvard University Press. [183]

LANGFORD, C. M. (1969), 'Birth control practice in England', *Family Planning*, 17, pp. 89–92. [153]

LARSEN, L. and KNAPP, R. H. (1964), 'Sex differences in symbolic conceptions of the deity', *Journal of Projective Techniques and Personality Assessment*, 28, pp. 303–6. [186]

LASAGNA, L., MOSTELLER, F., VON FELSINGER, J. M. and BEECHER, H. K. (1954), 'A study of the placebo response', *American Journal of Medicine*, 16, pp. 770–9. [98]

LAUMANN, E. O. (1969), 'The social structure of religious and ethno-religious groups in a metropolitan community', *American Sociological Review*, 34, pp. 182–97. [18, 167]

LAWRENCE, P. J. (1965), 'Children's thinking about religion: A study of concrete operational thinking', *Religious Education*, 60, pp. 111–16. [59]

LAZARSFELD, P. F., BERELSON, B. and GAUDET, H. (1944), *The People's Choice*. New York: Duell, Sloan & Pearce. [102]

LAZERWITZ, B. (1961a), 'Some factors associated with variations in church attendance', *Social Forces*, 39, pp. 301–9. [65, 67, 161]

LAZERWITZ, B. (1961b), 'A comparison of major United States religious groups', *Journal of the American Statistical Association*, pp. 568–79. [167]

LAZERWITZ, B. (1964), 'Religion and social structure in the United States', in L. Schneider (ed.), *Religion, Culture and Society*. New York: Wiley. [132, 168]

LAZERWITZ, B. (1970), 'Association between religio-ethnic identification and fertility among "contemporary" Protestants and Jews', *Sociological Quarterly*, 11, pp. 307–20. [160]

LAZERWITZ, B. and ROWITZ, L. (1964), 'The three-generation hypothesis', *American Journal of Sociology*, *69*, pp. 529–38. [28]

LEARY, R. H., MCNEES, J. E., and MAIER, C. S. (1960), Supplement on religious and political attitudes. *Harvard Crimson*, *55*, No 1. [35]

LEHMAN, E. C. JR. (1972), 'The scholarly perspective and religious commitment', *Sociological Analysis*, *33*, pp. 199–216. [90]

LEHMAN, E. C. JR. and SHRIVER, D. W. JR. (1968), 'Academic discipline as predictive of faculty religiosity', *Social Forces*, *47*, pp. 171–82. [88]

LEHMAN, H. C. and WITTY, P. A. (1931), 'Certain attitudes of present-day physicists and psychologists', *American Journal of Psychology*, *43*, pp. 664–78. [88]

LENSKI, G. E. (1953), 'Social correlates of religious interest', *American Sociological Review*, *18*, pp. 533–44. [32, 162, 171, 193]

LENSKI, G. E. (1963), *The Religious Factor*, revised ed. New York: Doubleday. [1, 6, 16, 18, 28, 29, 32, 81, 82, 84, 85, 86, 91, 101, 107, 112, 114, 161, 164, 168]

LESTER, D. (1972), 'Religious behaviour and attitudes towards death', in A. Goode (ed.), *Death and Presence*. Brussels: Lumen Vitae. [55]

LEUBA, J. H. (1925), *The Psychology of Religious Mysticism*. New York: Harcourt, Brace. [198, 199]

LEUBA, J. H. (1934), 'Religious beliefs of American scientists', *Harper's*, *169*, p. 297. [4, 88, 89, 90]

LEVENTHAL, H., SINGER, R. and JONES, S. (1965), 'Effects of fear and specificity of recommendation upon attitudes and behaviour', *Journal of Personality and Social Psychology*, *2*, pp. 20–9. [44]

LEVINSON, B. (1963), 'Some research findings with Jewish subjects of traditional background', *Mental Hygiene*, *47*, pp. 129–34. [94]

LIBERMAN, R. (1962), 'An analysis of the placebo phenomenon', *Journal of Chronic Diseases*, *15*, pp. 761–83. [98]

LIGHT, H. K. (1970), 'Attitudes of rural and urban adolescent girls toward selected concepts', *Family Coordinator*, *19*, pp. 225–7. [171]

LINDENTHAL, J. L., MYERS, J. K., PEPPER, M. P. and STERN, M. S. (1970), 'Mental status and religious behavior', *Journal for the Scientific Study of Religion*, *9*, pp. 143–9. [128, 130, 141, 143]

LIPSET, S. M. (1959), 'Religion in America: what religious revival?', *Review of Religious Research*, *I*, pp. 17–24. [17]

LIPSET, S. M. (1963), *Political Man*. New York: Doubleday. [101, 106]

LIPSET, S. M. (1964), 'Religion and politics in the American past and present', in R. Lee and M. Marty (eds), *Religion and Social Conflict*. New York: Oxford University Press. [106, 111]

LIPSET, S. M. and BENDIX, R. (1959), *Social Mobility in Industrial Society*. Berkeley: University of California Press. [85]

LOCKE, H. J. (1951), *Predicting Adjustment in Marriage*. New York: Holt. [158]

LOFLAND, J. and STARK, R. (1965), 'Becoming a world-saver: A theory of conversion to a deviant perspective', *American Sociological Review*, *30*, pp. 862–75. [38]

LOMBROSO, C. (1891), *The Man of Genius*. London: Walter Scott. [136]

LOMBROSO, C. (1911), *Crime. Its Cause and Remedies*, trans. H. P. Horton. London: Heinemann. [148]

LONG, D., ELKIND, D. and SPILKA, B. (1967), 'The child's concept of prayer', *Journal for the Scientific Study of Religion*, 6, pp. 101–9. [59]

LOUKES, H. (1961), *Teenage Religion*. London: SCM Press. [65]

LOVELAND, G. G. (1968), 'The effects of bereavement on certain religious attitudes', *Sociological Symposium*, 1, pp. 17–27. [54]

LOVELESS, E. and LODATO, F. (1971), 'Social control patterns and religious preference', *Sociological Analysis*, 28, pp. 226–8. [60]

LOWE, W. L. (1953), 'Psychodynamics of religious delusions and hallucinations', *American Journal of Psychotherapy*, 7, pp. 454–62. [135]

LOWE, W. L. (1954), 'Group beliefs and socio-cultural factors in religious delusions', *Journal of Social Psychology*, 40, pp. 267–74. [135]

LOWE, W. L. (1955), 'Religious beliefs and religious delusions', *American Journal of Psychotherapy*, 9, pp. 54–61. [135]

LUCKMANN, T. (1967), *The Invisible Religion*. New York: Macmillan. [27, 79]

LYND, R. and LYND, H. (1929), *Middletown*. New York: Harcourt, Brace. [162]

MCCANN, P. V. (1955), 'Developmental factors in the growth of a mature faith', *Religious Education*, May–June, pp. 3–11. [37]

MCCARTHY, T. J. (1942), 'Personality traits of seminarians', *Studies in Psychology of the Catholic University of America*, 5, No. 4. [99]

MCCLELLAND, D. C. (1955), 'Some social consequences of achievement motivation', *Nebraska Symposium on Motivation*. Lincoln, Nebraska: University of Nebraska Press. [83]

MCCLELLAND, D. C. (1961), *The Achieving Society*. Princeton: Van Nostrand. [82, 83]

MCCLELLAND, D. C. *et al.* (1953), *The Achievement Motive*. New York: Appleton-Century-Crofts. [78]

MCCLELLAND, D. C., RINDLISBACHER, A. and DE CHARMS, R. C. (1955), 'Religious and other sources of parental attitudes toward independence training', in D. C. McClelland (ed), *Studies in Motivation*. New York: Appleton-Century-Crofts. [82]

MCCOMB, S. (1928), 'Spiritual healing in Europe', *Mental Hygiene*, 12, pp. 706–21. [126]

MCCONAHAY, J. B. (1970), 'Attitudes of Negroes toward the church following the Los Angeles riot', *Sociological Analysis*, 31, pp. 12–22. [109, 169, 170]

MACDONALD, A. P., JR. (1969), 'Birth order and religious affiliation', *Developmental Psychology*, 1, p. 628. [31]

MCDONALD, L. (1969), *Social Class and Delinquency*. London: Faber & Faber. [150]

MCGUIRE, W. J. (1969), 'The nature of attitudes and attitude change', in G. Lindzey and E. Aronson (eds.), *Handbook of Social Psychology*. Reading, Mass.: Addison-Wesley. [39, 78]

MCKEEFERY, W. J. (1949), 'A critical analysis of quantitative studies of

229

religious awakening'. Unpublished Ph.D. thesis, Union Theol. Seminary and Teaching College. [61]

MACLEAN, A. H. (1930), *The Idea of God in Protestant Religious Education*. New York: Teachers College, Columbia University. [62]

MACRAE, D. (1954), 'A test of Piaget's theories of moral development', *Journal of Abnormal and Social Psychology*, 49, pp. 14–18. [122]

MAHESH YOGI, M. (1966), *The Science of Being and Art of Living*. London: International SRM. [50]

MAILLOUX, N. and ANCONA, L (1960), 'A clinical study of religious attitudes and a new approach to psychopathology', in H. P. David and J. C. Brengelmann (eds), *Perspectives in Personality Research*. London: International Union of Scientific Psychology. [135]

MALINOWSKI, B. (1925), *Science, Religion and Reality*. New York: Macmillan. [197]

MALZBERG, B. (1962), 'The distribution of mental disease according to religious affiliation in New York State, 1949–1951', *Mental Hygiene*, 46, pp. 510–22. [132, 145]

MARCUSE, H. (1964), *One Dimensional Man*. London: Routledge & Kegan Paul. [204]

MARINO, C. (1971), 'Cross-national comparisons of Catholic-Protestant creativity differences', *British Journal of Social and Clinical Psychology*, 10, pp. 132–7. [94]

MARSHALL, H. and ODEN, M. H. (1962), 'The status of the mature gifted individual as a basis for evaluation of the aging process', *Gerontologist*, 2, pp. 201–6. [67]

MARTIN, D. (1967), *A Sociology of English Religion*. London: Heinemann. [9, 11, 15]

MARTIN, D. and WRIGHTSMAN, L. S., JR. (1965), 'The relationship between religious behavior and concern about death', *Journal of Social Psychology*, 65, pp. 317–23. [55]

MARTY, M. E., ROSENBERG, S. E. and GREELEY, A. M. (1968), *What Do We Believe?* New York: Meredith Press. [173]

MARX, G. T. (1967), 'Religion: opiate or inspiration of civil rights militancy among Negroes?', *American Sociological Review*, 32, pp. 64–72. [108, 109, 110]

MARX, K. (1964), *Early Writings*. New York: McGraw-Hill. [191]

MARX, K. and ENGELS, F. (1957), *K. Marx and F. Engels on Religion*. Moscow: Foreign Languages Publishing House. [180, 192, 193, 201]

MASLOW, A. H. (1962), *Toward a Psychology of Being*. Princeton: Van Nostrand. [127, 207]

MASS OBSERVATION (1947), *Puzzled People*. London: Gollancz. [12, 13]

MASTERS, R. E. L. and HOUSTON, J. (1973), *The Varieties of Psychedelic Experience*. London: Turnstone Books. [47]

MASTERS, W. H. and JOHNSON, V. E. (1970), *Human Sexual Inadequacy*. London: Churchill. [157]

MATTHEWS, R. (1936), *English Messiahs*. London: Methuen. [136]

MAY, R. (1966), 'Sex differences in fantasy patterns', *Journal of Projective Techniques and Personality Assessment*, 30, pp. 576–86. [78]

MAY, R. (1969), 'Deprivation-enhancement fantasy patterns in men and women', *Journal of Projective Techniques and Personality Assessment*, *33*, pp. 464–9. [78]

MAYO, C. C., PURYEAR, H. B., and RICHEK, H. G. (1969), 'MMPI correlates of religiousness in late adolescent college students', *Journal of Nervous and Mental Disease, 149*, pp. 381; 385. [127]

MEADOW, A. and BRONSON, L. (1969), 'Religious affiliation and psychopathology in a Mexican-American population', *Journal of Abnormal Psychology, 74*, pp. 177–80. [131]

MECHANIC, D. (1953), 'Religion, religiosity, and illness behavior: the special case of the Jews', *Human Organization, 22*, pp. 202–8. [126]

MIDDLETON, G., ASHBY, D. W. and CLARKE, F. (1961), 'An analysis of attempted suicide in an urban industrial district', *Practitioner, 187*, pp. 776–82. [144]

MIDDLETON, R. and PUTNEY, S. (1962), 'Religion, normative standards, and behavior', *Sociometry, 25*, pp. 141–52. [150]

MIDDLETON, W. C. and FAY, P. J., (1940), 'Attitudes of delinquent and non-delinquent girls toward Sunday observance, the Bible, and war', *Journal of Educational Psychology, 32*, pp. 555–8. [150]

MILLER, D. R. and SWANSON, G. E. (1958), *The Changing American Parent*. New York: Wiley. [81, 82]

MILT, H. (1967), *Basic Handbook on Alcoholism*. Fair Haven, N.J.: Scientific Aids Publications. [145]

MISCHEL, W. (1968), *Personality and Assessment*. New York: Wiley. [80]

MOBERG, D. O. (1965), 'Religiosity in old age', *Gerontologist, 5*, pp. 78–87. [68, 69]

MOBERG, D. O. (1969), 'Theological self-classification and ascetic moral views of students', *Review of Religious Research, 10*, pp. 100–7. [147]

MOBERG, D. O. (1971), 'Religious practices', in Strommen (1971). [23]

MOBERG, D. O. and TAVES, M. J. (1965), 'Church participation and adjustment in old age', in A. M. Rose and W. A. Peterson (eds), *Older People and their Social World*. Philadelphia: F. A. Davis. [129]

MOL, H. (1970), 'Religion and sex in Australia', *Australian Journal of Psychiatry, 22*, pp. 105–14. [198]

MONAHAN, T. P. and KEPHART, M. M. (1954), 'Divorce and desertion by religious and mixed-religious groups', *American Journal of Sociology, 59*, pp. 454–65. [158, 159]

MOORE, T. V. (1936), 'Insanity in priests and religious', *Ecclesiastical Review, 95*, pp. 485–98, 601–13. [138]

MORETON, F. E. (1944), 'Attitudes to religion among adolescents and adults', *British Journal of Educational Psychology, 14*, pp. 69–79. [65]

MORPHEW, J. A. (1968), 'Religion and attempted suicide', *International Journal of Social Psychiatry, 14*, pp. 188–92. [144]

MOWRER, E. R. (1927), *Family Disorganization*. University of Chicago Press. [159]

MUELLER, S. A. (1971), 'The new triple melting pot: Herberg revisited', *Review of Religious Research, 13*, pp. 18–33. [85]

MYERS, J. K. and ROBERTS, B. H. (1958), 'Some relationships between religion, ethnic origin, and mental illness', in M. Sklare (ed.), *The Jews: Social Patterns of an American Group*. Chicago: Free Press. [133]

MYRDAL, G. (1944), *An American Dilemma*. New York: Harper. [108]

NASH, D. and BERGER, P. (1962), 'The child, the family, and the "religious revival" in suburbia', *Journal for the Scientific Study of Religion, 1*, pp. 85–93. [51, 54]

NATIONAL COUNCIL OF CHURCHES OF CHRIST IN THE USA, *Yearbook of American Churches*, 1900–1972. [3, 16, 17, 24]

NEL, E., HELMREICH, R., and ARONSON, E. (1969), 'Opinion changes in the advocate as a function of the persuasibility of his audience: a clarification of the meaning of dissonance', *Journal of Personality and Social Psychology, 12*, pp. 117–24. [45]

NELSEN, H. M. and YOKLEY, R. L. (1970), 'Civil rights attitudes of rural and urban Presbyterians', *Rural Sociology, 35*, pp. 161–74. [117]

NELSEN, H. M., YOKLEY, R. L. and MADRON, T. W. (1971), 'Rural-urban differences in religiosity', *Rural Sociology, 36*, pp. 389–96. [171]

NELSON, E. N. P. (1956), 'Patterns of religious attitude shift from college to fourteen years later', *Psychological Monographs*, No 424. Washington, D.C.: American Psychological Association. [65]

NELSON, M. O. (1971), 'The concept of God and feelings toward parents', *Journal of Individual Psychology, 27*, pp. 46–9. [185]

NEUMEYER, M. H. (1961), *Juvenile Delinquency in Modern Society*. Princeton: Van Nostrand. [149]

NEWCOMB, T. M. (1943), *Personality and Social Change*. New York: Dryden. [39]

NEWCOMB, T. M. and SVEHLA, G. (1937), 'Intra-family relationships in attitude', *Sociometry, 1*, pp. 180–205. [30, 32, 33, 74]

NEWSWEEK, 25 June 1973, 'When the spirit moves', *80*, pp. 85–6. [111]

NIEBUHR, E. R. (1929), *The Social Sources of Denominationalism*. New York: Holt. [167]

NIXON, R. M. (1973), Address by the president on live television and radio, 29 March 1973. Office of the White House Press Secretary, Washington, D.C. [27]

NOTTINGHAM, E.K. (1954), *Religion and Society*. NY: Doubleday. [193]

NUDELMAN, A. E. and NUDELMAN, B. E. (1972), 'Health and illness behavior of Christian Scientists', *Social Science and Medicine, 6*, pp. 253–62. [125]

NUNN, C. Z. (1964), 'Child-control through a "coalition with God"', *Child Development, 35*, pp. 417–32. [81]

NUNN, C. Z., KOSA, J. and ALPERT, J. J. (1968), 'Causal locus of illness and adaptation to family disruption', *Journal for the Scientific Study of Religion, 7*, pp. 210–18. [141]

NUTTIN, J. (1962), *Psychoanalysis and Personality*. New York: Sheed & Ward. [206]

OATES, W. (1949), 'The role of religion in the psychoses', *Journal of Pastoral Care, 3*, pp. 21–30. [135]

OATES, W. (1957), *Religious Factors in Mental Illness*. London: Allen & Unwin. [135]

232

ODHAM (1947), Unpublished report on survey of religious activity. Odham's Press. [3, 72, 73]

OGBURN, W. F. and TIBBITS, C. (1933), 'The family and its functions', Chapter 13 in *Recent Social Trends*. New York: McGraw-Hill. [171]

OLT, R. (1956), *An Approach to the Psychology of Religion*. Boston: Christopher. [61]

ORBACH, H. (1961), 'Aging and religion: church attendance in the Detroit metropolitan area', *Geriatrics*, *16*, pp. 530–40. [65, 67]

ORNSTEIN, R. E. (1973), *The Psychology of Consciousness*. San Francisco: Freeman.

ORPEN, C. (1972), 'A cross-cultural investigation of the relationship between conservatism and personality', *Journal of Psychology*, *81*, pp. 297–300. [116]

ORPEN, C. and VAN DER SCHYFF, L. (1972), 'Prejudice and personality in white South Africa: a "differential learning" alternative to the authoritarian personality', *Journal of Social Psychology*, *87*, pp. 313–14. [116]

ORUM, A. M. (1970), 'Religion and the rise of the radical White: the case of Southern Wallace support in 1968', *Social Science Quarterly*, *50*, pp. 674–88. [106]

OSARCHUK, M. and TATE, S. J. (1973), 'Effect of induced fear of death on belief in afterlife', *Journal of Personality and Social Psychology*, *27*, pp. 256–60. [55]

OSTOW, M. and SHARFSTEIN, B. (1954), *The Need to Believe*. New York: International Universities Press. [188, 195, 203]

OTTO, R. (1958), *The Idea of the Holy*. New York: Oxford University Press. [46]

PAHNKE, W. H. (1966), 'Drugs and mysticism', *International Journal of Parapsychology*, *8*, pp. 295–314. [48, 49]

PALLONE, N. J. (1964), 'Explorations in religious authority and social perception', *Acta Psychologica*, *22*, pp. 321–37. [38]

PARENTI, M. (1967), 'Political values and religious culture: Jews, Catholics, and Protestants', *Journal for the Scientific Study of Religion*, *6*, pp. 259–69. [105]

PARROTT, G. L. (1970), 'Who marches? A psychological profile of the San Francisco Moratorium crowd', *Proceedings of the Annual Convention of the American Psychological Association*, *5*, pp. 447–8. [108]

PARSONS, T. (1960), *Structure and Process in Modern Society*. Chicago: Free Press. [203]

PARSONS, T. (1966), 'Religion in modern pluralistic society', *Review of Religious Research*, *7*, pp. 125–46. [27]

PASCAL, G. R. and JENKINS, W. O. (1960), 'A study of the early environment of workhouse inmate alcoholics and its relationship to adult behaviour', *Quarterly Journal of Studies on Alcohol*, *21*, pp. 40–50. [147]

PATTERSON, S. (1969), *Immigration and Race Relations in Britain, 1944–1967*. London: Oxford University Press. [118]

PEARSON, G. B. and FERGUSON, J. O. (1953), 'Nun's melancholy', in
E. Podolsky (ed.), *Encyclopedia of Aberrations*. New York:
Philosophical Library. [138]

PETERSON, J. A. (1965), *Education for Marriage*, 2nd edn. New York:
Scribner's. [156, 157]

PFISTER, O. (1948), *Christianity and Fear*. New York: Macmillan.
[194, 195]

PHILP, H. L. (1956), *Freud and Religious Belief*. London: Rockliff.
[199]

PHOTIADIS, J. and SCHWEIKER, W. (1970), 'Attitudes toward joining
authoritarian organizations and sectarian churches', *Journal for the
Scientific Study of Religion*, 9, pp. 227–34. [174]

POBLETE, R. and O'DEA, T. F. (1960), 'Anomie and the "quest for
community": the formation of sects among the Puerto Ricans of
New York', *Sociological Analysis*, 21, pp. 18–36. [174]

POPE, L. (1942), *Millhands and Preachers*. New Haven: Yale University
Press. [204]

POPE, L. (1948), 'Religion and the class structure', *Annals of the
American Academy of Political and Social Science*, 256, pp. 84–91.
[167]

POPPLETON, P. K. and PILKINGTON, G. W. (1963), 'The measurement of
religious attitudes in a university population', *British Journal of
Social and Clinical Psychology*, 2, pp. 20–36. [34]

POTVIN, R. H. and SUZIEDELIS, A. (1969), *Seminarians of the Sixties:
National Survey*. Washington Center for Applied Research in the
Apostolate. [138]

PRATT, J. B. (1924), *The Religious Consciousness*. New York: Macmillan.
[40]

PRATT, K. C. (1937), 'Differential selection of intelligence according to
denominational preference of college freshmen', *Journal of Social
Psychology*, 8, pp. 301–10. [93]

PRESSEY, S. L. and KUHLEN, R. G. (1957), *Psychological Development
Through the Life Span*. New York: Harper. [61]

PSATHAS, G. (1957), 'Ethnicity, social class and adolescent independence
from parental control', *American Sociological Review*, 22, pp. 415–23.
[82]

PUGH, T. J. (1951), 'A comparative study of the values of a group of
ministers and two groups of laymen', *Journal of Social Psychology*, 33,
pp. 225–35. [170]

PUTNEY, S. and MIDDLETON, R. (1961), 'Rebellion, conformity and parental religious ideologies', *Sociometry*, 24, pp. 125–35. [32, 95, 105]

RANCK, J. G. (1961), 'Religious conservatism-liberalism and mental
health', *Pastoral Psychology*, 12, pp. 34–40. [98]

REES, D. G. (1967), 'Denominational concepts of God', M.A. thesis,
University of Liverpool. [188]

REIK, T. (1951), *Dogma and Compulsion*. New York: International
Universities Press. [199, 200, 201]

REISS, I. L. (1967), *The Social Context of Premarital Sexual*

Permissiveness. New York: Holt. [154, 156]

RHODES, A. L. (1960), 'Authoritarianism and fundamentalism of rural and urban high school students', *Journal of Educational Sociology*, *24*, pp. 97–105. [95]

RHODES, A. L. and NAM, C. B. (1970), 'The religious context of educational expectations', *American Sociological Review*, *35*, pp. 253–67. [86, 94]

RHODES, A. L. and REISS, A. J., JR. (1970), 'The "Religious Factor" and delinquent behavior', *Journal of Research in Crime and Delinquency*, *7*, pp. 83–98. [149]

ROBBINS, T. (1968), 'Eastern mysticism and the resocialization of drug users: the Meher Baba cult', *Journal for the Scientific Study of Religion*, *8*, pp. 308–17. [205]

ROBERTS, B. H. and MYERS, J. K. (1954), 'Religion, national origin, immigration and mental illness', *American Journal of Psychiatry*, *110*, pp. 759–64. [131]

ROBERTS, F. J. (1965), 'Some psychological factors in religious conversion', *British Journal of Social and Clinical Psychology*, *4*, pp. 185–7. [140]

ROBINSON, J. P. and SHAVER, P. R. (1972), *Measures of Social Psychological Attitudes*. Ann Arbor, Michigan: Institute for Social Research, University of Michigan. [4]

ROE, A. (1956), *The Psychology of Occupations*. New York: Wiley. [88, 137]

ROKEACH, M. (1960), *The Open and Closed Mind*. New York: Basic Books. [95, 96, 126]

ROKEACH, M. (1964), *The Three Christs of Ypsilanti*. New York: Knopf. [134, 137]

ROKEACH, M. (1969), 'Value systems in religion', *Review of Religious Research*, *11*, pp. 3–23. [120]

ROONEY, E. A. and GIBBONS, D. C. (1966), 'Social Reactions to "Crime without victims"', *Social Problems*, *13*, pp. 400–10. [120]

ROSE, A. M. (1956), *Mental Health and Mental Disorder*. London: Routledge & Kegan Paul. [133]

ROSEN, B. C. (1959), 'Race, ethnicity, and the achievement syndrome', *American Sociological Review*, *24*, pp. 47–60. [82, 83]

ROSENZWEIG, S. (1945), 'The picture-association method and its application in a study of reaction to frustration', *Journal of Personality*, *14*, pp. 3–23. [195]

ROSS, M. S. (1950), *Religious Beliefs of Youth*. New York: Association Press. [73]

ROSTEN, L. (1955), *A Guide to the Religions of America*. New York: Simon & Schuster. [3, 72]

ROUCEK, J. S. (1968), 'The special characteristics of the American Negro's church', *Sociologia Religiosa*, *11*, pp. 21–40. [169]

ROWNTREE, B. S. and LAVERS, G. R. (1951), *English Life and Leisure*. London: Longmans. [11, 76]

RUMMELL, H. S. (1934), 'Scholastic ranking of religious groups', *School Sociology*, *40*, pp. 286–8. [93]

SALES, S. M. (1972), 'Economic threat as a determinant of conversion rates in authoritarian and non-authoritarian churches', *Journal of Personality and Social Psychology*, *23*, pp. 420–8. [176]

SALISBURY, W. S. (1962), 'Religiosity, regional sub-culture and social behavior', *Journal for the Scientific Study of Religion*, *2*, pp. 94–101. [118]

SAMARIN, W. J. (1972) *Tongues of Men and Angels*. New York: Collier-Macmillan. [139]

SANAI, M. (1952), 'An empirical study of political, religious, and social attitudes', *British Journal of Psychology, Statistical Section*, *5*, pp. 81–92. [182]

SANFORD, R. N. (1973), 'Authoritarianism', in J. Knutson (ed.), *Handbook of Political Psychology*. New York: Jossey-Bass. [96].

SARGANT, W. (1957), *Battle for the Mind*. London: Heinemann. [41, 44]

SCHACHTER, S. (1959), *The Psychology of Affiliation*. Stanford, California: Stanford University Press. [194]

SCHACHTER, S. (1967), 'The interaction of cognitive and physiological determinants of emotional states', *Advances in Experimental Social Psychology*, *1*, pp. 49–80. [48]

SCHANCK, R. L. (1932), 'A study of a community and its groups and institutions conceived of as behavior of individuals', *Psychological Monographs*, *43*, No 195. [39]

SCHNEIDER, H. (1952), *Religion in Twentieth Century America*. Cambridge, Mass.: Harvard University Press. [166]

SCHOFIELD, M. (1965), *The Sexual Behaviour of Young People*. London: Longmans. [153, 154]

SCHOOL, M. E. and BECKER, J. (1964), 'A comparison of the religious beliefs of delinquent and non-delinquent Protestant adolescent boys', *Religious Education*, *59*, pp. 250–3. [150]

SCHROEDER, T. A. (1932), ' "Living God" Incarnate', *Psychoanalytic Review*, *19*, pp. 36–46. [198]

SCHUMAN, H. (1971), 'The religious factor in Detroit: review, replication, and reanalysis', *American Sociological Review*, *36*, pp. 30–48. [84]

SCHWARTZ, G. (1970), *Sect Ideologies and Social Status*. University of Chicago Press. [165, 177, 205]

SCHWEIKER, W. F. (1969), 'Religion as a superordinate meaning system and socio-psychological integration', *Journal for the Scientific Study of Religion*, *8*, pp. 300–7. [183]

SEAMAN, J. M., MICHEL, J. B. and DILLEHAY, R. C. (1971), 'Membership in orthodox Christian groups, adjustment and dogmatism', *Sociological Quarterly*, *12*, pp. 252–8. [97]

SELLIN, T. and WOLFGANG, M. E. (1958), *The Measurement of Delinquency*. New York: Wiley. [148]

SHAND, J. (1969), 'Report on a twenty-year follow-up study of the religious beliefs of 114 Amherst college students', *Journal for the Scientific Study of Religion*, *8*, pp. 167–8. [66]

SHAW, B. W. (1970), 'Religion and conceptual models of behaviour',

British Journal of Social and Clinical Psychology, 9, pp. 320–7. [141, 142]

SHAW, M. E. and WRIGHT, J. M. (1967), *Scales for the Measurement of Attitudes*. New York: McGraw-Hill. [4]

SIEGMAN, A. W. (1961), 'An empirical investigation of the psychoanalytic theory of religious behavior', *Journal of the Scientific Study of Religion*, 1, pp. 74–8.

SIEGMAN, A. W. (1963), 'A cross-cultural investigation of the relationship between introversion, social attitudes and social behaviour', *British Journal of Social and Clinical Psychology*, 2, pp. 196–208. [81]

SINCLAIR, R. D. (1928), 'A comparative study of those who report the experience of the divine presence and those who do not', *University of Iowa Studies in Character*, 2, No 3. [97]

SKOLNICK, J. H. (1958), 'Religious affiliation and drinking behavior', *Quarterly Journal of Studies on Alcohol*, 19, pp. 452–70. [145, 146, 147]

SLATER, E. (1947), 'Neurosis and religious affiliation', *Journal of Mental Science*, 93, pp. 392–8. [130, 131]

SLATER, E. and ROTH, M. (1969), *Clinical Psychiatry*, 3rd edn. London: Baillière, Tindall & Cassell. [134]

SMITH, H. S. (1972), *In his Image, But* . . . Durham, N.C.: Duke University Press. [116]

SMITH, M. B., BRUNER, J. S. and WHITE, R. W. (1956), *Opinions and Personality*. New York: Wiley. [39, 180]

SMITH, R. O. (1947), *Factors Affecting the Religion of College Students*. Ann Arbor, Michigan: Lane Hall. [38, 39]

SNYDER, C. R. (1958), *Alcohol and the Jews*. Chicago: Free Press. [145, 146]

SOCIAL SURVEYS (1964), *Television and Religion*. University of London Press. [12, 13, 66, 73, 155, 156, 168]

SPANGLER, J. D. (1971), 'Becoming a mystic: an analysis of developmental factors according to the Murray "need-press" theory', Ph.D. thesis, Boston University, cited by Clark (1971). [50]

SPELLMAN, C. M., BASKETT, G. D. and BYRNE, D. (1971), 'Manifest anxiety as a contributing factor in religious conversion', *Journal of Consulting and Clinical Psychology*, 36, pp. 245–7. [140]

SPENCER, A. E. W. (1966), 'The demography and sociography of the Roman Catholic community of England and Wales', in L. Bright and S. Clements (eds), *The Committed Church*. London: Darton, Longman & Todd. [9]

SPIRO, M. E. and D'ANDRADE, R. G. (1958), 'A cross-cultural study of some supernatural beliefs', *American Anthropologist*, 60, pp. 456–66. [33, 184, 185, 186]

SPOERL, D. T. (1952), 'The values of the post war college student', *Journal of Social Psychology*, 35, pp. 217–25. [74]

SPRAY, S. L. and MARX, J. H. (1969), 'The origins and correlates of religious adherence and apostasy among mental health professionals', *Sociological Analysis*, 30, pp. 132–50. [107]

237

SROLE, L., LANGNER, T., MICHAEL, S. T., OPLER, M. K. and RENNIE, T. A. C. (1962), *Mental Health in the Metropolis*, vol. I. New York: McGraw-Hill. [31, 127, 128, 132, 133, 140]

STARBUCK, E. D. (1899), *The Psychology of Religion*. London: Walter Scott. [38, 43, 62, 99, 195]

STARK, R. (1963), 'On the incompatibility of religion and science: a survey of American graduate students', *Journal for the Scientific Study of Religion*, *3*, pp. 3–21. [31, 90]

STARK, R. (1964), 'Class, radicalism and religious involvement in Great Britain', *American Sociological Review*, *29*, pp. 698–706. [28, 106, 111, 161, 163]

STARK, R. (1965), 'A taxonomy of religious experience', *Journal for the Scientific Study of Religion*, *5*, pp. 97–116. [48]

STARK, R. (1968), 'Age and faith: A changing outlook or an old process?', *Sociological Analysis*, *29*, pp. 1–10. [67, 68, 69]

STARK, R. (1971), 'Psychopathology and religious commitment', *Review of Religious Research*, *12*, pp. 165–76. [127, 128, 138]

STARK, W. (1967), *The Sociology of Religion*, vol. 2. London: Routledge & Kegan Paul. [165]

STEINBERG, S. (1973), 'The changing religious composition of American higher education', in C. Y. Glock (ed.), *Religion in Sociological Perspective*. Belmont, California: Wadsworth. [88]

STEMBER, C. H. *et al.* (1966), *Jews in the Mind of America*. New York: Basic Books. [113]

STENGEL, E. (1964), *Suicide and Attempted Suicide*. Harmondsworth: Penguin. [144]

STEPHEN, K. H. and STEPHAN, G. E. (1973), 'Religion and the survival of Utopian communities', *Journal for the Scientific Study of Religion*, *12*, pp. 89–100. [205]

STOKES, C. S. (1972), 'Religious differentials in reproductive behaviour: a replication and extension', *Sociological Analysis*, *33*, pp. 26–33. [160]

STONE, S. (1934), 'The Miller delusion: a comparative study in mass psychology', *American Journal of Psychiatry*, *91*, pp. 593–623. [134]

STOUFFER, S. A. (1955), *Communism, Conformity and Civil Liberties*. New York: Doubleday. [106, 120]

STOUFFER, S. A. *et al.* (1949), *The American Soldier, Vol. II. Combat and its Aftermath*. Princeton University Press. [52, 53]

STRAUS, R. and BACON, S. D. (1953), *Drinking in College*. New Haven: Yale University Press. [146, 147]

STRICKLAND, B. R. and WEDDELL, S. C. (1972), 'Religious orientation, racial prejudice and dogmatism: a study of Baptists and Unitarians', *Journal for the Scientific Study of Religion*, *11*, pp. 395–9. [115]

STROMMEN, M. P. (ed.) (1971), *Research on Religious Development*. New York: Hawthorn Books.

STRUENING, E. L. (1963), 'Antidemocratic attitudes in a Midwest university', in H. H. Remmers (ed.), *Anti-democratic Attitudes in American Schools*. Evanston, Illinois: Northwestern University Press. [112]

STRUENING, E. L. and SPILKA, B. (1952), 'A study of certain social and religious attitudes of university faculty members', *Psychological Newsletter*, *43*, pp. 1–17. [89]

STRUNK, O. JR. (1959), 'Perceived relationships between parental and deity concepts, *Psychological Newsletter*, *10*, pp. 222–6. [184]

SUMMERS, G. F., HOUGH, R. L., JOHNSON, D. P. and VEATCH, K. A. (1970), 'Ascetic Protestantism and political preference: a re-examination', *Review of Religious Research*, *12*, pp. 17–25. [105]

SWANSON, G. E. (1971), 'Life with God: some variation of religious experience in a modern city', *Journal for the Scientific Study of Religion*, *10*, pp. 169–99. [205]

SWENSON, W. M. (1961), 'Attitudes towards death in an aged population', *Journal of Gerontology*, *16*, pp. 49–52. [55]

SYMINGTON, T. A. (1935), *Religious Liberals and Conservatives*. New York: Columbia University Teachers College, Teachers College Contributions in Education No 640. [93, 98]

TART, C. T. (ed.) (1969), *Altered States of Consciousness*. New York: Wiley. [47]

TAYLOR, G. R. (1959), *Sex in History*. London: Thames & Hudson. [198]

TELFORD, C. W. (1950), 'A study of religious attitudes', *Journal of Social Psychology*, *31*, pp. 217–30. [54]

TERMAN, L. M. (1938), *Psychological Factors in Marital Happiness*. New York: McGraw-Hill. [157]

TERRY, R. L. (1971), 'Dependence, nurturance and monotheism: a cross-cultural study', *Journal of Social Psychology*, *84*, pp. 175–81. [33]

TEVAULT, R. K., FORBES, G. B. and GROMOLL, H. F. (1971), 'Trustfulness and suspiciousness as a function of liberal or conservative church membership: a field experiment', *Journal of Psychology*, *79*, pp. 163–4. [121]

THOULESS, R. H. (1923), *An Introduction to the Psychology of Religion*. Cambridge University Press. [67, 199]

THOULESS, R. H. (1935), 'The tendency to certainty in religious beliefs', *British Journal of Psychology*, *26*, pp. 16–31. [181]

THURSTON, H. (1951), *The Physical Phenomena of Mysticism*. London: Burns, Oates. [136, 190]

THURSTONE, L. L. and CHAVE, E. J. (1929), *The Measurement of Attitudes*. University of Chicago Press. [4]

TRENAMAN, J. (1952), *Out of Step*. London: Methuen. [148]

TRIANDIS, H. C. and TRIANDIS, L. M. (1960), 'Race, social class, religion and nationality as determinants of social distance', *Journal of Abnormal and Social Psychology*, *61*, pp. 110–18. [113]

TYGART, C. E. (1971), 'Religiosity and university student anti-Vietnam War attitudes: a negative or curvilinear relationship?', *Sociological Analysis*, *32*, pp. 120–9. [107, 108]

UNDERHILL, E. (1911), *Mysticism*. London: Methuen. [136]

UNWIN, J. D. (1934), *Sex and Culture*. London: Oxford University Press. [188]

BIBLIOGRAPHICAL INDEX

VERGOTE, A., TAMAYO, A., PASQUALI, L., BONAMI, M., PATTYN, A. and CUSTERS, A. (1969), 'Concept of God and parental images', *Journal for the Scientific Study of Religion*, *8*, pp. 79–87. [185, 186]

VERNON, G. M. (1968), 'Marital characteristics of religious independents', *Review of Religious Research*, *9*, pp. 162–70. [158]

VEROFF, J., FIELD, S. and GURIN, G. (1962), 'Achievement motivation and religious background', *American Sociological Review*, *27*, pp. 205–17. [84]

VON HENTIG, H. (1948), *The Criminal and His Victim*. New Haven: Yale University Press. [148]

WAGNER, H. R., FISHER, V. and DOYLE, K. (1959), 'Religious background and higher education', *American Sociological Review*, *24*, pp. 852–6. [91]

WALLACE, R. K. (1970), 'Physiological effects of transcendental meditation', *Science*, *167*, pp. 1751–4. [50]

WALLIN, P. (1957), 'Religiosity, sexual gratification, and marital satisfaction', *American Sociological Review*, *22*, pp. 300–5. [154, 198]

WALTERS, O. S. (1957), 'The religious background of 50 alcoholics', *Quarterly Journal of Studies on Alcohol*, *18*, pp. 405–16. [147]

WARDWELL, W. I. (1965), 'Christian Science healing', *Journal for the Scientific Study of Religion*, *4*, pp. 175–81. [125]

WARNER, L. W. (1961), *The Family of God*. New Haven: Yale University Press. [184]

WARREN, B. L. (1970), 'Socio-economic achievement and religion: the American case', *Sociological Inquiry*, *40*, pp. 130–55. [167]

WEATHERHEAD, L. D. (1951), *Psychology, Religion and Healing*. London: Hodder & Stoughton. [126, 136]

WEBER, M. (1904), *The Protestant Ethic and the Spirit of Capitalism*. London: Allen & Unwin, 1930. [82]

WEBER, M. (1922), *The Sociology of Religion*. Boston: Beacon Press. [181]

WEBSTER, H., FREEDMAN, M. and HEIST, P. (1962), 'Personality changes in college students', in N. Sanford (ed.), *The American College*. New York: Wiley. [37]

WECHSLER, H., DEMONE, H. W., THUM, D. and KASEY, E. H. (1970), 'Religious-ethnic differences in alcohol consumption', *Journal of Health and Social Behavior*, *11*, pp. 21–9. [145]

WEDEMEYER, B. (1949), 'Sexual factors in religious mysticism', *Persona*, *1*, pp. 10–12. [198]

WEIGERT, A. J. and THOMAS, D. L. (1972), 'Parental support, control and adolescent religiosity: an extension of previous research', *Journal for the Scientific Study of Religion*, *11*, pp. 389–93. [31]

WEINTRAUB, W. and ARONSON, H. (1968), 'A study of patients in classical psycho-analysis: Some vital statistics', *Journal of Nervous and Mental Disease*, *146*, pp. 98–102. [133]

WEISS, W. (1969), 'Effects of the mass media of communication', in G. Lindzey and E. Aronson (eds), *The Handbook of Social Psychology*, vol. 5. Reading, Mass.: Addison Wesley. [45]

240

WESTOFF, C. F. and RYDER, N. B. (1971), *Reproduction in the United States*. Princeton University Press. [154, 155]

WEYGANDT, W. (1926), 'Zur Psychpathologie der Sektenbildung', *Bekhterev 40th Anniversary Commemorative Volume*. [137]

WHELPTON, P. K., CAMPBELL, A. A. and PATTERSON, J. E. (1966), *Fertility and Family Planning in the United States*. Princeton University Press. [159, 160]

WHITAM, F. L. (1968a), 'Revivalism as institutionalized behavior: an analysis of the social base of a Billy Graham crusade', *Southwestern Social Science Quarterly*, 49, pp. 115–27. [42, 43]

WHITAM, F. L. (1968b), 'Peers, parents and Christ: interpersonal influence in retention of teen-age decisions made at a Billy Graham crusade', *Proceedings of the Southwestern Sociological Association*, 19, pp. 154–8. [38, 45]

WHITE, T. H. (1961), *The Making of the President 1960*. New York: Atheneum. [102]

WHITEMAN, P. H. and COSIER, K. P. (1964), 'Development of children's moralistic judgments: age, sex, IQ, and certain personal-experimental variables', *Child Development*, 35, pp. 843–50. [122]

WHITLOCK, F. A. and SCHAPIRA, K. (1967), 'Attempted suicide in Newcastle upon Tyne', *British Journal of Psychiatry*, 113, pp. 423–34. [144]

WHITT, H. P., GORDON, C. C. and HOFLEY, J. R. (1972), 'Religion, economic development and lethal aggression', *American Journal of Sociology*, 37, pp. 193–201. [143]

WICKHAM, E. R. (1957), *Church and People in an Industrial City*. London: Lutterworth. [166]

WILKE, W. H. (1934), 'An experimental comparison of the speech, the radio and the printed page as propaganda devices', *Archives of Psychology*, No 169. [46]

WILLIAMS, R. M. JR. (1956), 'Religion, value orientation, and intergroup conflict', *Journal of Social Issues*, 12, pp. 12–20. [115]

WILSON, B. R. (1955), 'Social aspects of religious sects: a study of some contemporary sects in Great Britain'. Unpub. Ph.D. thesis, London University. [43, 76, 77]

WILSON, B. R. (1961), *Sects and Society*. London: Heinemann. [125, 164, 176, 192]

WILSON, B. R. (1966), *Religion in Secular Society*. London: Watts & Co. [14, 17, 26, 27, 28, 57, 111, 166, 203, 204]

WILSON, B. R. (1970), *Religious Sects*. London: Weidenfeld & Nicolson. [25, 67, 165, 194]

WILSON, G. D. and PATTERSON, J. R. (1968), 'A new measure of conservatism', *British Journal of Social and Clinical Psychology*, 7, pp. 264–90. [95]

WILSON, G. E. (1956), 'Christian Science and longevity', *Journal of Forensic Science*, 1, pp. 43–60. [125]

WINGROVE, C. R. and ALSTON, J. P. (1971), 'Age, aging and church attendance', *Gerontologist*, 11, pp. 356–8. [66]

WINTER, G. (1962), *The Suburban Captivity of the Churches*. New York: Macmillan. [167]

241

WITTMAN, P. (1939), 'Developmental characteristics and personalities of chronic alcoholics', *Journal of Abnormal and Social Psychology*, *34*, pp. 361–77. [147]

WOODWARD, L. E. (1932), *Relations of Religious Training and Life Patterns to the Adult Religious Life*. New York: Columbia University Teachers College, Teachers College Contributions in Education No 527. [32, 33]

WRIGHT, D. (1971), *The Psychology of Moral Behaviour*. Harmondsworth: Penguin. [122, 123, 195, 196]

WRIGHT, D. and COX, E. (1967), 'A study of the relationship between moral judgment and religious belief in a sample of English adolescents', *Journal of Social Psychology*, *72*, pp. 135–44. [64, 74, 122]

WRIGHT, D. and COX, E. (1971), 'Changes in moral belief among sixth-form boys and girls over a seven-year period in relation to religious belief, age and sex differences', *British Journal of Social and Clinical Psychology*, *10*, pp. 332–41. [156]

YEARBOOK (from 1900), *Yearbook of American Churches*. National Council of the Churches of Christ in the USA. Later vols edited by B. Y. Landis. [16, 175]

YINGER, J. M. (1957), *Religion, Society and the Individual*. New York: Macmillan. [164, 203, 205]

ZAEHNER, R. C. (1957), *Mysticism, Sacred and Profane*. London: Oxford University Press. [48]

ZAEHNER, R. C. (1972), *Drugs, Mysticism and Make-believe*. London: Collins. [48]

ZELAN, J. (1968), 'Religious apostasy, higher education and occupational choice', *Sociology of Education*, *41*, pp. 370–9. [89]

Subject Index

abortion, attitudes to, 157
academic and scientific
  achievement, 87f
achievement motivation, 83f
acquiescence, 95
adjustment, 124f
adolescence, 59f
adolescent rebellion, 64
after-life, belief in, 12, 20f, 56
age, 58f
ageing, models of religious change
  in, 70
aggression, 78, 99
alcoholism, 145f
altruism and helping, 121f
anger, methods of handling, 99
anti-Negro attitudes, 113
anti-Semitism, 113, 116
anxiety, 126f
anxiety arousal, 44
articles about religion, 5, 23f
attendance, *see* church attendance
attitudes to religion, 3f, 19; sex
  differences in, 74f
authoritarian churches, 176f
authoritarianism, 94f

beliefs, 4, 12f, 19f; in adolescence,
  64; and class, 162f; in old age,
  69; sex differences, 73f
bereavement, 54f
Bible reading, 12

birth control, 154f
Blacks, *see* Negroes
brain hemispheres, 183

capitalism, 83
Catholics, 8f, 31f, 66, 76, 81f, 91f,
  101f, *see* denominations
childhood, 58f
child-rearing, 77f, 81f
Christian Science, 125f, 194f
church attendance, 3, 10f, 17f; in
  adolescence, 64; and class, 161f;
  in old age, 68; sex differences,
  72f
Church of England, 9
church groups, 12
church membership, 2f, 8f, 15f;
  sex differences, 71f
Church of Scotland, 9f
civil rights, 118f
clergy, 14f, 57; influence of, 110,
  117f; mental disorder in, 136f
cognitive need theories, 180f
college, effects of, 34f; norms of,
  35f
compassion, 120
conflicts, in adolescents, 62f; in
  students, 37
conservatism, religious, 93, 105f
conversion, 38, 40f, 59f, 139f, 195f;
  age of, 61; second, 67f; sudden,
  62

243

Routledge Social Science Series

Routledge & Kegan Paul   London and Boston

68–74 Carter Lane   London EC4V 5EL
9 Park Street   Boston   Mass 02108

Contents

*Authors wishing to submit manuscripts for any series in
this catalogue should send them to the Social Science Editor,
Routledge & Kegan Paul Ltd, 68–74 Carter Lane,
London EC4V 5EL*

● *Books so marked are available in paperback
All books are in Metric Demy 8vo format (216 × 138mm approx.)*

International Library of Sociology

General Editor   John Rex

GENERAL SOCIOLOGY

Barnsley, J. H. The Social Reality of Ethics. *464 pp.*
Belshaw, Cyril. The Conditions of Social Performance. *An Exploratory Theory. 144 pp.*
Brown, Robert. Explanation in Social Science. *208 pp.*
● Rules and Laws in Sociology. *192 pp.*
Bruford, W. H. Chekhov and His Russia. *A Sociological Study. 244 pp.*
Cain, Maureen E. Society and the Policeman's Role. *326 pp.*
Gibson, Quentin. The Logic of Social Enquiry. *240 pp.*
Glucksmann, M. Structuralist Analysis in Contemporary Social Thought. *212 pp.*
Gurvitch, Georges. Sociology of Law. *Preface by Roscoe Pound. 264 pp.*
Hodge, H. A. Wilhelm Dilthey. *An Introduction. 184 pp.*
Homans, George C. Sentiments and Activities. *336 pp.*
Johnson, Harry M. Sociology: *a Systematic Introduction. Foreword by Robert K. Merton. 710 pp.*
Mannheim, Karl. Essays on Sociology and Social Psychology. *Edited by Paul Keckskemeti. With Editorial Note by Adolph Lowe. 344 pp.*
Systematic Sociology: *An Introduction to the Study of Society. Edited by J. S. Erös and Professor W. A. C. Stewart. 220 pp.*
Martindale, Don. The Nature and Types of Sociological Theory. *292 pp.*
●**Maus, Heinz.** A Short History of Sociology. *234 pp.*
Mey, Harald. Field-Theory. *A Study of its Application in the Social Sciences. 352 pp.*
Myrdal, Gunnar. Value in Social Theory: *A Collection of Essays on Methodology. Edited by Paul Streeten. 332 pp.*
Ogburn, William F., and **Nimkoff, Meyer F.** A Handbook of Sociology. *Preface by Karl Mannheim. 656 pp. 46 figures. 35 tables.*
Parsons, Talcott, and **Smelser, Neil J.** Economy and Society: *A Study in the Integration of Economic and Social Theory. 362 pp.*
●**Rex, John.** Key Problems of Sociological Theory. *220 pp.*
Discovering Sociology. *278 pp.*
Sociology and the Demystification of the Modern World. *282 pp.*
●**Rex, John** (Ed.) Approaches to Sociology. *Contributions by Peter Abell, Frank Bechhofer, Basil Bernstein, Ronald Fletcher, David Frisby, Miriam Glucksmann, Peter Lassman, Herminio Martins, John Rex, Roland Robertson, John Westergaard and Jock Young. 302 pp.*
Rigby, A. Alternative Realities. *352 pp.*
Roche, M. Phenomenology, Language and the Social Sciences. *374 pp.*
Sahay, A. Sociological Analysis. *220 pp.*
Urry, John. Reference Groups and the Theory of Revolution. *244 pp.*
Weinberg, E. Development of Sociology in the Soviet Union. *173 pp.*

FOREIGN CLASSICS OF SOCIOLOGY

●**Durkheim, Emile.** Suicide. *A Study in Sociology. Edited and with an Introduction by George Simpson. 404 pp.*
Professional Ethics and Civic Morals. *Translated by Cornelia Brookfield. 288 pp.*
●**Gerth, H. H.,** and **Mills, C. Wright.** From Max Weber: *Essays in Sociology. 502 pp.*
●**Tönnies, Ferdinand.** Community and Association. (*Gemeinschaft und Gesellschaft.*) *Translated and Supplemented by Charles P. Loomis. Foreword by Pitirim A. Sorokin. 334 pp.*

SOCIAL STRUCTURE

Andreski, Stanislav. Military Organization and Society. *Foreword by Professor A. R. Radcliffe-Brown. 226 pp. 1 folder.*
Coontz, Sydney H. Population Theories and the Economic Interpretation. *202 pp.*
Coser, Lewis. The Functions of Social Conflict. *204 pp.*
Dickie-Clark, H. F. Marginal Situation: *A Sociological Study of a Coloured Group. 240 pp. 11 tables.*
Glaser, Barney, and **Strauss, Anselm L.** Status Passage. *A Formal Theory. 208 pp.*
Glass, D. V. (Ed.) Social Mobility in Britain. *Contributions by J. Berent, T. Bottomore, R. C. Chambers, J. Floud, D. V. Glass, J. R. Hall, H. T. Himmelweit, R. K. Kelsall, F. M. Martin, C. A. Moser, R. Mukherjee, and W. Ziegel. 420 pp.*
Jones, Garth N. Planned Organizational Change: *An Exploratory Study Using an Empirical Approach. 268 pp.*
Kelsall, R. K. Higher Civil Servants in Britain: *From 1870 to the Present Day. 268 pp. 31 tables.*
König, René. The Community. *232 pp. Illustrated.*
●**Lawton, Denis.** Social Class, Language and Education. *192 pp.*
McLeish, John. The Theory of Social Change: *Four Views Considered. 128 pp.*
Marsh, David C. The Changing Social Structure of England and Wales, 1871-1961. *288 pp.*
Mouzelis, Nicos. Organization and Bureaucracy. *An Analysis of Modern Theories. 240 pp.*
Mulkay, M. J. Functionalism, Exchange and Theoretical Strategy. *272 pp.*
Ossowski, Stanislaw. Class Structure in the Social Consciousness. *210 pp.*
Podgórecki, Adam. Law and Society. *About 300 pp.*

SOCIOLOGY AND POLITICS

Acton, T. A. Gypsy Politics and Social Change. *316 pp.*
Hechter, Michael. Internal Colonialism. *The Celtic Fringe in British National Development, 1536–1966. About 350 pp.*
Hertz, Frederick. Nationality in History and Politics: *A Psychology and Sociology of National Sentiment and Nationalism. 432 pp.*

Kornhauser, William. The Politics of Mass Society. *272 pp. 20 tables.*
Laidler, Harry W. History of Socialism. *Social-Economic Movements: An Historical and Comparative Survey of Socialism, Communism, Co-operation, Utopianism; and other Systems of Reform and Reconstruction. 992 pp.*
Lasswell, H. D. Analysis of Political Behaviour. *324 pp.*
Mannheim, Karl. Freedom, Power and Democratic Planning. *Edited by Hans Gerth and Ernest K. Bramstedt. 424 pp.*
Mansur, Fatma. Process of Independence. *Foreword by A. H. Hanson. 208 pp.*
Martin, David A. Pacifism: *an Historical and Sociological Study. 262 pp.*
Myrdal, Gunnar. The Political Element in the Development of Economic Theory. *Translated from the German by Paul Streeten. 282 pp.*
Wootton, Graham. Workers, Unions and the State. *188 pp.*

FOREIGN AFFAIRS: THEIR SOCIAL, POLITICAL AND ECONOMIC FOUNDATIONS

Mayer, J. P. Political Thought in France from the Revolution to the Fifth Republic. *164 pp.*

CRIMINOLOGY

Ancel, Marc. Social Defence: *A Modern Approach to Criminal Problems. Foreword by Leon Radzinowicz. 240 pp.*
Cain, Maureen E. Society and the Policeman's Role. *326 pp.*
Cloward, Richard A., and **Ohlin, Lloyd E.** Delinquency and Opportunity: *A Theory of Delinquent Gangs. 248 pp.*
Downes, David M. The Delinquent Solution. *A Study in Subcultural Theory. 296 pp.*
Dunlop, A. B., and **McCabe, S.** Young Men in Detention Centres. *192 pp.*
Friedlander, Kate. The Psycho-Analytical Approach to Juvenile Delinquency: *Theory, Case Studies, Treatment. 320 pp.*
Glueck, Sheldon, and **Eleanor.** Family Environment and Delinquency. *With the statistical assistance of Rose W. Kneznek. 340 pp.*
Lopez-Rey, Manuel. Crime. *An Analytical Appraisal. 288 pp.*
Mannheim, Hermann. Comparative Criminology: *a Text Book. Two volumes. 442 pp. and 380 pp.*
Morris, Terence. The Criminal Area: *A Study in Social Ecology. Foreword by Hermann Mannheim. 232 pp. 25 tables. 4 maps.*
Rock, Paul. Making People Pay. *338 pp.*
●**Taylor, Ian, Walton, Paul,** and **Young, Jock.** The New Criminology. *For a Social Theory of Deviance. 325 pp.*

SOCIAL PSYCHOLOGY

Bagley, Christopher. The Social Psychology of the Epileptic Child. *320 pp.*
Barbu, Zevedei. Problems of Historical Psychology. *248 pp.*
Blackburn, Julian. Psychology and the Social Pattern. *184 pp.*

●**Brittan, Arthur.** Meanings and Situations. *224 pp.*

Carroll, J. Break-Out from the Crystal Palace. *200 pp.*

●**Fleming, C. M.** Adolescence: Its Social Psychology. *With an Introduction to recent findings from the fields of Anthropology, Physiology, Medicine, Psychometrics and Sociometry. 288 pp.*

● The Social Psychology of Education: *An Introduction and Guide to Its Study. 136 pp.*

Homans, George C. The Human Group. *Foreword by Bernard DeVoto. Introduction by Robert K. Merton. 526 pp.*

● Social Behaviour: *its Elementary Forms. 416 pp.*

●**Klein, Josephine.** The Study of Groups. *226 pp. 31 figures. 5 tables.*

Linton, Ralph. The Cultural Background of Personality. *132 pp.*

●**Mayo, Elton.** The Social Problems of an Industrial Civilization. *With an appendix on the Political Problem. 180 pp.*

Ottaway, A. K. C. Learning Through Group Experience. *176 pp.*

Ridder, J. C. de. The Personality of the Urban African in South Africa. *A Thematic Apperception Test Study. 196 pp. 12 plates.*

●**Rose, Arnold M.** (Ed.) Human Behaviour and Social Processes: *an Interactionist Approach. Contributions by Arnold M. Rose, Ralph H. Turner, Anselm Strauss, Everett C. Hughes, E. Franklin Frazier, Howard S. Becker, et al. 696 pp.*

Smelser, Neil J. Theory of Collective Behaviour. *448 pp.*

Stephenson, Geoffrey M. The Development of Conscience. *128 pp.*

Young, Kimball. Handbook of Social Psychology. *658 pp. 16 figures. 10 tables.*

SOCIOLOGY OF THE FAMILY

Banks, J. A. Prosperity and Parenthood: *A Study of Family Planning among The Victorian Middle Classes. 262 pp.*

Bell, Colin R. Middle Class Families: *Social and Geographical Mobility. 224 pp.*

Burton, Lindy. Vulnerable Children. *272 pp.*

Gavron, Hannah. The Captive Wife: *Conflicts of Household Mothers. 190 pp.*

George, Victor, and **Wilding, Paul.** Motherless Families. *220 pp.*

Klein, Josephine. Samples from English Cultures.
　1. Three Preliminary Studies and Aspects of Adult Life in England. *447 pp.*
　2. Child-Rearing Practices and Index. *247 pp.*

Klein, Viola. Britain's Married Women Workers. *180 pp.*
　The Feminine Character. *History of an Ideology. 244 pp.*

McWhinnie, Alexina M. Adopted Children. *How They Grow Up. 304 pp.*

● **Myrdal, Alva,** and **Klein, Viola.** Women's Two Roles: *Home and Work. 238 pp. 27 tables.*

Parsons, Talcott, and **Bales, Robert F.** Family: Socialization and Interaction Process. *In collaboration with James Olds, Morris Zelditch and Philip E. Slater. 456 pp. 50 figures and tables.*

SOCIAL SERVICES

Bastide, Roger. The Sociology of Mental Disorder. *Translated from the French by Jean McNeil. 260 pp.*

Carlebach, Julius. Caring For Children in Trouble. *266 pp.*

Forder, R. A. (Ed.) Penelope Hall's Social Services of England and Wales. *352 pp.*

George, Victor. Foster Care. *Theory and Practice. 234 pp.*
    Social Security: *Beveridge and After. 258 pp.*

George, V., and **Wilding, P.** Motherless Families. *248 pp.*

●**Goetschius, George W.** Working with Community Groups. *256 pp.*

Goetschius, George W., and **Tash, Joan.** Working with Unattached Youth. *416 pp.*

Hall, M. P., and **Howes, I. V.** The Church in Social Work. *A Study of Moral Welfare Work undertaken by the Church of England. 320 pp.*

Heywood, Jean S. Children in Care: *the Development of the Service for the Deprived Child. 264 pp.*

Hoenig, J., and **Hamilton, Marian W.** The De-Segregation of the Mentally Ill. *284 pp.*

Jones, Kathleen. Mental Health and Social Policy, 1845-1959. *264 pp.*

King, Roy D., Raynes, Norma V., and **Tizard, Jack.** Patterns of Residential Care. *356 pp.*

Leigh, John. Young People and Leisure. *256 pp.*

Morris, Mary. Voluntary Work and the Welfare State. *300 pp.*

Morris, Pauline. Put Away: *A Sociological Study of Institutions for the Mentally Retarded. 364 pp.*

Nokes, P. L. The Professional Task in Welfare Practice. *152 pp.*

Timms, Noel. Psychiatric Social Work in Great Britain (1939-1962). *280 pp.*

●   Social Casework: *Principles and Practice. 256 pp.*

Young, A. F. Social Services in British Industry. *272 pp.*

Young, A. F., and **Ashton, E. T.** British Social Work in the Nineteenth Century. *288 pp.*

SOCIOLOGY OF EDUCATION

Banks, Olive. Parity and Prestige in English Secondary Education: a Study in Educational Sociology. *272 pp.*

Bentwich, Joseph. Education in Israel. *224 pp. 8 pp. plates.*

●**Blyth, W. A. L.** English Primary Education. *A Sociological Description.*
    1. Schools. *232 pp.*
    2. Background. *168 pp.*

Collier, K. G. The Social Purposes of Education: *Personal and Social Values in Education. 268 pp.*

Dale, R. R., and **Griffith, S.** Down Stream: *Failure in the Grammar School.* *108 pp.*

Dore, R. P. Education in Tokugawa Japan. *356 pp. 9 pp. plates.*

Evans, K. M. Sociometry and Education. *158 pp.*

●**Ford, Julienne.** Social Class and the Comprehensive School. *192 pp.*

Foster, P. J. Education and Social Change in Ghana. *336 pp. 3 maps.*

Fraser, W. R. Education and Society in Modern France. *150 pp.*

Grace, Gerald R. Role Conflict and the Teacher. *About 200 pp.*

Hans, Nicholas. New Trends in Education in the Eighteenth Century. *278 pp. 19 tables.*

● Comparative Education: *A Study of Educational Factors and Traditions.* *360 pp.*

Hargreaves, David. Interpersonal Relations and Education. *432 pp.*

● Social Relations in a Secondary School. *240 pp.*

Holmes, Brian. Problems in Education. *A Comparative Approach. 336 pp.*

King, Ronald. Values and Involvement in a Grammar School. *164 pp.*

School Organization and Pupil Involvement. *A Study of Secondary Schools.*

●**Mannheim, Karl,** and **Stewart, W. A. C.** An Introduction to the Sociology of Education. *206 pp.*

Morris, Raymond N. The Sixth Form and College Entrance. *231 pp.*

●**Musgrove, F.** Youth and the Social Order. *176 pp.*

●**Ottaway, A. K. C.** Education and Society: An Introduction to the Sociology of Education. *With an Introduction by W. O. Lester Smith. 212 pp.*

Peers, Robert. Adult Education: *A Comparative Study. 398 pp.*

Pritchard, D. G. Education and the Handicapped: *1760 to 1960. 258 pp.*

Richardson, Helen. Adolescent Girls in Approved Schools. *308 pp.*

Stratta, Erica. The Education of Borstal Boys. *A Study of their Educational Experiences prior to, and during, Borstal Training. 256 pp.*

Taylor, P. H., Reid, W. A., and **Holley, B. J.** The English Sixth Form. *A Case Study in Curriculum Research. 200 pp.*

SOCIOLOGY OF CULTURE

Eppel, E. M., and **M.** Adolescents and Morality: *A Study of some Moral Values and Dilemmas of Working Adolescents in the Context of a changing Climate of Opinion. Foreword by W. J. H. Sprott. 268 pp. 39 tables.*

●**Fromm, Erich.** The Fear of Freedom. *286 pp.*

● The Sane Society. *400 pp.*

Mannheim, Karl. Essays on the Sociology of Culture. *Edited by Ernst Mannheim in co-operation with Paul Kecskemeti. Editorial Note by Adolph Lowe. 280 pp.*

Weber, Alfred. Farewell to European History: *or The Conquest of Nihilism. Translated from the German by R. F. C. Hull. 224 pp.*

SOCIOLOGY OF RELIGION

Argyle, Michael and **Beit-Hallahmi, Benjamin.** The Social Psychology of Religion. *About 256 pp.*

Nelson, G. K. Spiritualism and Society. *313 pp.*

Stark, Werner. The Sociology of Religion. *A Study of Christendom.*
Volume I. *Established Religion. 248 pp.*
Volume II. *Sectarian Religion. 368 pp.*
Volume III. *The Universal Church. 464 pp.*
Volume IV. *Types of Religious Man. 352 pp.*
Volume V. *Types of Religious Culture. 464 pp.*

Turner, B. S. Weber and Islam. *216 pp.*

Watt, W. Montgomery. Islam and the Integration of Society. *320 pp.*

SOCIOLOGY OF ART AND LITERATURE

Jarvie, Ian C. Towards a Sociology of the Cinema. *A Comparative Essay on the Structure and Functioning of a Major Entertainment Industry. 405 pp.*

Rust, Frances S. Dance in Society. *An Analysis of the Relationships between the Social Dance and Society in England from the Middle Ages to the Present Day. 256 pp. 8 pp. of plates.*

Schücking, L. L. The Sociology of Literary Taste. *112 pp.*

Wolff, Janet. Hermeneutic Philosophy and the Sociology of Art. *About 200 pp.*

SOCIOLOGY OF KNOWLEDGE

Diesing, P. Patterns of Discovery in the Social Sciences. *262 pp.*

●**Douglas, J. D.** (Ed.) Understanding Everyday Life. *370 pp.*

●**Hamilton, P.** Knowledge and Social Structure. *174 pp.*

Jarvie, I. C. Concepts and Society. *232 pp.*

Mannheim, Karl. Essays on the Sociology of Knowledge. *Edited by Paul Kecskemeti. Editorial Note by Adolph Lowe. 353 pp.*

Remmling, Gunter W. (Ed.) Towards the Sociology of Knowledge. *Origin and Development of a Sociological Thought Style. 463 pp.*

Stark, Werner. The Sociology of Knowledge: *An Essay in Aid of a Deeper Understanding of the History of Ideas. 384 pp.*

URBAN SOCIOLOGY

Ashworth, William. The Genesis of Modern British Town Planning: *A Study in Economic and Social History of the Nineteenth and Twentieth Centuries. 288 pp.*

Cullingworth, J. B. Housing Needs and Planning Policy: *A Restatement of the Problems of Housing Need and 'Overspill' in England and Wales. 232 pp. 44 tables. 8 maps.*

Dickinson, Robert E. City and Region: *A Geographical Interpretation* *608 pp. 125 figures.*
The West European City: *A Geographical Interpretation. 600 pp. 129 maps. 29 plates.*
● The City Region in Western Europe. *320 pp. Maps.*
Humphreys, Alexander J. New Dubliners: *Urbanization and the Irish Family. Foreword by George C. Homans. 304 pp.*
Jackson, Brian. Working Class Community: *Some General Notions raised by a Series of Studies in Northern England. 192 pp.*
Jennings, Hilda. Societies in the Making: *a Study of Development and Redevelopment within a County Borough. Foreword by D. A. Clark. 286 pp.*
●**Mann, P. H.** An Approach to Urban Sociology. *240 pp.*
Morris, R. N., and **Mogey, J.** The Sociology of Housing. *Studies at Berinsfield. 232 pp. 4 pp. plates.*
Rosser, C., and **Harris, C.** The Family and Social Change. *A Study of Family and Kinship in a South Wales Town. 352 pp. 8 maps.*

RURAL SOCIOLOGY

Chambers, R. J. H. Settlement Schemes in Tropical Africa: *A Selective Study. 268 pp.*
Haswell, M. R. The Economics of Development in Village India. *120 pp.*
Littlejohn, James. Westrigg: *the Sociology of a Cheviot Parish. 172 pp. 5 figures.*
Mayer, Adrian C. Peasants in the Pacific. *A Study of Fiji Indian Rural Society. 248 pp. 20 plates.*
Williams, W. M. The Sociology of an English Village: *Gosforth. 272 pp. 12 figures. 13 tables.*

SOCIOLOGY OF INDUSTRY AND DISTRIBUTION

Anderson, Nels. Work and Leisure. *280 pp.*
●**Blau, Peter M.,** and **Scott, W. Richard.** Formal Organizations: *a Comparative approach. Introduction and Additional Bibliography by J. H. Smith. 326 pp.*
Eldridge, J. E. T. Industrial Disputes. *Essays in the Sociology of Industrial Relations. 288 pp.*
Hetzler, Stanley. Applied Measures for Promoting Technological Growth. *352 pp.*
Technological Growth and Social Change. *Achieving Modernization. 269 pp.*
Hollowell, Peter G. The Lorry Driver. *272 pp.*
Jefferys, Margot, *with the assistance of Winifred Moss.* Mobility in the Labour Market: *Employment Changes in Battersea and Dagenham. Preface by Barbara Wootton. 186 pp. 51 tables.*

Millerson, Geoffrey. The Qualifying Associations: *a Study in Professionalization. 320 pp.*
Smelser, Neil J. Social Change in the Industrial Revolution: *An Application of Theory to the Lancashire Cotton Industry, 1770-1840. 468 pp. 12 figures. 14 tables.*
Williams, Gertrude. Recruitment to Skilled Trades. *240 pp.*
Young, A. F. Industrial Injuries Insurance: *an Examination of British Policy. 192 pp.*

DOCUMENTARY

Schlesinger, Rudolf (Ed.) Changing Attitudes in Soviet Russia.
2. The Nationalities Problem and Soviet Administration. *Selected Readings on the Development of Soviet Nationalities Policies. Introduced by the editor. Translated by W. W. Gottlieb. 324 pp.*

ANTHROPOLOGY

Ammar, Hamed. Growing up in an Egyptian Village: *Silwa, Province of Aswan. 336 pp.*
Brandel-Syrier, Mia. Reeftown Elite. *A Study of Social Mobility in a Modern African Community on the Reef. 376 pp.*
Crook, David, and **Isabel.** Revolution in a Chinese Village: *Ten Mile Inn. 230 pp. 8 plates. 1 map.*
Dickie-Clark, H. F. The Marginal Situation. *A Sociological Study of a Coloured Group. 236 pp.*
Dube, S. C. Indian Village. *Foreword by Morris Edward Opler. 276 pp. 4 plates.*
India's Changing Villages: *Human Factors in Community Development. 260 pp. 8 plates. 1 map.*
Firth, Raymond. Malay Fishermen. *Their Peasant Economy. 420 pp. 17 pp. plates.*
Firth, R., Hubert, J., and **Forge, A.** Families and their Relatives. *Kinship in a Middle-Class Sector of London: An Anthropological Study. 456 pp.*
Gulliver, P. H. Social Control in an African Society: a Study of the Arusha, Agricultural Masai of Northern Tanganyika. *320 pp. 8 plates. 10 figures.*
Family Herds. *288 pp.*
Ishwaran, K. Shivapur. *A South Indian Village. 216 pp.*
Tradition and Economy in Village India: *An Interactionist Approach. Foreword by Conrad Arensburg. 176 pp.*
Jarvie, Ian C. The Revolution in Anthropology. *268 pp.*
Jarvie, Ian C., and **Agassi, Joseph.** Hong Kong. *A Society in Transition. 396 pp. Illustrated with plates and maps.*
Little, Kenneth L. Mende of Sierra Leone. *308 pp. and folder.*
Negroes in Britain. *With a New Introduction and Contemporary Study by Leonard Bloom. 320 pp.*

11

Lowie, Robert H. Social Organization. *494 pp.*

Mayer, Adrian C. Caste and Kinship in Central India: *A Village and its Region. 328 pp. 16 plates. 15 figures. 16 tables.*

Peasants in the Pacific. *A Study of Fiji Indian Rural Society. 248 pp.*

Smith, Raymond T. The Negro Family in British Guiana: *Family Structure and Social Status in the Villages. With a Foreword by Meyer Fortes. 314 pp. 8 plates. 1 figure. 4 maps.*

SOCIOLOGY AND PHILOSOPHY

Barnsley, John H. The Social Reality of Ethics. *A Comparative Analysis of Moral Codes. 448 pp.*

Diesing, Paul. Patterns of Discovery in the Social Sciences. *362 pp.*

●**Douglas, Jack D.** (Ed.) Understanding Everyday Life. *Toward the Reconstruction of Sociological Knowledge. Contributions by Alan F. Blum. Aaron W. Cicourel, Norman K. Denzin, Jack D. Douglas, John Heeren, Peter McHugh, Peter K. Manning, Melvin Power, Matthew Speier, Roy Turner, D. Lawrence Wieder, Thomas P. Wilson and Don H. Zimmerman. 370 pp.*

Jarvie, Ian C. Concepts and Society. *216 pp.*

Pelz, Werner. The Scope of Understanding in Sociology. *Towards a more radical reorientation in the social humanistic sciences. 283 pp.*

Roche, Maurice. Phenomenology, Language and the Social Sciences. *371 pp.*

Sahay, Arun. Sociological Analysis. *212 pp.*

Sklair, Leslie. The Sociology of Progress. *320 pp.*

International Library of Anthropology

General Editor Adam Kuper

Brown, Paula. The Chimbu. *A Study of Change in the New Guinea Highlands. 151 pp.*

Lloyd, P. C. Power and Independence. *Urban Africans' Perception of Social Inequality. 264 pp.*

Pettigrew, Joyce. Robber Noblemen. *A Study of the Political System of the Sikh Jats. 284 pp.*

Van Den Berghe, Pierre L. Power and Privilege at an African University. *278 pp.*

International Library of Social Policy

General Editor Kathleen Jones

Bayley, M. Mental Handicap and Community Care. *426 pp.*

Butler, J. R. Family Doctors and Public Policy. *208 pp.*

Holman, Robert. Trading in Children. *A Study of Private Fostering. 355 pp.*

Jones, Kathleen. History of the Mental Health Service. *428 pp.*
Thomas, J. E. The English Prison Officer since 1850: *A Study in Conflict.* *258 pp.*
Woodward, J. To Do the Sick No Harm. *A Study of the British Voluntary Hospital System to 1875. About 220 pp.*

International Library of Welfare and Philosophy

General Editors Noel Timms and David Watson

● **Plant, Raymond.** Community and Ideology. *104 pp.*

Primary Socialization, Language and Education

General Editor Basil Bernstein

Bernstein, Basil. Class, Codes and Control. *2 volumes.*
 1. *Theoretical Studies Towards a Sociology of Language. 254 pp.*
 2. *Applied Studies Towards a Sociology of Language. About 400 pp.*
Brandis, W., and **Bernstein, B.** Selection and Control. *176 pp.*
Brandis, Walter, and **Henderson, Dorothy.** Social Class, Language and Communication. *288 pp.*
Cook-Gumperz, Jenny. Social Control and Socialization. *A Study of Class Differences in the Language of Maternal Control. 290 pp.*
● **Gahagan, D. M.,** and **G. A.** Talk Reform. *Exploration in Language for Infant School Children. 160 pp.*
Robinson, W. P., and **Rackstraw, Susan D. A.** A Question of Answers. *2 volumes. 192 pp. and 180 pp.*
Turner, Geoffrey J., and **Mohan, Bernard A.** A Linguistic Description and Computer Programme for Children's Speech. *208 pp.*

Reports of the Institute of Community Studies

Cartwright, Ann. Human Relations and Hospital Care. *272 pp.*
● Parents and Family Planning Services. *306 pp.*
 Patients and their Doctors. *A Study of General Practice. 304 pp.*
● **Jackson, Brian.** Streaming: *an Education System in Miniature. 168 pp.*
Jackson, Brian, and **Marsden, Dennis.** Education and the Working Class: *Some General Themes raised by a Study of 88 Working-class Children in a Northern Industrial City. 268 pp. 2 folders.*
Marris, Peter. The Experience of Higher Education. *232 pp. 27 tables.*
 Loss and Change. *192 pp.*

Marris, Peter, and **Rein, Martin.** Dilemmas of Social Reform. *Poverty and Community Action in the United States. 256 pp.*

Marris, Peter, and **Somerset, Anthony.** African Businessmen. *A Study of Entrepreneurship and Development in Kenya. 256 pp.*

Mills, Richard. Young Outsiders: *a Study in Alternative Communities. 216 pp.*

Runciman, W. G. Relative Deprivation and Social Justice. *A Study of Attitudes to Social Inequality in Twentieth-Century England. 352 pp.*

Willmott, Peter. Adolescent Boys in East London. *230 pp.*

Willmott, Peter, and **Young, Michael.** Family and Class in a London Suburb. *202 pp. 47 tables.*

Young, Michael. Innovation and Research in Education. *192 pp.*

●**Young, Michael,** and **McGeeney, Patrick.** Learning Begins at Home. *A Study of a Junior School and its Parents. 128 pp.*

Young, Michael, and **Willmott, Peter.** Family and Kinship in East London. *Foreword by Richard M. Titmuss. 252 pp. 39 tables.*
The Symmetrical Family. *410 pp.*

Reports of the Institute for Social Studies in Medical Care

Cartwright, Ann, Hockey, Lisbeth, and **Anderson, John L.** Life Before Death. *310 pp.*

Dunnell, Karen, and **Cartwright, Ann.** Medicine Takers, Prescribers and Hoarders. *190 pp.*

Medicine, Illness and Society

General Editor W. M. Williams

Robinson, David. The Process of Becoming Ill. *142 pp.*

Stacey, Margaret, *et al.* Hospitals, Children and Their Families. *The Report of a Pilot Study. 202 pp.*

Monographs in Social Theory

General Editor Arthur Brittan

●**Barnes, B.** Scientific Knowledge and Sociological Theory. *About 200 pp.*

Bauman, Zygmunt. Culture as Praxis. *204 pp.*

● **Dixon, Keith.** Sociological Theory. *Pretence and Possibility. 142 pp.*

●**Smith, Anthony D.** The Concept of Social Change. *A Critique of the Functionalist Theory of Social Change. 208 pp.*

Routledge Social Science Journals

The British Journal of Sociology. *Edited by Terence P. Morris. Vol. 1, No. 1, March 1950 and Quarterly. Roy. 8vo. Back numbers available. An international journal with articles on all aspects of sociology.*

Economy and Society. *Vol. 1, No. 1. February 1972 and Quarterly. Metric Roy. 8vo. A journal for all social scientists covering sociology, philosophy, anthropology, economics and history. Back numbers available.*

Year Book of Social Policy in Britain, The. *Edited by Kathleen Jones. 1971. Published annually.*

Printed in Great Britain by Unwin Brothers Limited
The Gresham Press Old Woking Surrey
A member of the Staples Printing Group